Masaccio
and the Art of
Early Renaissance
Florence

BRUCE COLE

Masaccio and the Art of Early Renaissance Florence

INDIANA UNIVERSITY PRESS

Bloomington & London

This book was brought to publication with the assistance
of a grant from the Andrew W. Mellon Foundation.

Manufactured in the United States of America

Library of Congress Cataloging in Publication Data

Cole, Bruce, 1938–
    Masaccio and the art of early Renaissance Florence
    Bibliography: p.
    1. Art, Renaissance—Early Renaissance—Italy—Florence. 2. Art, Italian—Italy—
Florence. 3. Masaccio, Tommaso Guidi, known as, 1401–1428?—Influence. I. Title
N6921.F7C64   709′.45′51   79–2601
ISBN 0–253–12298–8   1 2 3 4 5 84 83 82 81 80

For
the Two Marvins

Contents

Contents

PLATES

Preface

As one concerned with the art of the Renaissance, I have found it strange that there has been no general history, in any language, of Florentine painting c.1375–c.1430. Although the period is universally considered one of the most seminal and important in Western art, there is no single volume to which the student or interested general reader can turn. Certainly, there are the large histories of Italian painting, such as those by Venturi or van Marle, but these tomes — sometimes hopelessly out of date—are often confusing to someone not closely acquainted with early Italian art.

In the following pages I shall discuss briefly the course of painting in Florence from the late Trecento to the fourth decade of the Quattrocento. I do not in any way claim that this book is exhaustive or definitive, because I know that such adjectives rarely apply with truth to historical studies and almost never to books dealing with the little-investigated artists and paintings of this volume. I have, instead, simply tried to describe only what I consider the genesis, evolution, and impact of the major artistic events of the time. It is my aim to give the reader a feeling for the stylistic dynamics of the crucial decades between the first works of Agnolo Gaddi and the death of Masaccio.

Masaccio is, of course, the most famous and in many ways the most important painter of the period. Consequently, I have devoted three chapters to him and have, to a certain degree, centered the book around his career. Like a number of other remarkable artists, he has often been studied without much reference to the art of his own time. I have tried to see him in the context of Florentine art of the late fourteenth and early fifteenth centuries.

The footnotes and bibliography have been planned to introduce the reader to the literature on the painting and sculpture of the period. They will, it is hoped, provide a starting place for those interested in pursuing further some of the more specific problems mentioned in the book.

If this volume succeeds only in giving the reader a sense of the vital complexity of this splendid era, its goal will have been reached.

No matter how many lonely days an author spends closeted with a manuscript, writing a book is not a solitary occupation. From first idea to printing one piles up intellectual debts. Mine are numerous and I am pleased to be able to make them public here.

In Florence, David Wilkins, Richard Goldthwaite, and Tony Molho were kind enough to exchange ideas with me, often in front of the paintings themselves. My time in Italy would have been greatly reduced without generous grants from the Samuel H. Kress Foundation, for which I am especially grateful to Mary Davis; the John Simon Guggenheim Memorial Foundation; and Indiana University.

Both in Florence and in Bloomington, first Scott Walker and then Helen Ronan provided invaluable assistance. I am also indebted to Ulrich and Gloria Middeldorf, Charles Mitchell, Carol Peters, Marilyn Hunt, Alfred David, and the staff of Indiana University Press.

Finally, I need to thank Heidi and Barry Gealt, whose love of painting both moved and taught me more than I can say, and Doreen, who made this book possible.

B.C.

Bloomington, Indiana
11 March 1979

Introduction

In the second half of the twentieth century, the painter works alone. Even if he has studied with another artist, he strives to create forms and ideas revealing no influence: originality is highly prized. In fact, works of art are often valued simply because they are like nothing else. Inspiration — the predecessor of originality — derives, we believe today, from some unfathomable source. Many would suggest that it is ultimately divine, but others — perhaps most others — think that it is generated solely from some complex mechanism set deep within the human mind.[1]

The assumptions about art and artist held by the residents of early Quattrocento Florence were decidedly different. They thought that the painter was a craftsman whose business it was to produce pictures. Artists hardly ever worked alone, but were associated in small cooperative organizations called *botteghe* (shops).[2] The notion that they were totally original or divinely inspired would have been rejected out of hand. There has been a radical change in ideas about how art is made; modern psychoanalytic theories of creativity would have made no sense in fifteenth-century Florence. Everyone then knew that artists took their styles from their teachers and that they gained inspiration from paintings and from the holy texts.

One cannot understand the most basic principles of the art of the late Trecento and early Quattrocento without knowing how artists of that time worked, how they were trained, and what they thought about their art. In fourteenth- and fifteenth-century Florence, the word *artist* does not seem to have been used generically: a man was called a *painter*, a *sculptor*, a *goldsmith*, or a *potter*, but not an *artist*. He was identified solely by his work. This lack of a label is indicative of the way people of the period viewed their painters: they were seen as artisans who labored on a specific craft that was important, but not more so than the work done by a saddlemaker or a tinsmith. True, there were several

notable examples — Giotto being the major one — of artists whose work cata-
pulted them to fame and wealth, but they were the rare exceptions.[3]

Not unnaturally, the artist's social and economic status coincided with society's valuation of his task. In Florence his position was certainly above the
manual laborer or wool worker but well below that of the city's well-to-do merchant, lawyer, or banker. He might be able to invest small sums in the shares of
the Florentine funded debt (the *Monte*) and own some humble property in the
country, but he could never live in a grand *palazzo* or have a splendid villa
outside the city.[4] Service in the government was open to him, but it was unlikely that he would rise above a middling level, or that he would occupy one of
the top posts in his guild, the Arte dei Medici e Speziali.[5] He probably rented
rather than owned the shop in which he worked. His sons might follow his
footsteps or pursue other careers of relatively equal social standing.

Painters began their trade in their early teens, when they were apprenticed
to the shop of an artist.[6] Here, along with other youths, they learned the many
skills needed, including grinding colors, preparing the gesso ground that covered the panels, applying the gold for backgrounds and haloes, making charcoal, and — what was very important — fashioning the scores of brushes used
by the artist for painting on the various surfaces. It was only after he had mas-
tered all these tasks that the apprentice could begin to paint.

The young apprentice (or *garzone*) was expected to be the master of several
media. Most likely his master's shop would be engaged in the painting of frescoes, panels, furniture, banners, shields, and many other items that are not now
associated with the painter's art.[7]

The painting of panels was a slow, exacting craft. Altarpieces of many shapes
and types — polyptychs, triptychs, diptychs, or simply single panels — were
needed for the high altars and individual chapels of the many churches. These
pictures came in many sizes and shapes, and varied from the humble to the
grandiose. Their subjects ranged from a simple Madonna and Child to complex
iconographic constructions that included dozens of saints and the depiction of
their legends.[8] Naturally the cost of an altarpiece was determined by how much
time, effort, and material were spent on it by the master and his apprentices.

Painters had very little to do with the complex task of building the panels or
making the frames. This job — which sometimes cost more than the actual
painting — was done by skilled carpenters. Then the artist had to prepare the
surface of the panel for the painting. This process was a slow one, for the wood
had to be covered so that it was not porous. A layer of linen and then coats of a
plasterlike material called gesso were applied; the latter had to be smoothed and
polished to form a dense, hard surface that would take the paint. After this

laborious work was finished a carefully worked-out charcoal design was applied to the gesso ground.[9] The panel was then gilded in the areas traditionally covered by gold leaf: the background, haloes, and decorative borders.

Finally the painting could begin. The normal medium was tempera. The pigments, derived from natural substances (roots, minerals, and the like), were ground into a fine powder and mixed with an organic vehicle — the yolks of eggs. Since the egg mixture was highly viscous, the painter had to work slowly, with small brushes, and painstakingly build up the paint surface from layers of underpaint to the finely worked top colors. From start to finish it was a job requiring great knowledge and skill, and it is no surprise to learn that apprentices stayed with their masters for years before they were ready to open their own shops.

Apprentices also helped with the painting of frescoes of many shapes and dimensions, from modest street-corner tabernacles of the Madonna to vast fresco cycles on the walls of churches. Of course, the painting of a fresco cycle took much more labor than even the most elaborate altarpiece. When the commission for a cycle was obtained, it was sometimes necessary to hire extra artists not normally attached to the shop. The shop was often an *ad hoc* unit, expanding when there was much work, contracting when there was little; it was at its largest when frescoes were being painted.

In its simplest definition fresco painting is the act of putting pigment suspended in a water vehicle on wet plaster; but, in fact. the making of a fresco is a very difficult job.[10] Frescoes were often to be put on walls that were of uneven stone or brick and unsuitable for painting. The walls had to be made realtively smooth by the application of a thick coat of plaster called the *arriccio*. On this surface was placed a full-scale design, executed first in charcoal and then in a brownish red pigment named *sinopia*.

This working procedure meant that the artist formed his ideas and designed his composition in actual size on the spot. Much of the wonderful physical relation that Trecento and early Quattrocento frescoes have with their surroundings comes from this basic working method, as does the coordination of style, space, and scale among all the individual parts of the cycles.[11] Certainly the painter referred to drawings on paper, but for the most part they seem to have been used only for details that needed to be worked out in a series of separate studies, a task not possible on the actual plaster.

The mid-Quattrocento saw a shift away from preparatory *sinopie* toward the use of cartoons. A series of small squared drawings were transferred to cartoons the actual size of the area to be painted. This change in procedure was probably brought about by the increased complexity of later frescoes, which had highly developed backgrounds containing numerous figures set in a perfectly plotted one-point perspective system. But the frescoes done from cartoons designed far away from the actual site lack the exciting relation with their surroundings and the spontaneity characteristic of the earlier wall paintings.[12]

Once the artist was satisfied with the *sinopia* design, he began to put on the last coat of plaster, called the *intonaco*. It was a very fine, thin layer on which the pigments, suspended in lime water, were applied. The plaster was not laid all at once, but in patches of varying size called *giornate*. Applied from the top down, these patches covered part of the *sinopia*. The remaining *sinopia* acted as a guide (to overall composition and scale) and enabled the artist to mesh his painting on the *intonaco* with the still-exposed underdrawing around it. But even in the final stage of fresco painting — the application of pigment to *intonaco* — the artist was on his own. With his preparatory drawing partially covered, he was faced with the task of beginning once again on a completely fresh patch of plaster.

Painting on the *intonaco* required considerable technical skill. The painter had to know the characteristics of each of his many colors. For instance, the same pigment could appear in slightly different values if it was applied to plaster patches that were not of the same degree of dryness.[13] If the brown for a mountain range were applied to a very wet *giornata* on one side of the fresco and to a relatively dry patch on the other, it might dry to two different values of brown. The fresco painter had to know at exactly which moment to apply his paint, and in order to achieve a consistency of color throughout the fresco, he had to finish the patch before it was too dry. Because the area of wet plaster had to be kept to a manageable size, the *intonaco* was laid on in a series of patches. This method of working also forced the painter to keep his shapes simple, so they could be fitted into the individual *giornate* with ease. Often the fresco was designed so that the edges of buildings, people, and mountains served as the junctures of large *giornate*, thereby eliminating — as much as possible — the need for the same color through a series of patches. This is a good example of technique influencing inspiration and, consequently, style.

The painting of frescoes was always a race against time. To put on pigment while the plaster was at an optimum state was the guiding principle. Large brushes, equal to the areas to be painted, were used to put in broad slashes of color at a rapid pace. One can imagine the precision and skill needed to organize, supervise, and paint a fresco as numerous artists stood together on narrow scaffolding — often far above the floor — each with a specific task and all working at top speed to complete the painting before the plaster dried.

This method of fresco painting is called true fresco, or *buon fresco*, as opposed to *fresco secco*, where tempera was put on dry plaster. The chemical bond formed by wet plaster and pigment makes true fresco a hard, durable surface. If the painter made a mistake he could correct it properly only by chipping out the dry plaster, putting in a new patch, and then repainting. Thus, he needed to be sure as well as quick.

Actually, most frescoes are a mixture of true fresco and *fresco secco*, for the many details of the landscape, architecture, and costume had to be put in with great care and so required the use of smaller brushes and a technique that allowed the painter more time. Many of the *secco* parts have flaked away, leaving the true fresco areas shorn of their enlivening details.

The many tasks involved in painting a fresco cycle could be handled only by a cooperative shop. When numerous artists had to labor on a single job, their painting had to be controlled by one man. It was the head of the shop who organized the work to be done and who designed it on both fresco and panel. For the execution of large or numerous commissions it was necessary to employ apprentices and helpers who could get the job done quickly. It was vital, however, that the result of all this cooperation not be a jumble of styles. To avoid that possibility, from the very beginnings of their own careers, apprentices were implored to make the style of their master their own; once they did, it was possible for a number of men to paint a large fresco cycle with no marked stylistic discrepancies.[14] Various hands probably worked on nearly every surface of frescoes and large panels; much the same was true of sculpture, where one artist might put in all the beards and another do all the facial features.[15]

So while it is possible to identify the hand and mind of an individual personality in the design of a work, one knows that its surface is most likely the cooperative effort of several hands. This highly collaborative manner of working, understood by any Florentine from the period covered by this book, is one of the major differences between the art of that time and ours.

The process of strict imitation as a way of learning created a progressive formation of new visual idioms from older ones, insuring, in most cases, the gradual transition of style from master to pupil and from generation to generation. To be sure, there were substantial changes, but they were mostly the slow movement of the new generation away from the work of its teachers. This is not true for two important artists of the period — Donatello and Masaccio — and thus their innovations are even more striking.

In many shops fresco and panel painting took up only a limited amount of time. Rather, most of the commissions were for what we would now consider utilitarian objects: the painting of armor, banners, wooden plates for new mothers (*deschi da parto*), drapery, and even various types of furniture.[16]

It was not considered demeaning for the artist to work on household items. There was no distinction — such as now exists — between the art of the utilitarian object and the painting of pictures. Painters of the Trecento and early Quattrocento would have felt quite comfortable painting the walls of a *palazzo* or decorating a shield for a Florentine merchant, and they would have thought it natural to receive a daily salary for their work, much like a mason or a carpenter. Again, one needs to know this to realize the vast difference between our perception of an artist and that held by the Florentines of the fourteenth and fifteenth centuries.

The Florentine artist had no romantic garret studio; his work was carried out in a *bottega*, which seems to have been physically just like the shops of many of his fellow artisans. It was a small room opened to the street, but it could be closed by wooden shutters and a single Dutch door. During working hours it was probably open, and passersby could see the artist working inside.[17] Painters did not work exclusively on commissions, for they had finished panels — usually small altarpieces — for sale in their shops. The customer could walk in and have his choice of several.[18]

For more important paintings, a contract was often drawn setting the obligations of both artist and patron. From extant documents we know that the patrons, not unnaturally, were anxious about cost (sometimes the actual price would be decided by an independent appraisal after the work was finished), quality of materials, and — since many painters were notoriously slow — completion date. Occasionally there was a clause stating that the artist must paint the work entirely with his own hands — an indication that at least some patrons wanted to get their full money's worth. In practice, however, it seems that the contracts were not terribly effective; for there are examples of pictures delivered late, and — in at least one case — the hands of assistants are clearly seen on an altarpiece whose contract bound the artist to work alone. The legalistic quality of these contracts and their numerous clauses reflect the businesslike manner in which the patrons dealt with the artists. Hardly anything could be further from the present-day relation between those who make works of art and those who buy them.[19]

In most cases the artist did not choose the subject he was to paint. Very likely that would be decided by the patron, or by the patron in consultation with a religious advisor, or by the authorities of the church for which the work was destined; actually very little is known about this process.[20] Thus the artist often had to work with a prescribed set of types. While he could rearrange the stock figures and props, he was seldom able to do away with them or replace them with new ones. The continuity in religious imagery is another reason for the gradual evolution of Trecento and Quattrocento painting. It also makes the study of the these pictures fascinating, for the variations on fixed types (sometimes interrupted by great innovators) have the subtle beauty of variations on musical themes. Such continuity and tradition are, of course, very alien to contemporary ideas in art.

Present-day attitudes toward paintings are very unlike those held by the patrons of the late Trecento and early Quattrocento. To a great extent art today has no utilitarian function; paintings are bought in art galleries almost solely for their visual excitement or for the prestige they give their owners. By contrast, in the fourteenth and fifteenth centuries pictures were almost always functional. Religious images had a special role, for they were intimately connected with liturgical rites: altarpieces were placed on altar tables before which the holy ceremonies were performed; frescoes decorated the walls of chapels; and carved and painted figures of sacred personages stood on the walls of the church, oratory, town hall, hospital, and tabernacle. Secular paintings were attached to chests and decorated banners, armor, and other useful items.

Religious paintings were didactic images of the miraculous legends of Christianity. They were not seen simply as stimulating compositions of color and line but as mysterious, profoundly moving icons thought to embody some of the awesome power held by the holy figures they portrayed. There are numerous instances of painted or carved images performing miracles, and men were executed for profaning the Madonna's likeness, even on a Florentine coin.[21] The idea (of prehistoric origin) that the image of a person or thing conveyed some supernatural part of him or it is a vital part of the art of the Trecento and Quattrocento. This idea is so alien to us that we must constantly remind ourselves that earlier onlookers really saw the frescoes and panels as the sacred, visual embodiments of active supernatural forces. They must have been thought of first as powerful iconic images and then as works of art. The very act of looking at an altarpiece must have carried with it a vast number of associations now lost.

The supernatural quality of the image was so powerful, so overwhelming, that very little was written about pictures as works of art.[22] Although artists are sometimes mentioned, there is seldom a discussion of the visual properties of their art; that does not take place until the sixteenth century. But there can be no doubt that the works were also appreciated for their splendid form and subtle variety, qualities that will be evident as we now turn to the paintings themselves.

Masaccio
and the Art of
Early Renaissance
Florence

I.

The Last Quarter of the Trecento

TWO DIFFERENT WAYS of understanding and painting religious drama are seen in Giotto's fresco of the *Raising of Lazarus* (Plate 1) from the Arena Chapel (c.1306) and Giovanni da Milano's picture of the same subject (Plate 2) in the Rinuccini Chapel, Santa Croce, Florence (c.1365).[1]

In the earlier work, the figure of Christ, although placed at the left, is the center of the drama. His isolated hand sparks the miracle. The area immediately surrounding it seems filled with a powerful charge that actually performs the raising. The apostles behind Christ, the figures holding Lazarus, and the imploring sisters of the dead man all look in his direction. The composition is tightly built around the belief that Christ, the human god, alone creates the great miracle.

To turn from the fresco by Giotto to the one painted by Giovanni da Milano is to leave one world for another. Gone are the ordered calm and immediate clarity of Giotto's work. Christ, framed by black mountains behind, now appears in the exact center of the picture, yet the drama does not really revolve around him. Although he is certainly a powerful presence, one does not sense that he works the miracle by himself; wraithlike, he looks more the manifestation of some supernatural power than the divine human of Giotto's fresco. His gesture and glance are unfocused; the miraculous force is defused when compared with the very specific source of energy found in the Arena Chapel. There is no direct communication between Christ and Lazarus as there was in the rhythmic groupings in the Padua fresco. Giovanni's Lazarus, nearly dragged from his tomb by the attendant figures, seems frightened as he looks over his shoulder toward the phantasmic, impassive, towering Christ. Lazarus, too, seems spectral as his white cloaked body glides silently out of the sarcophagus.

At either side of the picture groups of figures watch the event. To the left a

1. Giotto, *Raising of Lazarus*. Padua, Arena Chapel.

knot of bearded men stand uncomfortably wedged in a city gate. Although their
hands signify their surprise at the miracle, their unfocused gaze and the stiffness
of their gestures make their actions ritualistic. The joy shown by the sister of
Lazarus next to the standing men is also stilted. The group to Christ's right
lacks expression, being composed of blank faces and a dense mass of haloes.
The several groups do not relate to each other. This work is compositionally
well balanced, but it imparts a disjointed feeling because it is not tied together
emotionally. How different is this from the Arena Chapel *Raising of Lazarus*,
where the dramatic center is the psychological focus of the entire composition.

These two frescoes are indicative of the differences between two eras of Florentine painting. However, the individual artists' personal conceptions and predilections will account for difference in outlook, regardless of the period in which they worked. But even after this important qualification is made, there remain certain characteristics — seen in many other paintings from the two periods — that allow us to see each fresco as representative of a specific time in Florentine art.

The art of Giotto introduced a monumental, extremely human treatment of religious drama set within a pictorial milieu of crystalline clarity. Giotto shattered forever the old iconic, abstracted language of his artistic ancestors and made religious painting immediate and direct. In the decade or so after his death, Giotto's followers, while building on his revolutionary foundation, modified the dramatic content of his pictures by lessening the intense emotional fervor of his stories and by introducing many extraneous but enjoyable details into their work.

2. Giovanni da Milano, *Raising of Lazarus*. Florence, Santa Croce.

Until around 1350, they changed his idiom by forging compositions that are spatially more ambiguous and less tightly tied to the central drama of the story. There is also an overall tendency to de-monumentalize architecture and figures while developing light, gayer, slightly more pastel palettes. Although Giotto's late paintings — especially the Peruzzi Chapel frescoes — may have set the stage for such developments, it was such creative followers as Maso di Banco, Bernardo Daddi, and Taddeo Gaddi who brought them to fruition.[2] It is difficult to generalize on the reactions of Giotto's heirs to their great forerunner, since each took from him what he wanted. But even though these artists were not slavish imitators (on the contrary, their pictures are often highly inventive), their work more or less followed the major principles that Giotto had laid down as early as the first frescoes in the Arena Chapel.

The artists who came to the fore around 1350 were more removed from Giotto. When they began to work he was considered the most important artist Florence had ever produced, and pictures by an entire generation of painters strongly under his sway decorated the walls and altars of scores of Tuscan churches. Already he had become one of Florence's most important historical figures.

The men working in the 1350s — Andrea di Cione (called Orcagna), his brother Nardo, and Giovanni da Milano, to name three—created an art whose form and content often differed substantially from that of Giotto and his followers, as the comaprison just made between the frescoes of Giotto and Giovanni da Milano indicates.[3]

It has been suggested that the Tuscan economic and agricultural failures of the 1340s, combined with the plague of 1348, were responsible for the new style, but at the present stage of research no single solution to the problem — if indeed one exists — presents itself.[4] A study of the origins and development of the Florentine style that arose around mid-century is outside the scope of this book. It will be necessary, therefore, to limit discussion to several important works by the major painters of the generation c.1350 –1370 in order to determine the most salient characteristics of this pivotal period, between Giotto and his followers and the generation of painters that came to maturity after 1370.

Nardo di Cione is one of the most noteworthy figures from the decades of the mid-Trecento.[5] His beautiful, lyrical Madonnas and majestic, if somewhat hierarchical, frescoes were to influence Florentine painting for the rest of the century. Nardo began the Santa Croce triptych (Santa Croce Museum, Florence; dated 1365) representing the Madonna and Child flanked by SS. Gregory and Job (Plate 3), but it was completed by his younger brother Jacopo, who was a much inferior artist.[6] A comparison of this painting and Bernardo Daddi's San Pancrazio Madonna (Plate 4) of around 1340 (Uffizi, Florence) reveals some of

3. Nardo and Jacopo di Cione, Altarpiece, Florence. Santa Croce
Museum.

the differences that set Nardo's generation apart from that of Daddi and his
contemporaries.[7]

Nardo's Madonna is marked by an exclusiveness characteristic of several of
his works. The outline of the Madonna and Child is closed; they do not pene-
trate space, nor does space flow freely into their tightly packed forms. The basic
shapes of the two figures appear to be organized in a series of planes: the Madonna's knees form one, the knees of the Child another, and so forth. These
planes make movement back into space somewhat choppy and tend to be space-
denying rather than form-creating. In short, we do not easily enter into the
world of this lovely young Madonna and her son.

On the Madonna's left side and along the silhouette of Job the sharply folded
robes make a jagged pattern against the background gold. The technique differs from earlier Florentine painting in that there is no attempt to form smooth

4. Bernardo Daddi, San Pancrazio Altarpiece (detail). Florence, Uffizi.

transitions from figure to background space. In fact, there is an absolute dichotomy between the modeled, limited depth and surface of the saint's body
and the flat, gleaming gold.

Daddi's Madonna is more accessible and inviting. She is firmly and clearly
placed in the throne, and its projecting sides both flank her body and delineate
the space surrounding her. The circle of angels kneeling and standing around
the throne carve out space and direct the eye toward the central figure. The
corpulence and weight of this picture are missing from Nardo's panel, where
there is much bold, highly patterned material (on the carpet, on the Child's
robe, and on the throne seat) that breaks up the surface and makes the several
areas spatially ambiguous. There are patterns on the robes in Daddi's painting,
but they are not as large or as flat, and they are much more convincingly integrated into the construction of both figure and object. Daddi's picture repre-

5. Giotto's Shop, Bologna Polyptych. Bologna, Pinacoteca Nazionale.

sents one of the last examples of the idiom common to the first half of the Trecento. Although Daddi himself was to modify this style slightly, the San Pancrazio Madonna contains the spatial openness, stability, clarity, and directness that were often the hallmarks of the early followers of Giotto.[8]

Another example of the change in style between Nardo's generation and Bernardo's is found in a comparison of the Bologna polyptych (Plate 5; Pinacoteca, Bologna, signed "Giotto" but probably a product of his shop around 1335) and the S.S. Annunziata altarpiece (Plate 6; Accademia, Florence), painted c.1360 by Orcagna.[9]

Both altarpieces have a Madonna and Child in the central panel and two wings on each side. However the polyptych from Giotto's circle, albeit of lower quality, is more closely related to the spectator's world than is the SS. Annunziata altarpiece.[10] Its saints really seem to stand on the ground, while those in the later work appear to hover. Orcagna's saints are also more isolated, more lost in their individual thoughts and, consequently, less aware of the onlooker than are those of the Bologna altarpiece. Though quite monumental and brilliantly conceived, they have a brittleness that is characteristic of the period in which they were painted. This is not true of the Bologna saints, who move with a vigor, weight, and confidence typical of the first half of the Trecento.

6. Orcagna, Altarpiece.
Florence, Accademia.

The earlier Bologna Madonna is a compelling image who sits firmly centered in her throne. One senses her bulk through the rough triangle formed by the expansion of her body from head, to carefully articulated knees, down to the wide base created by the folded hem of her robe.

The extremely beautiful Madonna of the SS. Annunziata altarpiece does not project into the viewer's space; instead, the basic location of her form is somewhat ambiguous. Her position on the seat and in the picture's space is hard to define. Surrounded by a number of patterned fields and fronted by two hovering angels, she appears out of the spectator's reach. Her wistful face and wide, unfocused eyes seem to indicate that she is not conscious of our presence. The masklike faces of the surrounding saints are typical of Orcagna and his circle.

In this altarpiece there once again exists a strong separation between the figure and the space surrounding it. The texture of the figure, its shape, and its illumination still retain much of the softness and volume common to works from the first half of the century, even if they are now contained in a structure made up of more simplified planes. But the sharp outlines of the bodies — especially the saints' — set the figures apart from their background in a most jarring and space-denying fashion. The smooth transition between the plastic bodies and the background of early Trecento painting has been modified, and the figures now clash with their milieu.

In many of the pictures from the mid-century, including the SS. Annunziata altarpiece, the holy actors are more withdrawn, both physically and psychologically, than in earlier paintings; there is less communication between the various personages. Often the Madonna and the saints regard the spectator and one another aloofly; the openness and easy interplay of most of the works of the first half of the century have been suppressed.

Along with differences in composition, space, and figure construction, there also occur marked changes in color between the two generations of painters. In the Arena Chapel Giotto used a rather simple but highly effective palette of blues, reds, creams, yellows, and several other clear, highly saturated colors. His Bardi Chapel (c.1325) also has a limited range of saturated colors and a restrained use of bright accents, but by the time of his frescoes in the Peruzzi Chapel his ideas about color had changed. In this late fresco cycle (c.1330) there is a slightly greater range of color. More important, the paintings seem to have been less saturated, more pastel-like (they are badly damaged): pinks, greens, yellows, and light blues appear throughout, adding a note of fanciful brightness not found in any previous works. The older Giotto valued color not only as a building block in pictorial composition but also for its intrinsic decorative nature.

The followers of Giotto seem to have found inspiration in the Peruzzi frescoes rather than in the cycles of the Bardi or Arena chapels. Taddeo Gaddi and Bernardo Daddi, among others, enlivened their narratives and achieved a notable overall lightness with a palette containing numerous pastel blues, greens, and pinks. They also introduced large areas of white and cream into their frescoes. Shot colors (the highlights or shadows on one color are indicated not by employing white or by increasing or decreasing the color's value but by using another color) are also common in these pictures; the highlights of a blue, for instance, might be indicated by yellow or green or pink. These color preferences and harmonies are also found, in slightly more subdued form, in many of the tempera panels by Giotto's heirs. This palette is a perfect complement to the open and accessible forms of Giotto and the generation of painters that first adapted various parts of his style.[11]

The palette of Orcagna and his circle is, in many ways, different from that of the first half of the Trecento. Some of the carefully constructed color harmonies are abandoned, and in their place one finds a series of vividly contrasting colors. For example, instead of the gradual transitions from cream to brown to yellow, greens are placed next to sharp pinks and acid reds. Such juxtapositions energize the surface of the picture, sometimes making the reading of form and space quite difficult. The nature of the individual color also changes. In paintings executed from mid-century to around 1370 a number of smoky, highly saturated colors make jarring contrasts to large flat areas of patterned gold and cloth. In sizable frescoes, like those by Andrea da Firenze in the Spanish Chapel (Santa Maria Novella, Florence), the walls are enlivened with a wide range of colors (brown, green, rose, pink, yellow), which catch the spectator's glance and pull it jerkily across the wall. In Andrea's pictures, as in many other works from the period, color is not used as an aid in the construction of form but rather has its own life and rhythm. In many of the paintings by the first generation after Giotto, color is used almost exclusively in the service of shaping the human body or architecture, but in the period c.1350–1370 it is employed as a much more decorative element. In these later works various colors repeat across the surface of the painting, but these repeats are constructed without much consideration for the picture's narrative. This break between form and color parallels the increased formal and psychological disunity of Florentine painting.[12]

In the early 1370s, several important Florentine painters — including Agnolo Gaddi, Antonio Veneziano, Spinello Aretino, and Niccolò di Pietro Gerini — started their careers. This new generation of artists (which worked into the early Quattrocento) would help redirect the art of Florence away from the prevailing idiom of mid-century. But this development would not take place suddenly, for all these painters had grown up under the influence of Nardo and Orcagna and their circles. The painting of the 1350s and 1360s was the modern art of their youth, and its influence on them as young men immersed in the imitative workshop system cannot be overlooked.

Agnolo Gaddi seems to have been trained initially in the workshop of his father, Taddeo Gaddi (died 1366), a pupil of Giotto for several decades.[13] Agnolo is first recorded working as an assistant in Rome in 1369.[14] All his early painting has disappeared, but the *Coronation of the Virgin* (Plate 7; National Gallery, London; c.1380), one of his first extant panels, clearly reveals that his stylistic origins lay in great part in the the circle of Orcagna and his brother Nardo.

In the *Coronation* Christ and the Virgin seem to sit on a wide throne whose back forms a triangle behind the figures. One must say *seem* because the position of the two bodies is unclear and one is not really sure exactly how they are seated on the throne. They wear identical white robes with gold embroidery that form a patterned surface extending from the Virgin's shoulders, across her knees, over to Christ's knees, across the lower part of his body, and then upward to his back and shoulders. However, the figures themselves are separated in several ways: their bent bodies do not touch except where the patterned robes meet near the knees; they sit at opposite ends of the throne; their eyes do not make contact. The precise but unfeeling faces of the principal actors create a

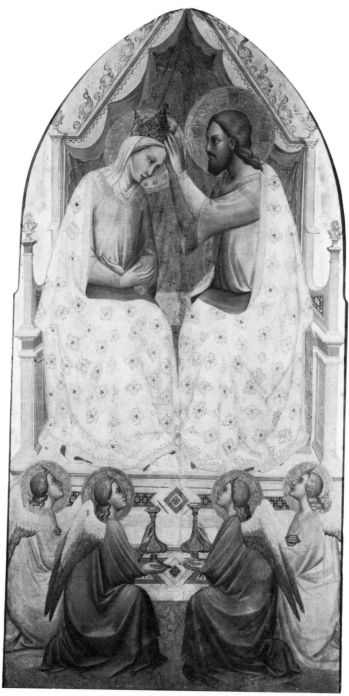

7. Agnolo Gaddi, *Coronation of the Virgin*. London, National Gallery.

riruallike atmosphere. The four angels kneeling below gaze reverently at the Virgin and Christ but seem to have little contact with the actual Coronation. They are not developed in space; the positions of their bodies only suggest but do not physically describe a semicircular arrangement. Gaddi has made only a minimal attempt to articulate their forms under the robes. The sharply folded garments follow the main outlines of the bodies beneath, but there is a feeling for flat pattern that is of greater importance. The arabesques of embroidered drapery exist more for their own decorative sake than as indicators of form underneath.

Another *Coronation of the Virgin* (Plate 8; now National Gallery, Washington, D.C.) was painted by Gaddi about ten years after the picture now in London. There are several notable changes between the two works indicative of an overall change in Florentine style. One of the most important is the scale. In the later picture the figures of Christ and the Virgin have been enlarged; instead of covering only half the surface of the panel, they now occupy about three-quarters of it. This change brings them closer to the onlooker and makes them more immediate. The throne has been done away with, and the two figures have been moved closer together. Christ and the Virgin are no longer so bent over; their actions seem much less ritualistic; there is more intimacy and warmth in their expressions and gestures. They are united by patterned white robes that now emphasize the nearness of the two bodies. In the London picture the cloth seems to exist only on the picture plane. On the Washington Virgin and Child the larger pattern now bends and pulls with the movement of the robes and conforms to the actions of the body beneath. There is a sense of the figure, for one observes the protrusion and recession of volumes in space. This new-found feeling for the weight and spatial existence of materials is seen in the cloth of honor behind the Virgin and Christ, which hangs heavily, folded over at the top, and now seemingly obeys the law of gravity.

The poses and attitudes of the Washington angels are very different from those of the London panel. The former make a semicircle broken only by the void in the middle giving access to the background. Their clear, lively movements and varied postures—note the overlapping of the bodies—are, like the Christ and Virgin, spatially well defined. The increased use of light and shade for modeling the faces and drapery also gives the figures a degree of corporeality lacking in the earlier picture.

The changes between the two paintings by Gaddi are interesting because they show that his work, which originated in the mid-Trecento idiom, developed into something quite different. While the earlier *Coronation* exhibits many of the characteristics of the circles of Orcagna and Nardo di Cione — a generally

8. Agnolo Gaddi, *Coronation of the Virgin*. Washington, National
Gallery of Art, Samuel H. Kress Collection.

9. Agnolo Gaddi, *St. John Baptizing the Philosopher and St. John Changing the Sticks and Stones*. Florence, Santa Croce.

closed figure construction with an ambiguous relation between figure and surrounding space and an isolated, distanced image—the later picture is more immediate, psychologically closer to the spectator, and less aloof. In the Washington picture the principal actors interact both with us and with the angels below to a much greater degree than in the London panel.

Gaddi's paintings of the legend of St. John the Evangelist in the Castellani Chapel, Santa Croce, Florence (c.1380) are the artist's first-known works in fresco, although he may have executed paintings in this medium earlier. In *St. John Baptizing the Philosopher and St. John Changing the Sticks and Stones* (Plate 9) Gaddi has created a rational, orderly picture. The two scenes are divided in the center by a pivotal group placed between the repeated figures of St. John; the division is further emphasized by the large church placed behind the central group. The figures at the sides facing or moving toward the center act as brackets, closing the composition at either end. Groups flanking the events in the left and the right halves of the picture form or suggest semicircular configurations. In other words, the fresco is full of solid, carefully planned geometric figures that give it order and stability.

Like the fresco painters of the early part of the century, Gaddi carefully constructed the background to create a limited spatial recession. He accomplished that by putting a wall behind the left side of the fresco and placing a low mountain range behind the right half of the picture. The figures themselves do not carve out much space and are located on a rather narrow strip of ground. All

10. Andrea da Firenze, Altar Wall. Florence, Spanish Chapel, Santa
Maria Novella.

this is done to keep the figures, architecture, and landscape up near the picture
plane. Fresco is wall painting, and the traditional approach to the medium
stressed its role as decoration that respected the basic solidity and flatness of the
surface it covered. The creation of deep pictorial space would have shattered its
decorative role by punching a fictive hole in the wall.

In his Castellani frescoes, however, Gaddi did not work in the tradition of his
immediate artistic ancestors, who had broken with the more rational and clear
compositions of Giotto, Taddeo Gaddi, and Daddi. For example, the frescoes
by Andrea da Firenze in the Spanish Chapel, painted in the 1360s, are very
different from Gaddi's Castellani pictures.[15]

In the first place, the division of the various stories on the walls of the Spanish
Chapel is often unclear (see Plate 10). On the altar wall are the *Way to Calvary*
(lower left), the *Crucifixion* (above the arch), and *Christ Harrowing Hell* (lower
right), but at first glance it seems to be a single huge, confused scene. Furthermore, one has the distinct impression that the narratives are not developed back
into some limited space behind the picture plane but up the surface of the wall.

Also perplexing are the sudden, marked shifts in scale. The city in the *Way to Calvary* is populated by tiny people who appear like toys against the figures in the procession. Andrea's disregard of rational spatial concepts is apparent in the cavalcade winding its way behind the wall of the city: Do the figures ride or walk? Where are they, and where are they going?

A multiplicity of forms confuses the spectator's eyes; scores of figures, many of them extraneous, appear in each episode. A wealth of highly visible detail — from the robe fold to architectural ornament — is everywhere. Color, distributed spasmodically, is not a helpful definer of form.

How different is Andrea's painting from Gaddi's Castellani fresco, a product of the following generation. The enigmatic, unsure quality of Andrea's work parallels many other pictures from around mid-century, while the more stable, more comprehensible construction of Gaddi's fresco is echoed by his Washington altarpiece and other painting from the last quarter of the century. In several major compositional components (shape, space, color), the Castellani fresco represents a remarkable change — a partial return to the older tradition of Florentine art.

In Gaddi's last fresco cycle, in the Cappella della Sacra Cintola in the Duomo at Prato, executed during the 1390s, the artist's style moved even further away from that of the generation preceding him.[16] In the Prato *Presentation of the Virgin* (Plate 11) Gaddi shows increased interest in the portrayal of space. Set at a slight diagonal to the picture plane, the temple gently recedes from the middle foreground toward the right background. The wall in the center background and the building to the left with the balcony are also placed at slight angles to the picture plane. Gaddi has taken great care to depict the inside of the structure; he is now very anxious to create a more complicated space. Architecture is used not only as a delineator of action but also as an integral part of the narrative with its own importance and interest. This exploration of the spatial complexity and individual nature of buildings is not unlike late works by Giotto and his followers, especially Taddeo Gaddi;[17] it also anticipates some of the more revolutionary investigations into the nature of objects in space that will occur during the early Quattrocento.

Gaddi's conception of the body has changed sharply from the Castellani Chapel. The figures are not quite as thin; and there is an increased interest in their mass moving through space. This new attitude is seen most clearly in the two kneeling girls at the lower right and in the three priests at the top of the stairs. Of course, not all the foreshortening is correct or entirely logical, but here Gaddi is struggling with problems that did not occupy or even interest the painters of the generation before him. This search for the convincing physical

11. Agnolo Gaddi, *Presentation of the Virgin*. Prato, Duomo.

delineation of solids in space is also a hallmark of many of Gaddi's artistic contemporaries.

In the Prato paintings there appears a new interest in a type of drama, reminiscent of the early years of the Trecento, that foreshadows some of the best religious narrative of the first decades of the Quattrocento. In contrast to many pictures from the middle of the century, the paintings now exhibit a real interest in human drama. Obviously concerned about their child, the Virgin's parents manifest their emotions through their postures and gestures. The Virgin looks back at them while mounting the steps toward the monumental priest, her uncertainty expressed by her location halfway up the stairs and by the duality of her situation as she moves forward while looking back. One feels that she will be welcomed kindly, however, for the middle priest — despite his being an imposing figure — extends his arms in a sign of greeting. A very different version of the same subject is Orcagna's relief (Plate 12) on the tabernacle in Or San Michele, Florence, carved during the late 1350s. The relief, which is

12. Orcagna, *Presentation of the Virgin.*
Florence, Or San Michele.

placed in a very different context than that of Gaddi's fresco, is an essay in frontality and isolation. The triangle made by the priest, the kneeling figures of Joachim and Anna, and the gridlike structure formed by the horizontals and verticals of the temple bring the objects up to the surface, creating an abstraction that almost overpowers the story. The Virgin appears on the steps in full frontal position as she turns her body away from the looming priest who mechanically blesses her. The relief is severely flat and rigid; it is almost as though the entire drama is a ritual centering on the small, isolated figure of the Virgin. The typically human qualities of the scene are surpressed in favor of a rather harsh visual symmetry.[18] Orcagna and Gaddi, two artists who are in many ways representative of their generations, have visualized and set down the same story in quite dissimilar ways.

Gaddi's development was paralleled by that of Spinello Aretino, a painter born around 1350 in the Tuscan town of Arezzo, southeast of Florence. We do not know with whom Spinello trained, but his master may have been an Aretine, since his first works, done during the 1370s, are located in Arezzo. He became a popular artist and was the recipient of several important commissions.[19] His earliest documented work still extant is the Monteoliveto altarpiece, which seems to have been commissioned originally for the convent of Santa Maria Nuova in Rome in 1384.[20] Like all of his known early pictures, it shows him clearly under the sway of the Florentine idiom (in the 1380s he matriculated in the Florentine painters guild), and one can deduce from its style that the young Spinello was influenced by Nardo di Cione and his closest followers.

The *Coronation of the Virgin* (Plate 13), the pinnacle originally above the main panel of the Monteoliveto altarpiece (now in the Siena Pinacoteca), is closer in style and spirit to Gaddi's Washington *Coronation* than to most works from around the mid-Trecento. The substantial figures of the Virgin and Christ form the focus of the composition as their arched bodies create an oval rhythm at the center of the panel. Because Spinello has carefully defined the various planes of their bodies, they have a noticeable spatial existence. There seems to be little doubt that he was aided here by a study of Giotto's style; the directness of the body gestures and the bulk of the forms would have been impossible without reference beyond Orcagna, back to the first few decades of the fourteenth century.[21]

There is still, of course, much of the style of the generation of artists active just before Spinello. The *mandorla* ringed by seraphim was popular in the painting of the third quarter of the Trecento; then it often blocked spatial recession while isolating the enclosed figures from the rest of the composition.[22] Spinello has denied it this function, for the angels at the bottom hold it as though it was some very weighty, tangible object overlapping their heads and haloes. This panel exhibits a harmony and unity lacking in most of the works from the 1350s and 1360s.

A later Madonna by Spinello (Plate 14), in St. Louis, demonstrates his increasing compositional mastery. Probably the center of a dispersed polyptych, this panel is remarkable for its straightforward simplicity. The large, monumental Madonna is the absolute center of the work, the object of all attention, including the spectator's. She is fixed in space by the strongly foreshortened throne, which acts as the visual anchor of her stable form. Her shape is opposed by the very corporeal Child, who twists through space while grabbing his mother's cloak. The picture is a subtle mixture of action and rest.

The foreshortened bodies of the two angels, unusually large in relation to the Madonna, lead the way into the picture's space as their upturned heads direct the onlooker's glance toward the mother and child. The angels' bulk and solidity are almost totally unprecedented in painting of the period c.1350–1375. Like Agnolo Gaddi, Spinello was fascinated by the movement of heavy figures through a definable space.

13. Spinello Aretino, *Coronation of the Virgin*.
Siena, Pinacoteca Nazionale.

The overall impression of Spinello's St. Louis panel is one of warmth, directness, and accessibility. The spectator feels in touch with the holy figures, who
occupy a comprehensible space related to his own world. This feeling is not
uncommon among many of the paintings produced during the first three or
four decades of the Trecento, and, in fact, the immediacy of Spinello's Virgin
has its origin in paintings from the first decades of the fourteenth century, such
as Giotto's great Ognissanti Madonna. Such direct imagery was often not a part
of the idiom of the mid-century paintings, where stylistic and psychological
barriers were erected to bar the spectator from too-close contact with sacred
images meant to be worshipped only from a distance. There can be little doubt
that pictures from the early Trecento aided Spinello in overcoming the isolation
and rigidity of the style that flourished just before his own.

14. Spinello Aretino, *Madonna and Child*.
St. Louis, St. Louis Art Museum.

Spinello's study of the masters of the early fourteenth century, especially Giotto, is apparent in several of his frescoes. In one of Spinello's last works, the *Submission of Barbarossa to Pope Alexander III* (Plate 15; Siena, Palazzo Pubblico; 1407), one sees the search for a simplified composition; if one compares it with any fresco from around the middle of the Trecento, it will be readily apparent that the story is here told with a minimum of figures and a sparing use of detail.

Each figure is a substantial being standing firmly and decisively on the ground; the columnar legs, thick arms, and broad backs describe men of weight and gravity. They are very different from the figures in Andrea da Firenze's Spanish Chapel cycle, where the much less substantial actors have an uncertain relation with the ground. Like Gaddi's personages in Prato, the figures in Spinello's fresco participate purposefully in the religious drama.

Spinello's use of color is similar to Gaddi's. A limited number of highly saturated colors, which aid in the building of form, are spread across the surface, creating a balanced, even coloration, very unlike the palette of many frescoes from the 1350s and 1360s, where color is often used in a much more decorative

15. Spinello Aretino, *Submission of Barbarossa to Pope Alexander III.*
Siena, Palazzo Pubblico.

manner. This disparity reveals certain attitudes toward painting. In the Siena fresco, Spinello has consciously striven for a clearly articulated, harmonious composition. To him, color was a tool; if used carefully, it could help form the bulk of the figures while balancing the narrative by a measured distribution of hue throughout the picture. But Spinello's goals were not those of the artists of Nardo's time, who were generally interested in a more distant and more formally complex imagery. Instead of using color as a building block for space and solid, they employed it to break up form and to deemphasize spatial volume. Once again it is apparent that Spinello (an artist of the generation of the 1370s) was intent upon redirecting painting away from the idiom of his predecessors and toward a new interpretation of the holy stories — an interpretation that depended in no small measure on the art of the early Trecento.

Slightly older than Agnolo Gaddi and Spinello, Antonio Veneziano was another important painter who worked during the last quarter of the fourteenth century.[23] He is first documented in Siena in the late 1360s, but there seems to be little doubt that he received his training in Florence, perhaps with Taddeo Gaddi or a follower of Maso di Banco.

Antonio's only signed work (dated 1388) is a panel of the *Flagellation of Christ* (Plate 16) in San Niccolò Reale, Palermo. Below the *Flagellation* is a long list of the members of the flagellant confraternity that commissioned it. This type of panel is rare, although there must have been others like it; flagellant societies, only marginally tolerated by Trecento civic authorities, were often disbanded.[24]

In the triangular format of the *Flagellation* Christ stands tied to a column that divides the space exactly in half. To either side are the flagellators, and at the ends of the triangle are the members of the confraternity, dressed in the hooded white robes usually worn by such societies. All the action takes place on a shallow ground plane that is stopped by the background gold. It is amazing to see how Antonio has worked within this very limiting shape. Instead of reinforcing the confining spatial possibilities of the triangle, he has chosen partially to negate them. The hooded figures have been turned into abstracted units that twist and turn into space: observe the way the figures to the right of the right flagellator are foreshortened, and note the contorted body of the man in the lower right corner who whips himself. Each of these forms creates a sizable amount of volume and space. The figures of Christ's tormentors are also wonderfully articulated. The body of the man on the right moves through space in a graceful, convincing fashion, his carefully delineated form clearly demonstrating that the action is taking place in a three-dimensional setting. Sometimes — in the hand of the flagellator to the left or in the hooded heads — the

16. Antonio Veneziano, *Flagellation of Christ*. Palermo, San Niccolò Reale.

figures actually overlap the punchwork of the border, creating the impression that they exist outside it, somewhere in front of the painted surface of the work.

The small figures in the medallions of the Palermo picture seem to be greatly influenced by works from the early Trecento. Their bulk, solidity, and unity are close to the style of Maso di Banco or of the early Taddeo Gaddi, two artists strongly under the spell of Giotto.[25]

The same concern for solidity and unity is seen in another of Antonio's panels (c.1390), which may represent the *Apostles at the Assumption* (Plate 17). In this fragment from an altarpiece (now in the Staatliches Lindenau-Museum, Altenburg),[26] Antonio is so concerned with foreshortening the faces that they are often flattened and awkward. Once again the field for the figures is very restricted; however, as in the Palermo *Flagellation*, one feels a considerable expansion of space as the apostles move backward. The overlapping of bodies, faces, and haloes acts as part of the bridge carrying the spectator's eye from the

17. Antonio Veneziano, *Apostles at the Assumption*(?). Altenburg, Staatliches Lindenau-Museum.

foot of Peter at the lower edge of the picture to the mountain range in the background.

The Altenburg saints are the cousins of those by Gaddi in Prato and by Spinello in Siena. Their broadly articulated bodies move in a slow, decisive fashion while their lionlike heads turn to look with serious concentration toward the now missing scene that was originally the center of the altarpiece. Antonio's brush has formed the entire surface of the panel with an economy that is indeed unusual. The basic simplification and abstraction of his forms are a harbinger of future Florentine art.

Antonio's pictures reveal that he was a very different artist than his immediate Florentine predecessors. His paintings in the Camposanto at Pisa — his only surviving frescoes — demonstrate that his straightforward narratives and formal directness are not a continuation of the more spatially constricted, ambiguous work of the painters of mid-century. His art has in it much of the same searching for simplicity and clarity (not always achieved) that one finds in the works of Spinello, Agnolo Gaddi, and several other painters of the same generation. By the 1370s all these men had received their training and had begun their first independent works. Collectively, their painting is a milestone in the history of Florentine art, for it exhibits a decided shift away from the style of mid-century, both back toward the early Trecento and forward into the new century. They moved the formal and psychological interpretation of religious drama and image from the iconic isolation of the circle of Orcagna to a new, more human, direct, and understandable world. And it is during the period in which they painted (the last quarter of the Trecento) that the stage was set for some of the most important developments of the coming century.

Agnolo Gaddi, Spinello Aretino, and Antonio Veneziano were the most innovative and progressive painters of their generation, but they do not represent all of Florentine art. There were others who evolved more slowly (or not at all) out of the idiom of the middle of the fourteenth century. Giovanni del Biondo and Niccolò di Pietro Gerini were two painters whose work demonstrates a more gradual movement away from the stylistic environment of the middle of the Trecento.

Giovanni del Biondo was slightly older than the artists just discussed; his name appeared on a work dated 1360, and he is mentioned in Florence from 1359.[27] He seems to have been an apprentice in the shop of Nardo di Cione, for in the late 1350s he painted several figures in Nardo's fresco cycle in the Strozzi Chapel, Santa Maria Novella, Florence. These rigidly frontal, wide-eyed saints are squarely within the idiom of his master. But in his later works his style shows a number of noteworthy changes. His charming *Madonna and Child* (Plate 18) in the Siena Pinacoteca (signed and dated 1377) is quite unlike

18. Giovanni del Biondo, *Madonna and Child*. Siena, Pinacoteca
Nazionale.

19. Giovanni del Biondo, *Annunciation*. Florence, Galleria
dell'Ospedale degli Innocenti.

anything from Nardo's circle, and its simple modesty recalls some of the most
intimate Madonnas of the early Trecento, such as Bernardo Daddi's or Taddeo
Gaddi's. In their closeness to the observer and in the plasticity of their rounded
shapes, the two figures are immediate and palpable, unlike most of Giovanni's
earlier work. The wonderful intertwining of the silhouettes, the wistful expression on the Virgin's face, and the infant pudginess of Christ make one think of
several Madonnas by Ambrogio Lorenzetti, the most innovative Sienese artist
of the early Trecento.

   As the century wore on Giovanni's work became more massive and direct. A
good example of a large altarpiece by him is the *Annunciation* (Plate 19), dated
1385, in the Gallery of the Ospedale degli Innocenti in Florence. Although still
quite flat, the Annunciation group moves in a spatially well defined room that
has its origins in the first part of the century, perhaps also in works by Ambrogio Lorenzetti that Giovanni may have known. In this gray architecture enlivened by pink and green decoration Giovanni strives to construct a simple, clear,
spatial milieu. His figure types are also straightforward but not always three-
dimensionally successful. For example, one feels that there has been a real at-

tempt to move the Virgin's body back into space and to make the angel's wing recede.

In the harmonious palette there is little of the clashing color seen in the art of Giovanni's teachers. Deep red, blue, mustard yellow, gray, and pink appear in large areas of the work. A gay, almost lighthearted, feeling emanates from the picture.

A basic clarity is apparent in the artist's handling of form: large areas of un-modulated color give the work a stability absent from much of the painting by the generation working around mid-century. The basis of Giovanni's idiom — his early training with Nardo — conditions every part of his art, but it is clear that in the Innocenti *Annunciation* he is striving for newer, more coherent ideals; ideals that he held in common with his fellow artists of the last quarter of the Trecento. Although Giovanni remained a spiritual pupil of Nardo to the end of his career, his work incorporates some of the developments seen in the evolution of Agnolo Gaddi, Spinello Aretino, and Antonio Veneziano. With Giovanni, however, the changes are never so severe or so far-reaching; his work remains as an enjoyable record of a basically conservative artist.

Like Giovanni del Biondo, Niccolò di Pietro Gerini seems to have been slightly older than the more progressive painters discussed above.[28] Since his early work exhibits the strong influence of Taddeo Gaddi, it is quite possible that he may have had some training in that artist's shop. Gerini is first mentioned in 1369 and heard of until 1415. He was a prolific painter, who often executed works in collaboration with other artists, and seems to have been a specialist in joint projects.[29] Collaboration by two independent masters was rare (as we shall see in chapter 5) and seems never to have taken place on single fresco cycles. Overall, Gerini's painting is perhaps the least attractive of the late Trecento artists' work; nonetheless it is important for what it reveals about the less-inventive painters of the last quarter of the fourteenth century in Florence.

Gerini's best panel is the large *Entombment and Ascension* (Plate 20), c. 1390, in the church of San Carlo dei Lombardi, Florence. In this extremely solemn work both scenes are represented with fitting restraint and dignity. The slow-weaving frieze of tall, elegant people across the picture plane sets the basic rhythm. The measured bending of heads, the interval of uplifted hands, and the space between the actors are constructed with some skill. The stiff, elongated Christ forms a prominent, rigid horizontal that complements the sarcophagus but contrasts with the much more varied vertical group behind. In the panel's gable is a fully frontal ascending Christ enclosed in a *mandorla*; his abstractly patterned robe and wide, staring, symmetrical eyes immediately recall works by Nardo di Cione and Andrea da Firenze.

However, on closer observation one can see that this seemingly stiff picture

20. Niccolò di Pietro Gerini, *Entombment and Ascension*. Florence,
San Carlo dei Lombardi.

contains several characteristics that we have associated with the more innovative of Gerini's contemporaries. Especially noteworthy are the broad foreshortened heads of the figures immediately behind Christ, where Gerini has attempted to project the forms both into and out of the picture's space. The extended bodies, draped in voluminous, complicated robes, have some weight, and their positions on the ground line seem certain.

A study of the palette is also revealing. The sharp red-orange of the Magdalene's robe or the pink of the figure at Christ's feet — and several other colors — are reminiscent of the colors of mid-century. But one does not feel that the colors or their combination are so visually grating or physically disturbing as those of Orcagna and his followers. There is in Gerini's painting a toning down of the harsher coloration of the previous generation of painters. His *Entombment and Ascension* is, in many ways, a picture standing between the idiom of the mid-Trecento and the new style of the years c.1375–1400.

A fresco cycle in San Francesco, Prato, seems to be Gerini's last work in that medium; its date is uncertain, but on the basis of its style it appears to be from the late 1390s. These paintings seem to clarify the artist's previous pictorial language. His ideas about the construction of narrative have changed; there is an overall simplification in both his use of space and the figures placed within it. A good example of this is found in the *Martyrdom of St. Matthew* (Plate 21), where Gerini has used architecture to define the various parts of the picture. To the left, the order for the saint's execution is given within an area backed by a large building whose bulk stops spatial movement and acts as a foil for the group of people standing before it. The martyrdom takes place at the right, within an open church placed very near the picture plane. This composition contrasts with the other side of the fresco, where the architecture appears only in the background. The strong positive-negative opposition between the two parts is smoothed by a soldier carrying the shield in the center; he blocks the void between the two sides and serves as a transition between them. The simple architecture conveys a strong sense of weight and place; the figures who occupy it are now quite large in proportion to it and to the overall size of the fresco. These size and scale characteristics are found in a number of other paintings from the late Trecento but are alien to most works from around the 1360s and 1370s.

Gerini has striven to achieve a simplification of his figure style. The praying saint, the fleeing man to his right, and the transitional figure with the shield — to name just three — are all conceived in an economical, broad manner. They are more organic than figures from Gerini's earlier works; there is even some attempt at a monumental, weighty treatment reminiscent of Agnolo

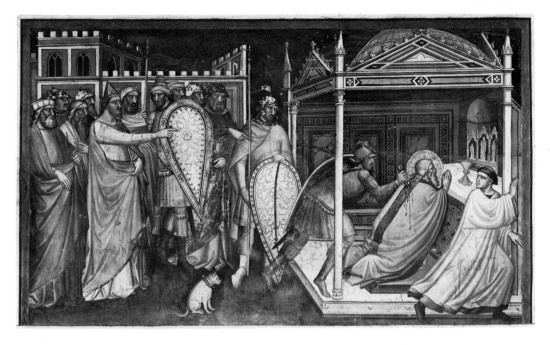

21. Niccolò di Pietro Gerini, *Martyrdom of St. Matthew.* Prato, San
Francesco.

Gaddi or Spinello Aretino. The stern figures with their straightforward movements are surely Gerini's response to the changing artistic climate of Florence
during the last decades of the Trecento.

The palette of this fresco cycle, like that of many contemporary works, also
shows a clarity and simplification. No longer are colors used as decoration, with
no ties to the formal constraints of narrative; instead they now work to define
the space and objects. The surfaces of the paintings are covered with shades of
pink, green, light purple, yellow, and some blue. Robes sometimes display shot
colors, and the architecture is often gray or pink or light green.

For many years the historical definition of the last quarter of the fourteenth
century has been unduly negative.[30] This period has been viewed as an artistically enervated one in which painters of little talent emptily repeated formulas
learned from their greater forerunners. Late Trecento painters are generally
considered the decadent ancestors of the important figures of the early Quattrocento. These ideas — which have remained basically unchallenged — are not
true, as any careful study of the best painters of the last twenty-five years of the
fourteenth century will reveal. There was considerable creativity as a few men
of talent redirected the painting of Florence away from the conception of reli-

gious art that had come to the fore during mid-century. These artists discovered their stylistic home not in the works of their teachers but in the works of their teachers' teachers. They looked back to the heroic years of the early Trecento, when the art of Florence was involved with the clear exposition of narrative and the creation of a very direct relation between the painted stories and those who prayed before them. This development from one idiom to another was gradual, for it was necessary for some painters — Agnolo Gaddi is a good example — first to free themselves from their early training, a task that took time given the workshop mentality common to all fourteenth-century artists.

By the end of the Trecento the style of the mid-century was no longer alive in Florence, and the new generation, which had destroyed it was itself giving way to yet another group of young painters. The older artists, however, left a vital legacy that would be utilized by their heirs. To see this as inconsequential is to misunderstand the artistic history of both the fourteenth and the fifteenth centuries.

II.

The Beginnings of the New Century: Painting c.1390-1420

DURING THE MATURITY of Agnolo Gaddi, Spinello Aretino, and Antonio Veneziano a new generation of artists was born. It was to be one of the most important in the history of Florence, for it included Lorenzo Ghiberti, Donatello, Nanni di Banco, Lorenzo Monaco, and Masolino, all of whom were destined to play key roles in the artistic history of the early Quattrocento. While these men were growing up, the modern idiom of their time was that of the last quarter of the Trecento. It was impossible for this art to have escaped their notice since their teachers were exponents of that very style. This fact has been often ignored, as some critics have sought to minimize the debt many artists of the early fifteenth century owed to the past in an attempt to make them appear more original than they really were. The corporate nature of the workship training that every artist received made borrowing and stylistic dependence necessary and natural. Without doubt some were more original than others, but nonetheless they all learned by copying; all were most conscious of their stylistic heritage as they fashioned works of traditional shape and function.[1]

This chapter will discuss the paintings of several artists who worked in Florence between roughly 1390 and 1420. For the most part, the style they brought into the new century was based on the late-Trecento idiom. The evolution away from the fourteenth century was slow but steady, and the art of the early 1400s contains much of the past.

Lorenzo Monaco was one of these artists.[2] There is a paucity of documentation concerning him, so the dates of his career and his chronological development are uncertain. It is generally supposed that he was born around 1370 and that he must have died around 1424. He was, as his name states, a monk, but he seems to have received his workshop training in a shop outside his own Camaldolese order. We do know that by 1391 he belonged to the monastery of Santa Maria degli Angeli in Florence and that a number of his commissions were destined for houses of his order. How his vocation affected his art is still unresolved, but certainly his vows and the practice of a monkish life must have had a profound impact on his conception of sacred art.

The *Agony in the Garden* (Plate 22; Accademia, Florence, originally in Santa Maria degli Angeli) appears to be among Monaco's earliest known works. The rocky background of the *Agony*, with its flinty, diagonal hills separating the space into individual units, is a direct borrowing from Agnolo Gaddi's Santa Croce Choir frescoes (completed about 1390), or something very similar. The strongly shifting scale — note how much larger Christ is than the figures in the foreground — and the division of the work by cliffs and a small stream into foreground and background make it likely that this panel dates from the last decade of the Trecento. The crisp, rather harsh facial features and sharply folded robes of Christ and the sleeping Apostles suggest the influence of Nardo di Cione (perhaps through the works of Niccolò di Pietro Gerini). Although this early work already demonstrates Lorenzo's considerable talent, it only hints at the stylistic path he was to follow later. After the stolid, expanded forms and choppy space of this picture, he was to create an elegant, fashionable style destined to have great effect on Florentine painting. He was soon to transfer the solid imagery of the generation of Agnolo Gaddi, Spinello Aretino, and Antonio Veneziano into a gracious, melodious, fantastic personal vision of celestial splendor.

The cut-out Crucifix (Plate 23) in the church of Santa Maria delle Vertighe, Monte San Savino (c.1415) is a good example of Lorenzo's later style.[3] We are at once struck by the fragile grace and weightlessness of the svelte, elongated Christ as he hangs on the cross. His isolation (there is no background of any sort and this type may be Lorenzo's invention) allows the artist to give free rein to his wonderful feeling for silhouette: the line extends from the sinuous arms (curving slowly where they meet the torso) down along the legs. Fascinated by the interplay of the body against the cross, Lorenzo has set up a number of strong rhythmic contrasts that enliven the work. Note, for instance, the relation between the horizontal of the cross bar and the diagonals formed by Christ's arms, and the way the gently curving legs contrast with the rigid vertical beam behind.

Monaco is in love with line. Not only does it play an important role in the overall shape of the figure, but Lorenzo's delicate handling of line lends an

22. Lorenzo Monaco, *Agony in the Garden*. Florence, Accademia.

23. Lorenzo Monaco, Crucifix. Monte San Savino,
Santa Maria delle Vertighe.

almost ethereal beauty to the loincloth or the hair or the fingers. A new sensibility is at work here. There is reason to suspect that Lorenzo was born in Siena, and it has been suggested that the great Sienese masters of line, such as Duccio or Simone Martini, may have influenced his work. There may be some validity to this theory although there can be no doubt that the basic foundation of Lorenzo's art is Florentine; and, in any case, it is not only in his art that such calligraphic interest is found during the early years of the Florentine Quattrocento.

While the basic vocabulary of the Monte San Savino Crucifix derives from the last years of the Trecento, the entire spirit of the work is quite different, as a comparison with Niccolò di Pietro Gerini's Crucifix (Plate 24), 1380, in Santa Croce, Florence, demonstrates.

Gerini's Christ is a heavy, bulky figure who sags limply on the cross; the silhouette is closed, the body echoing the vertical beam behind it. Musculature is indicated by rather rude contrasts of light and dark. The entire figure is completely under the control of gravity and is totally devoid of life.

24. Niccolò di Pietro Gerini, Crucifix. Florence, Santa Croce.

By contrast Lorenzo's Christ is a delicate, agile being. His body moves out into space much more, while a number of strong rhythms work within the figure itself; note the angles of the head and the legs. The Monte San Savino Christ is much thinner, more elongated, and more delicate than Gerini's. The latter seems more solid and earthbound, while Lorenzo's Christ appears almost to hover before the cross.

The loincloth is a good point of contrast between the two paintings. In Niccolò's, its filmy folds hug the body. In Lorenzo's work it seems to have a wind-blown life of its own, as it twists and turns away from Christ's hips, setting up yet another system of rhythms in this already rhythmically complex painting. Nowhere else in the picture does Lorenzo have an opportunity to express his feelings for line so freely; the loincloth is perhaps its most compelling element.

Nuance is one of the trademarks of Lorenzo's style. The beautiful modeling of the body and its remarkably subtle transitional passages between light and dark contrast strongly with the heavy-handed articulation of light on Gerini's

25. Lorenzo Monaco, Altarpiece. Florence, Accademia.

Christ. The fineness of the facial features, hair, and beard of Lorenzo's Christ make Gerini's (and most other Trecento pictures) look clumsy by comparison.

Although Lorenzo is a creature of the late Trecento, he has broken away from a great deal of the serious, monumental — occasionally overheavy — quality so characteristic of much of that art. His figures have a grace and lightness not seen in Florentine painting before his time, yet they are solid, three-dimensional beings with a corporeal existence. But so enlivened are they by Lorenzo's sensitive use of line and shape that they often appear to be from some magical world.

There is in all Lorenzo's art a rigorous control of line, color, and light that produces images of exquisite beauty. His pictures portray a somewhat distanced, idealized conception of Christianity in which delicate beings act with great restraint, dignity, and — above all — grace. This style, which Lorenzo invented, may be the result of his constant contemplation of otherworldly matters through the devotional literature and sermons that he read and heard every day.

One of Monaco's most noteworthy polyptychs (dated 1410, Accademia, Florence) depicts the *Madonna and Child with Angels* (Plate 25) flanked by two saints on each of the side panels. In the pinnacles above the panels, the Angel and Madonna of the Annunciation bracket the blessing Christ. This splendid altarpiece has a swaying elegance. The curves of the bodies and the drapery set up a slow, sensuous, restrained rhythm across the surface. Lorenzo has perfect control of line and interval. Every facet of the work is carefully constructed; observe the way the gold is formed into exquisite abstract patterns, perhaps the panel's most beautiful passages.

Lorenzo's attitude toward form is both sophisticated and relentless. The tense, ever-moving expansion of the cloth of honor, the outline of the Madonna's dress, and the shape of the robes of each saint are miracles of tightly held energy. The line is so carefully refined and charged and the entire surface is so finely wrought that at times it seems not quite the product of a human hand.

Ultrarefined also is the palette, which perfectly complements the panel's forms. The Madonna wears a pearl gray tunic with a light green scarf under a blue mantle lined with gold. The angels behind wear green robes, which form a harmonious color link to the golden cloth of honor. The two saints closer to the Madonna wear dusty rose-violet robes — John's makes a subtle contrast to his gray-green hair shirt — while the outside saints are dressed in white and pearl gray. All the figures stand on a red carpet embroidered with gold. One feels that each color has been chosen only after much thought and with a mind to its place in the carefully honed composition. The nature of the colors, their delicate highlighting with white, and their role in the composition are marvels of originality and refinement. From the elegant use of pattern to the position of a finger or the tilt of a head, this work is painstakingly composed. Seldom in the history of Western art has an artist as sensitive to the most basic formal components of painting appeared, or one more sophisticated in combining line, light, and color.

The *Adoration of the Magi* (Plate 26), 1422, now in the Uffizi, reveals the breadth of Lorenzo's last works. Here the fantasy hinted at in the Monte San Savino Crucifix dominates the picture. Against a background of dusky gray mountains (which erupt out of the earth) appears the great train of the Magi; its members — some well over twelve heads high — are among the most fashionable to appear in a Florentine *Adoration*. Like princes of some fairy-tale court, with swaying, mannered poses, long beards, and sumptuous clothes, they pay homage to Mary and Christ. Their richly colored robes (of pink, green, blue, rose, red, gold, and violet) and weird hats form a multicolored pattern that moves the eye across the picture's surface.

Although there is certainly a foreground and a background in this painting,

26. Lorenzo Monaco, *Adoration of the Magi*. Florence, Uffizi.

Lorenzo has done away with the rocky space dividers used in the Accademia *Agony in the Garden*. Here space is much more compressed. The figures occupy a narrow foreground plane that seems to be pressing against the writhing mountains in the background. The scene is unreal, as the high mountains — one with a tiny toy castle — rise up somewhere just behind the tall foreground figures. The open, strongly foreshortened shed at the left projects out into the viewer's space and then recedes sharply into the distance, its smooth pink walls setting up a highly dynamic motion having very little to do with the rest of the picture's space. These unconnected spatial elements help give the *Adoration* a sense of disjunction, which was exactly the artist's intent.

The crowded, confused scene of elegant, brightly colored figures in costly finery set before the craggy gray mountains strikes a new note in Florentine painting. Not since the thirteenth century had there appeared such a range of color and form, nor had the overall feeling of an individual painting been quite so fantastic. Lorenzo's art was to become very popular; he was, as we shall see, to have many followers who, like himself, were widely patronized. The entire last quarter of the Trecento had been sober and straightforward. It is surprising, therefore, that Lorenzo, who was certainly the product of that period, introduced into the art of Florence a style that is exotic, often ethereal, highly fashionable, and, above all, fantastic. How did that happen? It has been suggested that he was influenced by the International Gothic Style, but that label is nearly meaningless. Certainly there were works being produced in other parts of Europe that have some similarities with Lorenzo's — the elongation of figures, for instance. But most of these shared characteristics are simply surface resemblances that tell one little about the roots, development, and essence of a particular style. The real foundation on which Lorenzo built his art was his early training in a workshop. To imply that his mature idiom arose from some amorphous combination of disparate national styles grouped under the name International Gothic is to misunderstand the evolution of a Florentine artist trained in the localized, cooperative workshop system.

The Bartolini Salimbeni Chapel in Santa Trinita, Florence, contains what is, in all likelihood, Lorenzo Monaco's last works. The chapel is one of the very few in Florence that still contain, in unaltered form, most of their original decoration. It is fronted by a splendid Trecento gate of wrought iron, its walls are covered by Monaco's frescoes of the *Legend of the Virgin*, and its altar is graced by a beautiful panel of the *Annunciation*, also from Lorenzo's hand.[4]

Painted sometime around the mid-1420s, the chapel documents Monaco's last style through his only sizable extant work in fresco. Many panels from the period c.1400–1420 survive, but there exist for the same period only a handful of chapels with fresco cycles. It is not certain whether this is the result of later destruction or of a paucity of commissions. Since the contemporary Brunelleschi churches of Santo Spirito and San Lorenzo do not have large private chapels of the Duecento and Trecento type, which were meant to be covered with frescoes, there seems to be reason to suspect that the fashion for frescoes, prevalent during the preceding century, was now out of date. In fact, during the rest of the century few chapels were built for fresco decoration, and the majority of large Florentine cycles were produced to redecorate chapels covered by Trecento frescoes. In any case, there was a decided decline of commissioned frescoes, which is noteworthy even if its exact cause cannot be determined.

In the chapel's centerpiece, the *Annunciation* (Plate 27), a young angel clothed in a wildly folded rose-violet robe gracefully announces Christ's coming.

27. Lorenzo Monaco, *Annunciation*. Florence, Santa Trinita.

The angel's large wings make a sweeping upward pattern while their glorious colored feathers of blue, gray-blue, maroon, and pink spread across the panel's surface. The Virgin looks up from her book and lightly touches her chest in a wonderfully mannered gesture of surprise. Her blue robes lined with yellow form broad curvilinear patterns around the base of the pink chair as beautiful as those made by the angel's wings.

Alive with subtle interval and carefully wrought decoration, the picture attracts and holds the spectator's attention. The shapes formed in the gold background by the angel's silhouette; the verticals and horizontals of the house; and the striking relation between the organic, elongated bodies and the rigid verticals and horizontals of the trees and architecture in the distance enliven the work. Patterns are seen everywhere: on the floor, in the haloes, on the drapery, on the building. Monaco's palette is slightly more restricted here than in the Uffizi *Adoration of the Magi*; soft, warm, dusky rose-violets, blues, pinks, and grays are the predominant colors in the *Annunciation*.

28. Lorenzo Monaco. *Meeting at the Golden Gate*. Florence, Santa
Trinita.

Each *predella* scene is a jewel of miniature fantasy. In the *Visitation*, *Nativity*,
Adoration, and *Flight into Egypt*, graceful, elongated figures with small heads
and heavy, swinging robes act out the sacred dramas.

In the frescoes of the Bartolini Salimbeni Chapel, depicting the legend of the
Virgin, one sees a slightly more restrained Lorenzo Monaco. The fantasy still
remains in the *Meeting at the Golden Gate* (full of reminiscences of Taddeo
Gaddi's fresco of the same subject in the Baroncelli Chapel[5]), where Joachim
and Mary come together before a Jerusalem surrounded by a pink wall and
filled with strange tall towers of pink and gray (Plate 28). To the left, set in a
sea stretching to the horizon, is an island occupied by a pink castle. The yellow,
red-orange, blue, brown, and gray of the figure's robes all play subtly against
the pink wall in the background.

In the *Marriage of the Virgin* (Plate 29), Monaco is fascinated by interval.
The figures are spread frieze-like across the entire width of the picture, their
bodies closely arranged in a measured, harmonious fashion that complements
the calculated progression of the arches of the building in the background. Only
around the actual ceremony is the space opened as the lithe Virgin, robed in

29. Lorenzo Monaco, *Marriage of the Virgin.* Florence, Santa Trinita.

white, is wed to a Joseph clad in dusty yellow. The turning of heads in different directions and the slow, careful gestures of the figures keep the onlooker's eye moving across the fresco's surface. Pink, green, gray, yellow, and white predominate; and the slow march of the highly original, marvelously varied colors attracts one as much as the narrative itself.

Lorenzo Monaco's only extant frescoes, the Bartolini Salimbeni paintings, reveal that he was capable of creating remarkably exciting decorative works on a large scale. It is true that these pictures do not utilize the bold potential inherent in their medium, but that does not prevent them from being masterpieces. The overall composition of both the altarpiece and the frescoes, however, seems slightly more restrained, a little less fantastic than Monaco's previous work, perhaps indicating that in the last phase of his career he was moving away from the svelte, more fashionable style of his earlier pictures.

Monaco's taste did not run to the dramatic; he was more impressed by the exotic setting of craggy black-gray cliffs, fancy costume, and gracious celestial creatures. His paintings contain a world of splendid refinement, grace, and fashion; a world that was to be shared by a number of artists of his generation. His style had an overwhelming impact on his contemporaries, who were awestruck

30. Rossello di Jacopo Franchi, *Madonna del Parto*.
Florence, Palazzo Davanzati.

by its beauty, but it could not last outside the almost pristine purity of Lorenzo's pictures. It was soon to give way to other, more diluted modes of pictorial representation.

Rossello di Jacopo Franchi was one of Monaco's best and most delightful followers.[6] He was born in the 1370s (he was almost an exact contemporary of Monaco) and had a long and active career. His earliest extant works seem to date from the first decade of the Quattrocento and he is documented painting through the 1440s.

In Rossello's *Madonna del Parto* (Plate 30; Palazzo Davanzati, Florence), the central image of the pregnant standing Madonna glancing sideways at the on-looker is a wonderful expression of controlled, elongated grace with none of the tense feeling of ultrarefinement of every form and surface found in Monaco's work. The attenuated body is clothed in a pink tunic under a blue-black mantle

31. Master of the Bambino Vispo, Altarpiece. Würzburg,
Martin von Wagner-Museum.

and capped by a delicate, homey face and waves of blond hair. Here Lorenzo's style is domesticated and made slightly less elegant.

Two gracious, youthful angels dressed in blue robes hold up a red cloth of honor, which makes swinging abstract shapes in the background. Below, either side, kneel two tiny figures (perhaps the picture's donors; the woman on the right is obviously pregnant) imploring the gentle Madonna for help, help that the spectator is certain they received from such a kindly image.

The Davanzati *Madonna del Parto* of c.1420 is an excellent example of the work of a very close follower of Lorenzo Monaco. Rossello — either by accident or, more likely, by design — has deemphasized some of the more formally aloof aspects of Monaco's style, thus making his own painting more intimate and accessible. Such a modification is not at all unusual among Monaco's many charming but less-talented contemporaries.

Named after his lively infant Christs, the Master of the Bambino Vispo (an unidentified artist who worked in Florence during the early decades of the Quattrocento) was another of the first painters to be heavily influenced by Lo-

renzo Monaco.[7] This is evident in his altarpiece (Plate 31), c. 1420, of the
Madonna and Child with SS. Margaret, Andrew, Peter, and Mary Magdalen
in the Martin von Wagner-Museum, Würzburg. The serene Virgin surrounded
by a *mandorla* of angels is reminiscent of some of the Madonnas by Monaco.
The angels, whose slim, elongated bodies are clothed in yards of sweeping
drapery, are also heavily indebted to his idiom. Their positions help create a
believable space; the viewer's eye moves from the seated musicians in the fore-
front, back to the angels who twist into space at the edge of the arm rest (the
right one has his back daringly turned to us), and then stops at the rearmost
figures staring adoringly at the Virgin and Child. The throne type is quite an
ancient one and is first found painted in the early years of the fourteenth century.
As we have seen, the late Trecento witnessed a renewed interest in Giotto and
his contemporaries, so the occurrence of Giottesque types is not unusual; even
a highly innovative painter like Masaccio was to borrow from the early fourteenth century.[8]

Monaco's style is reflected again in the saints in the side wings of the
Würzburg painting. These elegant but substantial beings are nearly as finely
wrought as those by Monaco himself. And their soft faces, heavy-lidded eyes,
wavy hair, and graceful necks make them almost as attractive. The Master of
the Bambino Vispo has not forgotten his training, however — which must have
been with an artist of the generation c.1375–1400 — for these side saints also
remind one of the substantial beings painted by Spinello and by Agnolo Gaddi
just a decade or so before the Würzburg altarpiece. Throughout his career the
Master of Bambino Vispo remained somewhere between the solidity of the late
Trecento and the new-found grace of his principal influence, Lorenzo Monaco.

Like the Master of the Bambino Vispo, the artist who painted the *Madonna
and Child* (Plate 32) now in the Cleveland Museum of Art was a close contemporary of Lorenzo Monaco. Called the Master of 1419 after the date on the
Cleveland panel, he seems to have studied and worked in Florence during the
first quarter of the Quattrocento.[9]

One of the most striking aspects of the Cleveland picture (the center of a now
dispersed altarpiece) is its color, which is both extremely lively and typical of
Monaco and the artists influenced by him. The flat gray throne acts as an effective foil for the blue of the Virgin's robe, the orange-red of her mantle, and the
bright yellow and pink-lavender of the child's garments. Each carefully chosen
hue subtly works against the others to create an extremely lively flow of color
across the panel's surface. The base, back, and arm rest of the throne and the
floor are decorated with yellow, blue, green, and brown veined marble. At the
base of the panel is an abstract pattern of red and blue-green lines set against
white, and behind the throne one sees the expanse of gold background. All

32. Master of 1419, *Madonna and Child.*
Cleveland, The Cleveland Museum of Art,
Gift of the Hanna Fund.

these colors and patterns make the painting vivid and exciting. The bright, happy palettes of this and a number of other works painted under Monaco's sway during the first three decades of the Quattrocento are among the most innovative in the history of Florentine painting. The combination of white, yellow, blue, red, pearl-gray, and pink, to name just some of the many colors, complements the elegant forms used during the first years of the new century. The nature of the colors, their juxtaposition, and the way they are employed by Monaco's contemporaries are quite different from the practice of the previous artistic generation, which had a more sober, less varied sense of color.

The Madonna by the Master of 1419 is one of the graceful women common to many of the Florentine works done under Monaco's influence. Her oval face, elegantly curved shoulders, shapely hands, and finely molded, solid knees curve into and out of space, establishing her physical presence. The painter's strong interest in abstract patterns formed by the slow, carefully controlled swing of line is seen in the arabesque formed by the hem of the Virgin's cloak, in the fold pattern near her knees, and in the arm rests of her throne. Such a use of line is most characteristic both of Monaco and of his best followers.

The spirit of many of these works is harder to define than their form. Although their figures are most fashionable and splendidly wrought, many are wistful and melancholy. As in the Cleveland panel, the Virgin is usually preoccupied, lost in some distant thought, unaware of the serious Child on her lap or the self-conscious, mannered saints in the side panels. The exquisite style created by Monaco and his followers is, in many ways, the art of the connoisseur. It seems aimed, more than any other Florentine idiom (except, perhaps, that of painting done during the first quarter of the Cinquecento), toward an audience that appreciated a subtle, somewhat mannered play of form; a bright, original palette; and a sumptuous elegance. There is a loss of narrative power in the works of Monaco and his followers, for as beautiful as they are, they do not contain the seriousness and moral vigor of the paintings of the Trecento masters. Rather, they often seem to be the most perfect vision of a fairy-tale world divorced from the human and spiritual drama of Christianity. We do not know what it was in society that made such a style so popular that it dominated Florence until around 1430. Perhaps the audience that commissioned it was more interested in the beauty of its style than in the high moral and intellectual message so typical of most earlier Florentine painting. The popularity of Monaco and his followers is an anomaly because it represents a diversion from an old, highly characteristic mode of Florentine painting, a mode far from the splendid, exotic, elegant world created by Monaco.

During the first years of the Quattrocento the work of another group of artists shows a slow evolution from the style of the late Trecento to the idiom of Monaco and his closest followers. Like Lorenzo di Niccolò, Mariotto di Nardo, the Straus Master, and Giovanni Toscani, most of these painters were not as talented as Monaco but they are important nevertheless, for their art represents a gradual transition between two important Florentine idioms. In their first panels and frescoes they were most sensitive to the painting of their teachers, but then they slowly fell under the spell of the more *au courant* style around them. The paintings of these once popular masters of only limited talent are a good index of the changing artistic taste of Florence.

Lorenzo di Niccolò was born during the late 1370s or early 1380s and has been documented from 1392 to 1411. He was probably trained by Niccolò di Pietro Gerini, with whom he painted a number of joint commissions.[10] Lorenzo appears to have been a rather prolific artist who executed a number of altarpieces for important locations.

Lorenzo's *Coronation of the Virgin* (Plate 33), 1402, now in San Domenico, Cortona, was on the high altar of the Church of San Marco in Florence until it was replaced by a painting by Fra Angelico. The Cortona picture is very elaborate: it has three central panels filled with figures, a painted superstructure,

33. Lorenzo di Niccolò, *Coronation of the Virgin.*
Cortona, San Domenico.

pilasters with rows of saints, and a *predella*. Such large altarpieces came into vogue during the early years of the Quattrocento; the largest, perhaps, is Monaco's gigantic *Coronation of the Virgin* (1413), once in Santa Maria degli Angeli but now in the Uffizi.[11] The fashion for such huge works was not to last, and by the 1430s and 1440s altarpieces on the whole were again smaller and less grandiose.

In the Cortona *Coronation* Lorenzo has managed to keep the complex composition in check. The symmetry of the various parts of the altarpiece and the clear disposition of the figures in space stabilize the work. Lorenzo's close acquaintance with the late Trecento, in general, and Niccolò di Pietro Gerini, in particular, is apparent in the figure types, the articulation of the predella narratives, and the overall composition of the main panels. This is not surprising because in 1402 Niccolò was still alive, as was Spinello Aretino; and Agnolo Gaddi had been dead only six years. While Lorenzo's stylistic origins are ob-

34. Lorenzo di Niccolò, *Coronation of the Virgin*. Florence, Santa
Croce Museum.

vious, he has already forged his own idiom, which is a variant on the solid,
rather monumental types of Gaddi and Gerini. Dressed in voluminous robes,
the Cortona figures are firmly placed in space. There is a new sharpness foreign
to the masters of the late Trecento: robes are more metallic, facial features
crisper, and movements slightly more mannered and less direct. There is a
slackening of the rugged, sometimes overly dramatic force common to the generation before Lorenzo. In part, this change is due to the influence of Monaco;
the figures of prophets between the main panels and the pinnacles are certainly
reminiscent of that artist, and it seems likely that by 1402 Lorenzo di Niccolò
had already come into contact with Monaco's work.

By 1410, the date inscribed below the central figures of Lorenzo's *Coronation
of the Virgin* (Plate 34) in Santa Croce, Florence, the artist was more fully
under the sway of Monaco. A comparison with the Cortona *Coronation* of eight
years before reveals just how much the style of Lorenzo di Niccolò had

changed. The Santa Croce altarpiece is not as compartmentalized; there is much more communication between the side wings and the central scene. The scalar and spatial relationships between the Santa Croce Christ and Virgin and the saints flanking them are much more intimate than in the Cortona *Corona-tion*. The basic shape of the altarpiece has also changed. The painting in Santa Croce is proportionally wider, and the arches are now topped by cusps containing Christ, the *Annunciation*, and prophets. These cusps had just come into fashion when this altarpiece was painted, and similar ones are seen on Lorenzo Monaco's later *Adoration* in the Uffizi. Their flamboyant shapes well suit the curvilinear style of the altarpieces by the two Lorenzos.

The Christ and the Virgin from Lorenzo di Niccolò's Santa Croce *Coronation* are quite different from the same figures of the earlier, Cortona altarpiece. They are more elongated and lithe and create more movement. Their voluminous robes wind around their bodies in a series of sinuous, sharp-edged folds. In fact, the sumptuous drapery is more important in the stylistic makeup of the Santa Croce panel. Note the splendid cloth of honor behind the central pair, the heavy material hanging from Christ's upheld arm, the brocaded floor covering, and the angels' weighty robes. During the early fifteenth century Florence was one of Europe's leading finishers of woolen cloth, and a considerable number of her citizens were engaged in some aspect of this trade. Throughout the history of Florentine art there is an emphasis on the depiction of cloth, but in the first years of the Quattrocento one finds a particular interest in its portrayal. One can imagine that many of the Florentines who stood before Lorenzo's painting must have surveyed the cloth with a knowing eye to its color, weight, finish, and cost.[12]

Monaco's sway in the Santa Croce *Coronation* can best be seen in the elegantly posed saints in the wings, especially Lucy and John the Evangelist, to the left of the central panel. Their oval faces, long necks, elongated bodies, and weighty, complex robes seem directly inspired by Monaco. Also new is the slightly mannered, melancholic feeling emanating from the side saints, the same wistful air previously seen in Monaco's work. The overall complexity of the Santa Croce panel, its unification, and its elegant but removed inhabitants demonstrate a substantial change in Lorenzo di Niccolò's art. At the same time, they document the strong influence of Monaco's style, an influence that was to touch a number of other artists.

One of them was Mariotto di Nardo, a close contemporary of Lorenzo di Niccolò. Documented between 1394 and 1424, Mariotto was probably trained by someone still very much under the influence of Orcagna and his circle.[13] It may have been Jacopo di Cione, the younger brother of Orcagna and Nardo, a conservative minor artist who worked up to the end of the Trecento.[14]

35. Mariotto di Nardo, Altarpiece. Villamagna, San Donnino.

Among Mariotto's earliest surviving work is a polyptych (Plate 35) with the Madonna and Child surrounded by saints in the church of San Donnino at Villamagna near Florence, which appears to date from the mid-1390s. As in the later *Coronation* by Lorenzo di Niccolò in Santa Croce, one observes the growing tendency, begun during the late Trecento, toward the unification of the entire altarpiece. In Mariotto's picture the ancient triptych form has begun to give way to a single unified panel; the old subdivisions between panels are preserved only by the foliated capitals next to the figures of those saints nearest the Virgin. This increasing desire for unity may signify that the painters and their patrons were psychologically no longer satisfied with the older altarpiece types in which the several side wings were physically separated from the center panel. Now the side saints really seem to be in the presence of the Madonna and to exist in the same time and space.

For the 1390s Mariotto's figures are old-fashioned. St. John the Baptist, for example, retains some of the stiffness and exclusiveness of the mid-Trecento.

36. Mariotto di Nardo, Altarpiece. Formerly London, Hatton Garden
Church; Central panel, Minneapolis Institute of Arts.

His dark, masklike face and unstable hovering position over the ground plane
are ultimately derived from works such as Orcagna's Strozzi altarpiece. In fact,
the basic spatial orientation of the figures flanking the Madonna is not far removed from the SS. Annunziata altarpiece discussed in chapter 1. It is strange,
consequently, that such an out-of-date figural style should appear in a painting
that is rather up to date in its overall composition, especially when one consid-
ers that many of the changes in Florentine painting between 1375 and 1420
occur in the figure rather than in the composition.

Mariotto's *Coronation of the Virgin* (formerly at Hatton Garden Church, London; the center panel is now in the Minneapolis Institute of Arts,) is dated
1408. Before the polyptych was dismantled the spiral colonnettes of a nine-
teenth-century frame (visible in Plate 36) masked the fact that originally space
flowed across the altarpiece's surface in a manner similar to that of the San
Donnino di Villamagna altarpiece. But in the *Coronation* the saints now stand
in better proportional relationship to the central actors and there is a more
confident handling of the figures, all of whom sit or stand more firmly in space
than those in the earlier altarpiece.

Some of the saints in the Hatton Garden altarpiece show the early influence
of Lorenzo Monaco: St. John the Evangelist, at the far right, is more elongated,
has a proportionally smaller head, and twists in space more than any figure from

37. Mariotto di Nardo, *Trinity with Two Donors*. Impruneta, Collegiata.

the San Donnino di Villamagna painting. The complexity of the robes is also indicative of this new influence, which seems to have started just at the time this picture was painted. Perhaps the most direct borrowing is apparent in the angels, whose swinging poses, heavy and complexly folded drapery, and tiny heads are taken almost directly from some work by Lorenzo Monaco.

The shot color of the angels' robes and the alternation and saturation of certain colors (yellow, green, red) are characteristic of many of the palettes of the first years of the Quattrocento.

In 1418, ten years after the completion of the Hatton Garden *Coronation*, Mariotto dated the *Trinity with Two Donors* (Plate 37) in the Collegiata at Impruneta, near Florence. Here the influence of Lorenzo Monaco is now quite strong. The Christ is an extremely crude variant of the Monte San Savino Crucifix type by Lorenzo Monaco. The robe of the wooden God the Father cascades earthward, its twisting hem making a silhouette that owes much to the sinuous line of Lorenzo. Although Mariotto has tried to be up to date, this Monaco influence is uncomfortably grafted onto what is still a basically mid-Trecento style. The frontal face of God the Father, with its vacant, symmetrical eyes, comes directly from Nardo di Cione, as does the still uncertain spatial location of the figure. Mariotto was not as adaptable as Lorenzo di Niccolò, nor could he completely leave the older idiom in which he was trained.

Bicci di Lorenzo (1373–1452) was another Florentine who was firmly bound to an older style at the beginning of his career.[15] His earliest idiom was based on the works of painters active during the last decades of the Trecento. His well-documented paintings offer a fascinating glimpse into his evolution. While his style never escaped from its conservative base, it absorbed the influences of many of his most prominent contemporaries. Consequently his work mirrors (and often helps to date) many of the major stylistic events that took place as he pursued his career. Bicci was an extremely popular artist, perhaps because his cautious nature endeared him to many Florentines who were wealthy enough to commission works of art. But his paintings were done not only for locations in Florence; he had an extensive audience in some of the small Tuscan cities, and it is possible that his shop specialized in the production of pictures for these more *retardataire* locations. Throughout the Trecento and the early Quattrocento there were Florentine artists — such as Jacopo del Casentino, Giovanni del Biondo, Bicci's son Neri, and Benozzo Gozzoli — who appealed to the taste of provincial centers. This phenomenon, which has never been investigated, may prove to be important for our understanding of how developments in the major artistic centers were perceived by those living in less urban settings.

Bicci's first dated work (1414) is an *Annunciation* with saints (Plate 38) in the church of Santa Maria Assunta at Stia, a provincial town in the Tuscan countryside east of Florence. Its triptychlike shape is already rather old-fashioned for its date, and while there is some attempt to integrate the wings with the central panel, the colonnettes and the scale differences between the side saints and the figures of the *Annunciation* make for disharmony rather than unity.

The saints in the wings are still late Trecento in type. Their basic configuration is certainly dependent on the model of someone like Agnolo Gaddi, even though this painting was done eighteen years after his death. This influence is apparent everywhere, but especially in the St. John the Evangelist on the extreme right, whose long, narrow face and flowing beard seem to be heavily indebted to Gaddi.

The *predella* stories of the legends of SS. Michael and John come almost straight from the Trecento. The use of hills to divide space and the drawing of narrative action across nearly the entire surface of the panels reveal Bicci's uncomplicated adoption of the art of the previous generation. His old-fashioned painting in Stia must have appealed to those who longed for a traditional, easy to understand style; this, in turn, must be one of the reasons that a mediocre

38. Bicci di Lorenzo, *Annunciation*. Stia, Santa Maria Assunta.

artist like Bicci received so many commissions. He periodically updated his style, but that never obscured the fact that he always grafted new fashions onto a basically conservative idiom.

Two other painters who worked during the early decades of the Quattrocento are worth studying for what their paintings reveal about the major artistic currents of the first twenty years of the century and because their work demonstrates the high quality of many of the minor painters of the period.

Giovanni Toscani (who until very recently was known as the Master of the Griggs Crucifixion) was born in 1372 and lived until 1430.[16] His triptych (c.1425) with the Madonna, Child, and SS. Jerome and Catherine (Plate 39) in the Galleria of the Ospedale degli Innocenti, Florence, is a good example of his enchanting work. The delicate, beautiful Madonna occupies a seat covered with gold flowers, set against a red background. Her wistful glance is directed away from the spectator as her chubby son turns to bestow a mannered, self-conscious blessing. There is a prettiness about the Madonna — who is fashion-

39. Giovanni Toscani, Altarpiece. Florence, Galleria
dell'Ospedale degli Innocenti.

ably attired in a full blue robe draped over what was once a pink dress — that
is at once lighthearted and captivating. Such lilting softness is certainly derived
from Lorenzo Monaco.

Monaco's style is also seen in the side figures, especially in the graceful Catherine, whose silhouette creates a subtle pattern against the gold background.
The slow, elongated line that forms the crown, forehead, nose, neck, and arms
in the flowing pink-rose robe makes a perfect complement to the elegant Madonna. The composition is completed by the kneeling Jerome (dressed in a red
robe that totally envelopes his body), whose rightward turn mirrors the pose of
Catherine across the panel.

It is quite likely that Giovanni studied with a painter strongly under the sway
of Agnolo Gaddi, for there are certain elements (mostly in the facial types) that
are reminiscent of that artist in the Innocenti triptych, but it is Lorenzo Monaco
who exerted the strongest influence. In Giovanni's painting and in the works of
a number of other artists of the very early Quattrocento, Monaco's style overwhelmed and destroyed the influence of Gaddi, which had been so strong at the
end of the Trecento and in the first few years of the next century.

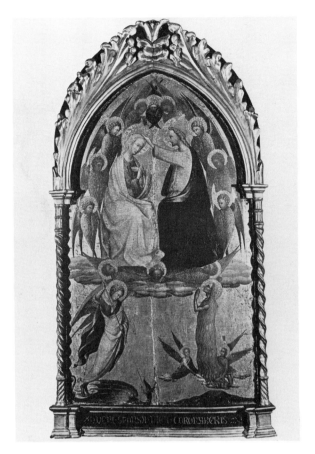

40. Straus Master, *Coronation of the Virgin*. Florence, Galleria
dell'Ospedale degli Innocenti.

The second of these fine minor painters is known as the Master of the Straus
Madonna after a picture by him formerly in the Straus Collection. His small
Coronation of the Virgin (Plate 40) with SS. Michael and Mary Magdalen
(c.1410) in the Galleria of the Ospedale degli Innocenti, Florence, is another in
a series of notable panels documenting the transition between the late Trecento
style and the new, more lyrical world created by Lorenzo Monaco.[17]

The panel's palette is striking. The Virgin's light blue robes (patterned with
gold) contrast strongly with the deep blue of Christ's mantle and the pink of his
tunic. Around the Virgin and Christ flutters a mandorla of cherubim and seraphim of alternating red-orange and blue.

Below, St. Michael dispatches the dragon with an easy elegance as the sin-

uous Mary Magdalen looks toward the *Coronation*. All the figures, especially
the lower ones, are marvels of carefully controlled line and silhouette. Like the
triptych by Giovanni Toscani in the same gallery, the picture has a delicacy and
a sweetness that captivate and then charm the onlooker.

In the Madonna's body, facial features, and hands, the Master of the Straus
Madonna reveals a specific debt to Agnolo Gaddi and the works from his late
shop. But in the svelteness of the figures, in the handling of line to construct
forms of great elegance, and in the cool, restrained color, the artist demonstrates
his profitable study of Lorenzo Monaco. The overall mood of the small Innocenti *Coronation* is not that of the serious milieu of the late Trecento but of the
fashionable and elegant religious stories painted by Lorenzo Monaco and his
close followers. The latters' works lack Monaco's brilliance in handling line and
color but they compensate for that by being more approachable, more homey,
and not so exquisitely demanding. The Innocenti *Coronation*, like the triptych
by Giovanni Toscani, certainly demonstrates the considerable skill of some of
the little masters of the early Quattrocento. Their painting seems to exist half
in the style of the late Trecento, half in the newer idiom of Monaco. And, in
fact, the panels of both the Straus Master and Giovanni Toscani are quite representative of several talented, but not terribly innovative, artists who followed
in the wake of the great figures of the early Quattrocento.

Gentile da Fabriano was an innovative and important artist. He was born at
Fabriano in the Marches in east-central Italy around 1380 and worked in various areas before arriving in Florence in 1422.[18] Gentile may have received his
first training in the Marches, where strong influences of Florentine, Sienese,
and other styles were present. Before 1422 he had painted works in the
Marches, Venice, and Brescia, so when he entered Florence he was already a
fully formed artist who had had considerable experience with the idioms of
several different locations in the Italian peninsula.

The Strozzi *Adoration of the Magi* (Plate 41) dated May 1423, is Gentile's
first — and most famous — Florentine painting. The altarpiece, commissioned
by the prominent citizen Palla Strozzi for the church of Santa Trinita, is now in
the Uffizi. When the picture was first set up in Santa Trinita it must have
created a sensation, for nothing like it had ever been seen in Florence. It is,
above all, a gorgeous work. The spectator's eye is captured by the abundance
of its form, its color, its gold, and its elaborate frame. Enclosed within three
arches — the remnants of the old triptych type — Gentile has painted the jour-
ney and the adoration of the Magi. A vast cavalcade of mounted figures winds
from the left background to the left foreground, where the Magi adore Christ;
each member is a detailed unit whose particular color and shape separate him
from the surrounding forms. The distant landscape is occupied by planted

41. Gentile da Fabriano, *Adoration of the Magi*. Florence, Uffizi.

fields, walled cities, and mountains crested by tiny castles. Before a gray-green sea the star signals the birth of Christ to the three golden Magi.

The foreground is alive with people, horses, dogs, monkeys, and birds. Great visual excitement is created by the movement into and out of space of the gray and brown horses in the right foreground. One gets a sense of confusion and noise as the scores of individual figures go about their many tasks. Gentile's *Adoration* is quite different from any contemporary Florentine picture, for there is a crowded, busy, hurried feeling about it that is at odds with the taste of the city.

Compared with the Strozzi *Adoration*, Lorenzo Monaco's contemporary Uffizi *Adoration* has fewer figures and a much more unified, compressed landscape background. Both Gentile and Monaco are concerned with the depiction of a fantastic world, but there are basic differences in their ideas on the creation of figures and the space they inhabit. In Lorenzo's panel the elegant actors are solidly constructed; one understands their positions in space and their movement through it; they seem firmly set within the landscape. Some of the objects in Gentile's picture (the horses, for example), while very solid, are often spatially ill defined. The young magus in the middle foreground is a sturdy figure, but he seems to be hovering instead of standing. Frequently figures appear almost flat. It is, on the whole, a rather uneven painting, for while some of the details are very three-dimensional (the Virgin's knees) and strongly foreshortened, others are flat and unmodulated (for instance, the heavily patterned robe of the kneeling magus). This formal conflict may result from Gentile's recent contact with the monumental tradition of Florentine art and his adaptation of it for parts of his painting.

There remains throughout Gentile's *Adoration* a feeling for minute observation that is really quite alien to Florentine art. The detailed portrayal of landscape, the very careful attention to the depiction of animals, and the particular rendering of the individualized costumes set it apart from the much more abstracted work of Florentine painters. The dispassionate realism of Gentile's painting betrays a non-Florentine sensitivity. The many details, the large number of figures, the abundance of peripheral visual material are not characteristic of the Florentines.

The Strozzi *Adoration of the Magi* is a brilliant *tour de force* of color and gold. The gray and brown horses and the reds, blues, and browns of the robes are punctuated by the strong reds of the turbans and stockings worn by the foreground figures. The gold, blue, and red brocades of the robes of the middle foreground figures draw attention to and activate the center of the picture. In the foreground other passages of gold (the horses' gear, the haloes, the crowns, the dove above Joseph) are conspicuously placed. These areas are echoed

by the considerable amount of gold used in the pilasters and cusps of the frame.
The patron of this most ostentatious panel undoubtedly wanted to show that it
had cost him a lot of money. In a number of contracts for panels of the fourteenth
and fifteenth centuries almost more attention is paid to the type and quality of
material to be used than to the painting itself.[19] Often the gold had to be the
finest or the lapis lazuli the most expensive. This type of materialistic mentality
seems to have been responsible for the splendor of Gentile's altarpiece.

Perhaps the most beautiful and inventive passage in the painting is the central *predella* of the *Flight into Egypt*. Here, on a more informal scale, one sees
Gentile's great interest in the depiction of the world, which he may have ac-
quired in the north, where acute studies from nature played an important role.
The holy family flees toward Egypt through a deep, convincing landscape with
blooming orange trees, a verdant hillside, and a white, blue, and pink town
complete with turreted wall. The rhythmic figures seem to glide silently along
the gravel path leading upward toward the town. But Gentile's mind is much
more on the detail than on the whole. We see each stone in the path, the leaves
of every tree, and the complex architecture of the city's buildings, just as in the
Adoration we observed the careful rendering of swords, spurs, and robes. A
most sophisticated treatment of light is seen in the *Flight*: the tops of the low
mountains are bathed in golden sunlight while the valleys are cast in dark, cool
shadows. There is a feeling of a particular time of day — a dewy early morn-
ing — not found in any contemporary Florentine painting. This sense of moment, like Gentile's specificity and his love of anecdotal detail, probably also
derives from a close study of northern Italian painting; and surely it was this
attention to minutiae, within the framework of an elegant style, that must have
fascinated several important patrons.

But there are also similarities between Gentile's style and that of Monaco and
his followers that must have made the former's work not totally foreign to the
Florentines of the 1420s. The fantastically inventive quality of the Strozzi *Adoration* with its many figures, distant views, and sumptuously clad figures is
similar in spirit to several works by Monaco. Both artists are involved with the
highly decorative quality of silhouette, line, and color. They take a similar approach to the figure, stressing mannered, self-conscious poses. They also share
a taste for a languorous, otherworldly atmosphere that removes stress from religious drama and places the sacred stories in the realm of some gorgeous, elegant, and exotic fable.

As we shall see in chapter 7, it was not a case of Gentile's style influencing
the future of Florentine painting, but of Florentine painting changing the
course of the remainder of Gentile's career. His art must have been immediately
popular in Florence, for he was given a number of other noteworthy commis-

sions; but by the time he had completed the Strozzi *Adoration*, he had already fallen under the spell of contemporary Florentine art. He was not alone in this development, for a similar stylistic evolution may be observed in the work of his contemporary Masolino da Panicale.

Although Masolino is one of the most famous painters of the early Quattrocento, almost nothing is known about the important dates in his career.[20] He was born in Panicale, a minuscule town in the Arno valley that once existed near San Giovanni Valdarno, the birthplace of Masaccio. The date of Masolino's birth is often given as 1383, but on the basis of inconclusive documentation. His entry into the Florentine Arte dei Medici e Speziali (the painters' guild) took place in 1423. Artists seem to have joined the guild when they were ready to begin independent work; that is, during their early twenties. If such were the case with Masolino that would place his birth around 1400, but there is very little evidence to support such a speculation. The rest of Masolino's life is also poorly documented. We know that in 1424 he was paid for painting a fresco cycle of the True Cross for a religious confraternity in Empoli.[21] During the second half of the 1420s he may have gone to Hungary to work for the *condottiero* Pippo Spano, and his presence is recorded in Florence in 1428.[22] By the end of the decade he appears to have left Florence for good. His later work (to be discussed in chapter 7) is preserved in Rome and in the rather remote Lombardy town of Castiglione Olona; the dates of these commissions are uncertain.

Masolino's only dated panel (1423), now in the Bremen Kunsthalle, is possibly his earliest extant work. An elaborate frame encloses the rather small picture of the *Madonna of Humility* (Plate 42), an old Madonna type probably invented by Simone Martini during the first years of the Trecento. Masolino seems to have had some trouble setting the Madonna in space. Although placed before a pillow (seen on the left), she does not really appear to rest on it, and it is not clear if she is sitting or squatting. This lack of clarity is partially due to the damaged condition of the Madonna's blue robe, which has lost almost all its modeling; the flatness of this area deprives the picture of the strong space-creating surface it had originally. But even with this damage, it is clear that Masolino has handled the spatial location of the figure awkwardly; this may indicate that the painting is an early work.

The outline of the Madonna dominates the panel. From her headdress to her shoulders, to the elegant curves of the gold-bordered hems of her robe and around her feet, the sinuous line enlivens the edge of her form. Her wonderfully defined blue silhouette makes a bold contrast with the gold background while at the same time it shapes the gold into a striking, abstract pattern.

If the gracious Madonna were to stand she would certainly strike one of the

42. Masolino, *Madonna of Humility*. Bremen, Kunsthalle.

43. Shop of Lorenzo Monaco, *Madonna of Humility*. Washington, National Gallery of Art, Samuel H. Kress Collection.

mannered poses of Lorenzo Monaco's figures. Her oval face with its delicate features clearly derives from Monaco, as does the contrast of her blue robe with the orange-red tunic beneath it. The gleaming gold and the marblelike floor also contribute to the splendid effect.

In another *Madonna of Humility* (Plate 43; National Gallery, Washington, D.C., dated 1413), attributed to Lorenzo Monaco but, in all likelihood, a shop work of very high quality, are the origins of Masolino's Bremen panel. Obviously Masolino closely studied works like this one, painted ten years before his own. The basic articulation of his figures, his feeling for line, and the delicacy and sweetness of his faces all arise from Monaco's idiom. Even the smallest details of hair, hands, and facial features owe something to the Washington Madonna.

While Monaco's idiom is responsible for the basic formal vocabulary of the Bremen Madonna, it has not been taken over without some change. The sweeping lines and great elongation have been toned down; although elegant, Masolino's Madonna is not quite as mannered or as attenuated as the earlier shop work in Washington.

It is worth repeating that even though there are changes from the canon of

Monaco' style, the very basis of Masolino's idiom still comes directly from Monaco. Nothing in Masolino's earliest known work suggests that his style derives
from the late Trecento; unlike the work of Mariotto di Nardo and of Lorenzo di
Niccolò, Masolino's painting does not show a gradual shift from the world of
Gaddi and Gerini to that of Monaco. It seems almost certain from the stylistic
evidence of the Bremen panel that Masolino's apprenticeship must have begun
while the sway of Monaco was strongest in Florence. Consequently, one can
cautiously postulate that his first training took place during the early years of
the Quattrocento and that the picture in Bremen is among his first works as an
independent artist.

A comparison between the Christ child in the Bremen and Washington pictures reveals another difference between Masolino's and Monaco's styles. In the
former he is robust, childlike, roly-poly — note the dimpled behind — while in
the latter he is frail, gracefully elongated, and rather wistful. Throughout his
career Masolino was like a stylistic sponge soaking up influences from various
artists. He could modify his style with ease. So it is possible that his more
robust, strongly modeled child may reflect the very early sway of yet another
painter — the young Masaccio. Masaccio's influence on Masolino will be more
apparent and intense in later paintings, but it is interesting to note here that it
may be at work as early as 1423, the year of Masolino's entry into the Florentine
painters' guild.

A number of small fresco quatrefoils with saints from the intradoes of the
entrance to the chapel of Sant'Elena in Sant'Agostino, Empoli, are among the
few surviving fragments of Masolino's work there in 1424.[23] The fluidity and
softness of these half-length figures immediately recall the work of Lorenzo
Monaco, Rossello di Jacopo Franchi, and the Master of the Bambino Vispo.
The long, flowing beards, curly blond locks, and heavy-lidded eyes make a
perfect Monaco-like complement to the heavy robes and gently mannered poses
that express the languorousness of the Empoli saints.

Among all the graciousness of the saints there is another hint of a new influence working on the impressionable Masolino. The fierce-looking old saint
(Plate 44) with the gray beard (Peter?) seems to manifest a more serious, vigorous spirit. The staring eyes and tense pose of the sturdy figure may once
again — a year after the Bremen *Madonna of Humility* — document the sway
of Masaccio, whose art was to play a decisive role in Masolino's career.

The period c.1390–1420 was one of important artistic activity. The older
painters of these three decades took the foundation of their style from the artists
of the last quarter of the Trecento, who had deflected the course of Florentine
painting away from the harsh idiom of the mid-Trecento. But those working in

44. Masolino, *Saint Peter* (?). Empoli, Sant'Agostino (Santo Stefano degli Agostiniani).

the first decades of the Quattrocento did not carry on unaltered the heritage of the late fourteenth century. Under the influence of one powerful figure, Lorenzo Monaco, the sturdy, monumental, and increasingly direct idiom of artists like Agnolo Gaddi, Antonio Veneziano, and Spinello Aretino was modified into a much more elegant, fabulous, and exotic style. It was Lorenzo Monaco who set the mood of the first twenty years of the new century; his radiantly beautiful paintings influenced the work of almost every Florentine artist. By around 1420, however, two new forces had appeared on the Florentine scene. One was Masaccio, whose artistic presence was first felt in the city early in the third decade of the Quattrocento, as the child from Masolino's Bremen Madonna and the Empoli saints seem to suggest. The other was the sculpture of Donatello, the most brilliantly innovative and dramatic to appear in Florence. It is to this artist and his contemporaries that we now turn.

III.

The Beginnings of the New Century: Sculpture c.1390-1420

MUCH HAS BEEN WRITTEN about early Italian painting and early Italian sculpture, but seldom has the symbiotic relation between the two been discussed. To treat each medium in isolation presupposes that painters looked only at painting and sculptors were interested exclusively in sculpture. Of course, that was not the case; in all periods artists are fascinated by works of art produced in every medium. The visually sensitive respond to and borrow from visual sources of every type. Consequently, in discussing the history of painting in Florence during the period c.1375–1430 it is necessary to consider the work of several sculptors of the highest talent who were working side by side with the painters in that physically small city.

In Florence painting started earlier than sculpture.[1] One can trace an indigenous school of painters from the second half of the Duecento onward, but the first native sculptors do not seem to have been active, in any important way, before c.1350. During the years c.1290–c.1350, the great sculpture of Florence was produced by foreigners: Arnolfo di Cambio, Tino di Camaino, and Andrea and Nino Pisano.[2]

One of the first noteworthy Florentine sculptors was Orcagna, whose painting style was discussed in chapter 1.[3] His major work of sculpture is the tabernacle (finished 1359) in Or San Michele, Florence — a huge, elaborate structure, as much architecture as sculpture (Orcagna was also *capomaestro*, a position roughly equivalent to architectural foreman, of Orvieto Cathedral). It was built to house a painting by Bernardo Daddi, which was the last in a line of copies of a famous miracle-working Madonna destroyed by fire in the Duecento.

The large relief of the *Dormition and Assumption of the Virgin* (Plate 45) from the Or San Michele tabernacle gives an insight into Orcagna's style. There are two narrative levels. In the lower one, the Virgin is placed in the sarcophagus. Deeply carved but flattened figures watch the event, the bulk of their broadly formed bodies making an arc back into space. Their deliberate gestures, the movement of their heads, and their strongly carved facial expressions indicate that they are moved by the scene taking place before them. This emotional display is complemented by a clear, highly expressive treatment of the body, its gesture, and the space in which it acts. Orcagna's composition seems strongly influenced by the *Dormition* from Giotto's shop (Plate 46), then in the church of Ognissanti, which was probably one of the most famous pictures in Florence.[4] Orcagna's debt to the great master of the early Trecento is much more obvious here than in the Strozzi altarpiece (Santa Maria Novella, Florence), although the figurative language of the latter would have been impossible without Giotto. Perhaps the *Dormition* is closer to Giotto because the hardness of the marble forced Orcagna to execute the figures in broad, simplified forms (like Giotto's) that exist in actual space. On the altarpiece Orcagna could create shapes that easily defy gravity and are, therefore, spatially ambiguous.

Above the Or San Michele *Dormition* is the *Assumption*, where the Virgin appears in a *mandorla* supported by the outstretched hands of the flanking angels. At the lower left St. Thomas gropes for the *cintola* (belt), which the Virgin throws to him. The entire scene is backed by a complex pattern of gold, green, red, and blue marble inlays that blocks the spatial recession seen in the *Dormition* and makes the figures placed on it seem two-dimensional. Thomas appears to kneel on thin air; his powerfully wrought body is without a spatial anchor. The spatial and formal differences between the levels of the *Dormition* and the *Assumption* seem to represent Orcagna's compositional solution to the representation of two different spheres: the natural and the supernatural. If so, such a response is very like his solution to the spatial and compositional problems of the Strozzi altarpiece, where the *predelle*, representing historical events, are more firmly fixed in space than are the iconic assembly of saints in the upper panel. Whatever Orcagna's intention in the Or San Michele *Dormition* and *Assumption*, he has produced a masterpiece of mid-Trecento sculpture, one in which figures of great purpose and dignity solemnly participate in the somber drama.

Orcagna's massive figures with their dramatic gestures, often created by the twisting of their bodies, are fundamentally indebted to Giovanni Pisano, who influenced Andrea Pisano, the sculptor, who, in turn, seems to have impressed Orcagna the most.[5] So the stylistic heritage of the *Dormition* as well as its compositional source are ultimately derived from the early Trecento.

45. Orcagna, *Dormition and Assumption of the Virgin*. Florence, Or San Michele.

46. Giotto's Shop, *Dormition of the Virgin*. Berlin, Staatliche Museen.

Orcagna's style in painting and sculpture had a powerful effect on several sculptors working during the second half of the Trecento. One of them was Jacopo di Piero Guidi, the likely author of a *Prophet with Two Angel Musicians* (Plate 47; Museo dell'Opera del Duomo, Florence) carved around 1385.[6] If the Prophet is compared with St. John the Baptist from the SS. Annunziata polyptych in the Accademia (discussed in chapter 1), one sees how much alike are the stiff, fully frontal figures. The exclusive, closed silhouettes, relieved only slightly by the folds of material jutting out into space, are also very similar.

47. Jacopo di Piero Guidi, *Prophet with Two Angel Musicians*. Florence, Museo dell'Opera del Duomo.

48. Giovanni d'Ambrogio, *Prudence*. Florence, Loggia dei Lanzi.

Although the Duomo Prophet lacks a head, there is still the strong feeling, expressed by the rigidly held body, that he is aloof and withdrawn. Much the same is true of the angels, whose elongated bodies and masklike, expressionless faces are close in spirit and form to the angels from the Accademia picture. All these are iconic beings, who make little effort to acknowledge the spectator or his world. Guidi, it is interesting to note, seems to have been more impressed with Orcagna as a painter than as a sculptor, for his Prophet contains little of the spatial or volume-defining character of the *Dormition* from Or San Michele.

Another close tie between sculptors and painters existed during the closing years of the Trecento, when statues for the façade of the Duomo and for the Loggia dei Lanzi (the huge arched structure in the Piazza della Signoria) were being commissioned. Interestingly enough, painters were given the task of designing the statues, which were then to be carved by sculptors. One of the most important of the latter was Giovanni d'Ambrogio, a Florentine documented between 1366 and 1418, roughly the same time that Spinello Aretino was active.[7] Giovanni's period of training must have occurred shortly after Orcagna's death, and his career extended through some of the most important years of Lorenzo Monaco's activity.

49. Agnolo Gaddi, Altarpiece. Florence, Gallerie, Contini Bonacossi
Collection.

Giovanni's figure of *Prudence* (Plate 48) on the Loggia dei Lanzi was designed by Agnolo Gaddi in 1386.[8] The exact nature of the designs that the
painters made for sculptors is unknown because none have survived. However,
a preliminary sketch by Agnolo Gaddi, which must have been intended for a
figure of *Justice* (also to be placed on the Loggia dei Lanzi), indicates that the
painters were probably responsible for the basic design of the figures, but we
do not know whether the finished drawing (if indeed there was one) was very
detailed. In any case, the carved *Prudence* by Giovanni is stylistically close to a
late work by Agnolo Gaddi (dating from the 1390s), the Madonna and Child
(Plate 49) from a polyptych once in San Miniato al Monte but now in the
Contini Bonacossi Collection, Florence. They share certain structural similarities: the closed silhouettes of the seated figures, which make them independent
units separated from the background; the line of the shoulders; the strong protrusion of the knees from beneath heavy material; the long, oval face perched
on top of the cylindrical neck. Some of this resemblance must be due to Gaddi's
drawing, but part of it must also be attributed to the influence of the painter's
style on Giovanni.

50. Giovanni d'Ambrogio, *Annunciation*. Florence, Museo dell'Opera
del Duomo.

Occasionally painters and sculptors seem to exert little discernable influence on each other, but at certain times one or the other group appears to be the dominant stylistic force. In the late Trecento many sculptors worked in a style strongly indebted to contemporary ideas in painting, perhaps because much of the sculpture was designed by painters or because of the compelling spatial and compositional developments in painting during the last quarter of the century. Whatever the reason, during this time the sculptors do not seem to have been responsible for many of the important new stylistic trends.

The nearly life-sized, pinkish-brown marble *Annunciation* group (Plate 50) in the Museo dell'Opera del Duomo, Florence (which may formerly have been on the Duomo's Porta della Mandorla) is another work strongly under the influence of contemporary painting. Not documented, the Virgin and Angel have been attributed to Giovanni d'Ambrogio on stylistic grounds. Indeed, the softly modeled surfaces of the figures, the cutting of the robes, and the construction of the facial features resemble the *Virtues* by Giovanni on the Loggia dei Lanzi.[9]

The elegant, swaying movement of the angel (whose gesture is echoed by the rhythmic curves of his voluminous robes) is mirrored by the gently uplifted hand of the Virgin, who looks toward the holy figure with hesitation. The manner in which the robes respond to the bodies underneath and the way that the bodies themselves are articulated reveal a sophistication and talent rare in Florentine sculpture before the early years of the Quattrocento. In fact, the wonderfully carved faces and classically inspired cutting of the hair remind one of works made in the early fifteenth century; and it has been suggested that the two statues might indeed come from the first years of the Quattrocento.

In the *Annunciation* group the robes have an especially pictorial quality. The broad, pliant folds form highlighted ridges and deep pools of shadows that create softly rippling effects of light and dark, not unlike those found in many contemporary paintings. Even some of the details, such as the deeply cut diagonal slash just above the right foot of the Virgin, often occur in painted robes of the late Trecento. The painterly feeling of the *Annunciation* figures reminds one of early works by Lorenzo Monaco.

The *Annunciation* group (Plate 51) from Lorenzo Monaco's polyptych in the Accademia, Florence, contains a number of resemblances to the Duomo *Annunciation*. The closest link is the hardest to describe — a gentle, poignant communication between the lithe figures who, with calm and dignity, acknowledge each other's presence, understanding the great message just spoken. Also very similar is the composition of the slightly fleshy, exquisitely proportioned faces of all four figures. The handsome stone Virgin's subtly modeled face, with its delicate nose and slightly open mouth, is framed by a crown of wavy hair closely resembling the hair of Lorenzo Monaco's Virgin.

51. Lorenzo Monaco, *Annunciation*. Florence, Accademia.

The Duomo figures are neither as elongated nor as elegant as the personages from the altarpieces; nor are their stances so complex, their drapery quite so wonderfully wrought. The greater sobriety of the Duomo group does not rule out the possibility of Monaco's influence; rather, the statues may reflect his sway well before the Accademia *Annunciation* of c.1420 (?). The Duomo figures might, in other words, echo a period of Monaco that is nearly lost and that can be inferred only by postulating a less-developed style than that seen in his *Annunciation*, a style more like the early Accademia *Agony in the Garden*, discussed in chapter 2.

The *Annunciation* group seems to date from the beginning of Lorenzo Ghiberti's period of major activity. One of the most famous sculptors of the Florentine Quattrocento, Ghiberti was born in Florence in 1378, just about the time that the painters destined to dominate the last quarter of the Trecento were starting their first independent commissions.[10] He studied first to be a goldsmith, but in his autobiography (contained in a series of historical, stylistic, and theoretical observations called *I Commentari*, written toward the end of his career) Ghiberti states that he was painting in Pesaro when he received news of a competition for a new set of bronze doors for the main entrance of the Baptistery in Florence.[11] It is not known with whom Ghiberti studied painting, but surely it must have been someone of Agnolo Gaddi's generation. It is fascinating to speculate on what Ghiberti's earliest experiences with art were; he was 23 when he entered the famous competition for the Baptistery doors. By that time he must have had a nearly fully formed style that was, in all likelihood, very close to the idiom of the group of late-Trecento painters and sculptors just discussed.

The 1401 competition for the east doors of the Baptistery held by the Arte di Calimala (the wool refiners guild) has often been seen as a central event in the history of Florentine art. It was not. There had been and were to be other competitions for important commissions; the one for the Baptistery doors was by no means unique.

What is known about the six sculptors who submitted bronze reliefs of the prescribed size, shape (quatrefoil), material (bronze), and subject (*The Sacrifice of Isaac*) does not lead one to believe that their works were revolutionary. New styles are not formed overnight, nor are they the result of events like a competition. To see the competition of 1401 as a major turning point in Florentine art is to misunderstand the city's stylistic history. Since the training of all the artists involved took place during the late Trecento, their competition panels must have shown a great debt to the idiom of that time, as do the works of Giovanni d'Ambrogio and the *Annunciation* group from the Duomo. For the most part, Florentine art is characterized by gradual shifts from one style to another. This is the logical result of the workshop system, where each pupil was strongly encouraged to copy the idiom of his teacher and to make it his own. None of this was changed by the event of 1401.[12]

In Ghiberti's competition relief (Plate 52; now in the Bargello, Florence) the expansion of space is rigidly held in check. The scene is set against a flat, unyielding area of dark bronze that emphasizes the solidity of the relief. Ghiberti knew that if the reliefs (there were to be 28) were to be a success, they would have to express the function of the door as a solid entity that closed the Baptistery. Thus the flat backs of each relief not only had to stop spatial development but, in their metallic hardness, make the figurative part of each scene appear applied to its background, just as each quatrefoil seems (and in fact is) applied to the huge door it decorates. The figures and architecture are further separated from the back of the relief by their gilding, which coloristically sets them apart from the dark surrounding bronze.

The major spatial rhythms of Ghiberti's competition relief are diagonal. The spectator's eyes follow the development of the narrative from the man standing in front of the donkey, over the rocky ledge, to the group of Isaac and Abraham, and finally up to the hovering angel. It, like other flying angels on the doors, is intended to appear from deep space (notice the low-relief clouds out of which it flies); but Ghiberti has held down the illusion, and the figure looks almost stuck on the surface of the relief. The implied diagonal running from the lower-left to the upper-right lobes is intersected by another diagonal formed by the rocky ledge running from upper left to lower right. (As we have seen from Lorenzo Monaco's Accademia *Agony in the Garden*, such ledges were commonly used as space dividers in late Trecento painting.) In his major compositional rhythms Ghiberti has carefully avoided deep space while cunningly arranging the predominant compositional movements across, instead of into, the relief.

The other surviving competition relief, by the sculptor and architect Filippo Brunelleschi, reveals a similar desire to avoid deep space and to keep the composition consistent with the function of the door; but fundamentally it lacks the fluidity and easy grace of Ghiberti's narrative essay.[13] One can also assume that the other artists who entered the competition were equally interested in striking a balance between the narrative and decorative functions of their bronze panels. It is true that Ghiberti's relief is technically sophisticated, a fact that would not have been overlooked by the hard-headed Florentine businessmen judges who would have had cost very much in mind. But his *Sacrifice of Isaac* is miracu-

52. Lorenzo Ghiberti, *The Sacrifice of Isaac*. Florence, Bargello.

lously both a beautiful abstract door decoration and a clear, flowing exposition of a dramatic story. Surely it was because of this almost seamless combination of the decorative and narrative elements of his bronze that Ghiberti was chosen.

The same men who commissioned Ghiberti must have considered his style to be well within the acceptable boundaries of the day; this is especially pertinent because the doors (finished in 1424) were to decorate one of Florence's most famous public buildings. In fact, Ghiberti's style was up to date, and a survey of his bronze narratives reveals that his idiom has a number of parallels in contemporary Florence.

Ghiberti's *Annunciation* relief (Plate 53) brings to mind the stylistic world that saw the genesis of works such as the Duomo *Annunciation* group and Lorenzo Monaco's *Agony in the Garden*. The gentle, quiet mood of Ghiberti's *Annunciation* and its graceful elongated figures who make beautifully mannered gestures cannot but remind one of the Duomo group. Like those wonderful statues, Ghiberti's Angel and Virgin respond to each other in an intimate, moving way. The angel, who has not yet alighted, extends his hand in blessing while the Virgin draws back into her small house. The diagonals of the bodies are softly contradicted by the curves of the quatrefoil lobes and the horizontals and verticals of the architecture. The geometry of the setting is brilliantly played against the supple organic bodies, a trait found throughout Ghiberti's reliefs.

Of course, the fashionable grace of the scene resembles the work of Lorenzo Monaco: the attenuated body of the Virgin with its small head and delicate facial features would not be alien to a panel by him, nor would the long sweeping folds of the Virgin's dress or the angel's complex robes. Works like Lorenzo Monaco's Accademia *Annunciation* are recalled by the vibrant, carefully shaped void between the two bronze figures and by the brilliantly calculated adjustment to, and contrast with, the shape of the frame. While it is probable that the painted *Annunciation* is later than the bronze version, their community of spirit demonstrates that their authors had the same stylistic concepts and clearly understood each other's work. In Trecento and Quattrocento Florence, borrowing from other artists was considered the best way to improve one's art. So even though it is quite likely that paintings by Monaco had a profound effect on Ghiberti, it is just as plausible that Ghiberti's sculpture influenced Monaco. This artistic interchange was common; painters and sculptors took what they liked and could use from the works of others throughout their careers.

Because no exact dating is possible for the conception or execution of the Baptistery door reliefs, no precise chronological parallels can be made with contemporary painting. However, by the time the work on the doors was begun

53. Lorenzo Ghiberti, *Annunciation*. Florence, Baptistery.

54. Lorenzo Ghiberti, *Adoration of the Magi*. Florence, Baptistery.

(c.1403), Monaco was already an established artist. Perhaps then, one might be correct in supposing some influence from him (and from his first followers) on the youthful Ghiberti.

Nowhere is the Monaco–Ghiberti connection more evident than in the *Adoration of the Magi* (Plate 54). It is the spirit of Ghiberti's relief rather than any borrowed motif that recalls Monaco. Monaco's Uffizi *Adoration* is probably later than Ghiberti's relief, so it is even possible that Monaco might have drawn some inspiration from the bronze. Whatever the exact stylistic relationship between the two, the feeling of exotic fantasy they provoke is quite similar. Ghiberti's beautifully dressed, attenuated men observing the action occuring in the foreground seem to belong to the race of highly mannered people in Monaco's *Adoration*. Equally alike are the melancholy gazes, tightly curled tresses, and long, flowing beards.

In his relief Ghiberti does not have Monaco's control over drapery. Although the bronze figures often reveal the bulk of their bodies beneath their robes (note the leg and knee of the bearded magus, or the back of the kneeling magus), their drapery has a rhythm of its own, which catches the spectator's eye, nearly diverting it from the story. Here the complex stances and swinging drapery remind one more of the Master of the Bambino Vispo or the Master of 1419 than of Lorenzo Monaco.

In the Baptistery reliefs Ghiberti's style resembles that of a painter. The additive process of modeling the quatrefoils in wax before they were cast in bronze is more like putting paint on a panel than the subtractive action of carving stone. The softness of Ghiberti's forms, his use of extremely low relief to suggest the disappearance of objects into space (always, however, rigidly controlled), and the incredibly subtle transitions between the convexity and concavity of the surface are painterly in nature.

In his *Commentari* Ghiberti includes a capsule history of art. His appreciation of Giotto, Duccio, and several other Trecento painters (especially the Sienese, whose use of line he must have admired) reveals that he studied their work with care. As a painter, his observation of the old masters was only natural, but Ghiberti was also a conservative artist who never abandoned his ties with the past. The majority of his narratives utilize traditional iconographic arrangements, while the strong memory of the Sienese painter Duccio and the sculptor Andrea Pisano (the author of the first set of Baptistery doors in the 1330s) permeates his pictorial thought. Ghiberti is a complex artist whose work is composed of many elements: his training as a goldsmith and as a painter, a deep respect for the past, and an elegant, fashionable style. To understand Ghiberti's accomplishments and his position in Florentine art, all these things should be kept in mind so that the artist is seen in the context of his own background and times. He should not be viewed as a man caught between the stylistically vague terms *Gothic* and *Renaissance* (as has so often been done), but should be recognized as one of the finest representatives of an indigenous Florentine style that flourished during the first several decades of the Quattrocento.

The bronze *St. John the Baptist* (Plate 55), Ghiberti's first known full-round figure, was begun some time around 1413 for the church of Or San Michele. During the early fifteenth century, this church became one of the principal repositories of Florentine sculpture. Each of the important guilds was assigned a niche to be filled with a bronze or marble statue of its patron saint.[14] The niches are on the outside of the building, high above street level. Ghiberti's statue of St. John, placed within a fussy niche, was commissioned by the Calimala, the same guild that oversaw the Baptistery door competition.

The graceful, swaying articulation of the gaunt desert saint and his measured

55. Lorenzo Ghiberti, *St. John the Baptist.*
Florence, Or San Michele.

relation to the niche are wrought with care. Every complex rhythm of the great loops of drapery, hair shirt, and beard is alive and wonderfully exciting. But once again painting springs to mind. A glance at the St. Peter from the altar-piece by the Master of the Bambino Vispo at Würzburg demonstrates that this artist and Ghiberti are working along similar lines. In the attenuated intersections of the various axes of the body and in the self-conscious bearing of the refined figures there is a special affinity between sculptor and painter. The large, soft folds that rise in light from shadowy troughs created by the deep creases, or the bony, mobile faces — partially covered by the tightly curled beards — testify to a shared artistic outlook.

Giovanni d'Ambrogio, the sculptor of the Duomo *Annunciation* (if he is not Giovanni), and Lorenzo Ghiberti are the best of the Florentine sculptors to emerge from the stylistic world of the late Trecento, and they represent the highest level of this development. To see what the works of popular (and thus important), but less accomplished, sculptors of the period are like, one needs to turn to Bernardo Ciuffagni's or Niccolò Lamberti's Evangelist statues for the façade of the Duomo. These figures are especially interesting because they can

56. Niccolò di Piero Lamberti,
St. Mark. Florence, Museo
dell'Opera del Duomo.

be compared with two others that were commissioned about the same time but
were carved in an entirely different spirit: Donatello's *St. John the Evangelist*
and Nanni di Banco's *St. Luke*.

Lamberti (c.1370–1451) was a Florentine who spent much time working in
Venice.[15] His *St. Mark* (Plate 56; now in the Museo dell'Opera del Duomo) for
the Duomo façade was commissioned in 1408. Like the other statues, it is a
nearly life sized seated marble figure and was placed in a niche on the façade.
Lamberti, however, did not compensate for the distance between the statue and
the observer below. His many fussy, sharp details could not have been seen from
the ground: the intricate folding of the hems, the circles of material over the
right shoulder, and the curled, patterned beard must have been nearly invisible.
Lamberti simply conceived and carved the figure as though it were to be seen
from close up.

There is also no attempt to establish communication between the figure and
the observer (such a linkage was an important part of the three other figures
destined for the façade). In fact, there is very little connection between the

57. Bernardo Ciuffagni, *St. Matthew.*
Florence, Museo dell'Opera
del Duomo.

statue's various elements: the position and articulation of the body are not clear;
one senses no organic ties between its parts; and it is impossible to see exactly
where the leg connects to the knee or the arm to the shoulder. There is no
definable relation between the material covering the body and the body itself.
The swirls, twists, and knots of the heavy cloth have an exclusively decorative
existence; there are few logical or coherent rhythmic passages from part to part.

Even though the figure was not finished until 1415, it shows little sign of the
stylistic developments of the early Quattrocento. Instead, it harks back to
Agnolo Gaddi and Spinello Aretino. Its rather feeble attempts at grandeur are
not inspired by Lamberti's contemporaries, but by some of the more monumental and sober painters of the late fourteenth century; and there even remains a
trace of the stiffness and rigidity of the mid-Trecento style. The rigid pose and
closed silhouette of the figure remind one of something created by a follower of
Nardo.

Bernardo Ciuffagni (1381–1457), our other representative of more middling
Florentine sculpture of the early Quattrocento, was commissioned in 1410 to

do the *St. Matthew* (Plate 57) for the Duomo façade.[16] One glance tells us that a new spirit is at work here. This statue is more direct and coherent than Lamberti's, and it is obvious that Ciuffagni took the spectator's viewpoint into consideration. He has elongated the torso to compensate for the optical distortion that occurs when the figure is seen from the street. This seemingly simple difference (which stems from Donatello) between Ciuffagni's and Lamberti's Evangelists is actually quite important, for it is indicative of a desire to create closer ties between the spectator and the work of art.

In contrast to Lamberti's *St. Mark*, Ciuffagni's statue is a marvel of integration and simplicity. The overall fussiness of Mark's robes has been replaced by a reduced rendering of heavy drapery, one that reveals much more of the workings of the body underneath. The connections between the various parts of the body and their potential for action are clearer and stronger: note how the drapery pulls over the knees and the way the right arm appears through the robes; now one feels the layers of material. The relation between the simplified drapery and the body and the organic articulation of the body itself make the statue more plausible; and since the figure appears more real it seems physically and psychologically nearer the spectator.

The saint's face is an organic whole, echoing the unity of the entire figure. The eyes look downward (originally toward the street and the viewer); and the head is tilted slightly in the same direction, as though the figure is acknowledging something outside its own immediate space. The stylized beard (more natural than the decorative, stuck-on beard of the *St. Mark*) surrounds a subtly modeled face.

Part of the difference between Lamberti's and Ciuffagni's statues can be attributed to the artists' relative skills as marble carvers. Without doubt, Ciuffagni was a rather good sculptor while Lamberti was not. But the essential disparities between their Evangelists stem not only from skill or style. There was a strong desire on Ciuffagni's part to fashion a unified dynamic body with implications outside itself, to create a simplified, convincing figure that is in touch with the spectator. In the art of Florence that is something very new; its invention cannot be credited to Ciuffagni, however, but to that supreme genius, Donatello. For on the façade of the Duomo there was once placed yet another Evangelist: the *St. John* (Plate 58) commissioned from Donatello in 1408, which, upon its completion, became one of the landmarks of Florentine art.

Donatello, whose full name was Donato di Betto Bardi, was probably born between 1383 and 1386. His first experience with the art of his day must therefore have been with the works of Agnolo Gaddi, Spinello Aretino, and their contemporaries.

Some time between 1404 and 1407 Donatello worked on the Baptistery

58. Donatello, *St. John the Evangelist*. Florence, Museo dell'Opera del
Duomo.

doors in the shop of Lorenzo Ghiberti.[17] His first independent commissions seem to have come around the time of the Duomo *St. John the Evangelist* (1408). Soon he was engaged on a number of important statues for the Duomo and Or San Michele that were to occupy him during the second decade of the century. His *St. John* was preceded by a *David* (Plate 59) for the Duomo (commissioned in 1408, completed in 1409; now in the Bargello, Florence), which serves as a good introduction to the slightly more developed style of the Evangelist figure.

The *David*, carved in a warm, grayish-pink marble, is more vivid than any work discussed thus far. One is taken aback by the tense carriage of the body and the alert face. The figure seems animated from within, awake and aware of the world around. It is vibrant, endowed with the potential for action. By so energizing the figure Donatello has made a statue different from any of its Trecento predecessors; it is no longer just the image but the personality and presence of David.

The *David* also relates to the area around it in a new way. The body and the head move along slightly different axes, forming a decided movement within the figure. As the arms curve outward from the torso they allow space to enter the confines of the body: the contours are broken and opened. Donatello has thus fashioned two significant areas of void within the framework of the figure. David's robe (which may have been recut by Donatello after the statue was finished) descends slowly but decisively from the left hand, creating yet another deviation from the vertical and a further intrusion into the surrounding void. By pushing the figure out into the spectator's environment, Donatello forges a new rapport between observer and holy figure.

The *David* exhibits a nervous energy that is consistent with what he has just been through (Goliath's head is at his feet) and with Donatello's obvious desire to make him interact with the onlooker. The sinuous development of the arms and legs; the tilted head with its somewhat startled, almost quizzical expression; the long, twisting neck; and the contradicting movements of arm, legs, and drapery folds make the figure appear tense, about to move into our world. The *David* is alive with varying rhythms: the long, slow sweep of the robe down the legs; the sharper, twisting folds around the waist; the shorter, deeper folds on the chest and left sleeve — each calculated to activate the form.

No artist develops out of a stylistic vacuum; all are sensitive to the art of their ancestors. It is sometimes hard to discover the source of inspiration of a genius, for the workings of his fertile, subtle mind can almost totally transform borrowed sources and stylistic influences. This is especially true of Donatello. The *David*, his first extant work, is already nearly a seamless whole, the result of the integral style of his youth. However, there are some just-discernible traces of

59. Donatello, *David*. Florence, Bargello.

the influences on him. The elegant carriage of the figure, the sweeping robe, and the self-confident air are reminiscent of Lorenzo Monaco, the artist of the Duomo group, and Lorenzo Ghiberti. The suave, refined members of the train in the Uffizi and in the Baptistery door *Adorations* seem to be distant cousins of the marble *David*. This is only natural, for when Donatello was carving the figure, Lorenzo Monaco's and Ghiberti's styles held sway in Florence; and it was with Ghiberti that Donatello had been employed a few years before he began the *David*.

While the youthful works of all great masters owe a debt — obvious or subtle — to older artists, their later work may set the stylistic pace of their times or even soar above it, moving with a rhythm all its own. This latter development is well exemplified in Donatello, for several years after the marble *David* his work was indebted mainly to his earlier sculpture as the chain reaction of his own style propelled him forward.

Much of what was first conceived and then carved in the *David* was shortly to reappear in the marble *St. John the Evangelist* (Museo dell'Opera del Duomo, Florence), of 1408. Of the four figures executed for the façade, it is Donatello's that first catches and holds the spectator's eye, for it (even more than the *David*) has a radiating presence. The patent power of the figure is expressed in the large hands, the strong shoulders, and the eyes' fiery glance. Although in repose, the *St. John* seems about to rise, as he moves his large head slightly to the viewers' left (implying that the object of his interest is behind us to our left) in the opposite direction of the turn of his legs. This shifting between the head and the body charges the figure with potential movement and keeps it from becoming a static entity like Lamberti's *St. Mark*.

Donatello has taken great care in his bold, dynamic design of the *St. John* to accommodate the needs of the viewer (making adjustments similar to those Ciuffagni attempted in his own Evangelist). The elongation of the chest and neck and the strong forward tilt of the head compensate for the optical distortion that would occur when the statue was put in place above the street. The almost abstracted treatment of parts of the figure — the large units that define the knees, the folds around the waist, and the vast, nearly flat chest — would also be easy to see and understand from below. Even the very nature of the broad carving indicates Donatello's desire to make the figure seem coherent. From the street, the articulation of the planes of the body and the wide, rather roughly shaped folds would be clearly comprehensible. The wealth of detail that characterized Lamberti's figure (and much of previous Florentine sculpture) has been abandoned in favor of a composition at once simple and readily intelligible.

The shock that Donatello's contemporaries felt when they saw the marble *David* was probably equalled when they first glimpsed the *St. John*. Never before in the history of Florentine sculpture had there been such a tense, electric image. The clarity of its form and its potential for action are not matched by any earlier statue in the city. As they gazed at the stern face and flowing beard or looked at the great hands now slack, but obviously full of strength, they must have felt themselves in the presence of something human rather than, as in the past, before some iconic, unapproachable holy apparition. Here was a man like themselves — perhaps more terrible and powerful — but a man nevertheless. One later admirer certainly understood the concentrated, economical method by which Donatello was magically able to make marble into an animated being: when Michelangelo began to carve his *Moses* (now in San Pietro in Vincoli, Rome) the memory of the Duomo *St. John* must have been in his mind.

About five years after beginning the *St. John*, Donatello was at work on a statue for the north side of Or San Michele, the marble *St. George* (Plate 60) commissioned for a niche with a carved *predella* owned by the guild of armorers (the Arte dei Spadai e Corazzai). At first glance the George (now in the Bargello) looks lost in his large niche, surrounded by a considerable expanse of space. But the isolation plays a vital role in the meaning of the figure. Unlike David, George is not already a victorious hero; his battle with the dragon is yet to come. The void surrounding his form fixes the figure as the solid, solitary center of the entire composition.

The widespread legs form a stable base for the tensed body. The sturdy shoulders and armored torso are turned frontward, while the head, set on a graceful neck, cranes forward, staring out behind the spectator. But the figure is not rigid; one senses the continual adjustment and balance necessary to maintain the tense, alert pose.

The *St. George* is not self-sufficient; to be understandable and complete it must interact with its immediate milieu, with the space around and before it, for its psychic and physical strength is concentrated on events yet to come. Standing in front of this figure, one feels compelled to turn around to find the object of George's anxious stare. Figure and spectator are now involved in the same space, time, and action.

The drama expressed by the position and posture of St. George is also shown on his youthful face. Its vitality results from Donatello's complete understanding of the structure of the head and his uncanny ability to realize it in stone. One feels the solid structure of the forehead, under the taut, creased skin; the hardness of the jaw; and the rigidity of the nose. But — and this is one of the splendors of Donatello's art that make their embryonic appearance in the marble

60. Donatello, *St. George*. Florence, Bargello.

David — all this underlying structure is seen (or perhaps *sensed* is a better word) through a layer of skin that itself has another texture and feeling. For the first time in Florence a sculptor has been able to depict the textural differences between an ear lobe and a nose, between the pliability of a lip and the boniness of an eye socket. Never before had Florentines seen a face so well articulated, so convincingly real. With understanding and skill Donatello has created a visage that echoes and complements the emotions expressed by the body.

The *St. George* and the other early works by Donatello are landmarks, for they introduced a new type of religious imagery. The art of Florence from the late Duecento through the early Quattrocento is characterized by the increasing realism of religious figures and drama. This development was not an unbroken Darwinian evolution, and it was not without numerous deviations, but beginning with Cimabue and Giotto, there was an increasing movement away from the hieratic, iconic images of Duecento art.[18] Yet, the past stylistic and iconographic development of sacred images could not have prepared Florentines for the vitality and immediacy of the *St. George*. That statue broke the ancient barrier that still existed between the spectator and the holy figures and stories in the beginning of the fifteenth century.

Just below the *St. George* is a stone *predella* (Plate 61) carved by Donatello in *rilievo schiacciato*, an extremely subtle low relief. In his first extant narrative the artist depicts figures in movement in a scene filled with high dramatic action. In the center, St. George on horseback kills the dragon. As his mount rears in fright, the saint puts all his weight behind the spear he thrusts into the monster. George and the body of the horse are carved in medium relief, but from the neck upward, the horse is rendered very shallowly. Undoubtedly this device was used to suggest movement of the horse back into space, but it does not work well, and the illusion of the aerial perspective is not achieved. The unsuccessful attempt seems to indicate two things: that Donatello had little experience with this type of relief, and that he was striving for what can only be called a painterly treatment of space. Painters can indicate objects receding into space by making them less distinct; and the use of this aerial perspective was to become commonplace in the first half of the Quattrocento, although it was not employed much before the St. George *predella*.

Donatello uses painterly concepts in other parts of the *predella*: the flying cloak and horse's mane; the wind-blown robes of the princess standing to the right; and the arcade, which moves in an illusionistic manner back into space along two converging orthogonals. The background itself is in very low relief; windswept trees scratched in the marble's surface are barely visible, and stumpy hills are lost in the atmospheric haze of deep space. Donatello could have uti-

61. Donatello, *St. George*, Predella. Florence, Bargello.

lized a higher relief for his *predella*, but he must have felt that the technique of *rilievo schiacciato* would allow him the spatial and pictorial goals he wished and which he could achieve only by using the illusionistic methods of painting.

Although he has utilized a painterly technique here, it does not appear that Donatello has borrowed it from any particular artist. While Lorenzo Monaco's landscape backgrounds are fantastic and mysterious — like the deep space in the St. George *predella* — they are not nearly as weird, atmospheric, or illusionistic as Donatello's. Even Ghiberti, who also borrowed much from painting, never allowed the space of his doors to become so realistic that it threatened their solidity. Donatello was in the vanguard of the development of aerial perspective. The St. George *predella*, which was to have a profound effect on later artists, both painters and sculptors, exemplies the unity of sculpture and painting during the early Quattrocento.

That Donatello was commissioned (and paid) to do these statues indicates his patrons' approval of his new conception of art. Since the publication of Jacob Burckhardt's famous *The Civilization of the Renaissance in Italy* in the middle of the nineteenth century, the early Quattrocento has been seen as the seedbed of modern individuality, the period in which the ego triumphed over the collective mentality of earlier times. While Burkhardt's chronology for this development has been challenged, his theories seem to remain valid.[19] In the late Trecento and early Quattrocento there are indeed signs that men wished, more and more, to record their deeds and thus endow their names with at least a certain amount of immortality. Histories (of both cities and men), memoirs, and paintings of donor portraits become more frequent. During this time particular personalities and specific motivations of the important figures emerge. No longer was life seen as predestined; man began to take a new interest in his world, which he now saw as a less anonymous, less hostile, more hospitable place. Florentines started to think of their environment as a civil, beautiful setting for their daily activities.

So when Donatello created his new, highly accessible and strikingly live images, he was in many ways responding to contemporary feelings about man and his place in the world. After the 1420s several other artists were also able to break with the iconic tradition of the past and forge a new imagery that would tie strongly individualized sacred figures to those who worshipped them. This new breed of religious hero was the contemporary of the Florentines, who were then becoming increasingly conscious of their own individuality.[20]

Concomitant with this development were the beginnings of town planning on a consistent, sustained basis. Men of the early Quattrocento wished to control their environment and make it serve their own needs. In painting after c.1420 religious drama is increasingly depicted in the streets and squares of Florence. By making his city the center of his spiritual world, man brought the sacred and the mysterious to earth while at the same time making his own environment a holy place.[21] Ultimately, perhaps, this phenomenon is the result of the concrete Florentine mind, which always strove to make things measurable and understandable.

In the next chapter we will see how many formal elements of Masaccio's pictures (one-point perspective, light, modeling) tie the painted images to the spectator's world. Although this new-found realism is easier to create in painting than in sculpture, it first developed in the latter. It was in the work of Donatello that the traditional modes of religious expression and representation were broken and the way was opened for iconographic and stylistic developments that would eventually give new meanings to the sacred stories.

Naturally, the impact of these first works by Donatello was strongly felt in Florence. We have already seen the early influence of his *St. John* on Ciuffagni's *St. Matthew*. Another sculptor who was touched by these innovations was Nanni di Banco, a Florentine who was probably born in the 1370s and was, therefore, a slightly older contemporary of Donatello's. Nanni's death in the 1420s cut short a promising career, which had started only in the first decade of the Quattrocento.[22]

62. Nanni di Banco, *St. Luke.*
Florence, Museo dell'Opera
del Duomo.

Nanni's *St. Luke* (Plate 62), begun in 1408 (Museo dell'Opera del Duomo, Florence), is another in the series of seated Evangelists commissioned for the Duomo façade. The basic structure of its body and the relation of one part to another are often awkward. The expansive chest does not seem properly connected to the torso; the knees appear isolated as they press against the layers of cloth. There is a flatness about the figure common to much late-Trecento sculpture but always alien to the fluid, highly developed articulation of all Donatello's early figures. Nanni was undoubtedly aware of Donatello's *St. John* (or at least its basic design), for St. Luke's expansive arms, large hands, and tilted head with stern, downcast eyes are surely indebted to it. Also similar is the figure's potential for action; the Evangelists of both men seem endowed with a spiritual force almost unequaled by any other works from the period.

.Nanni's debt to the style of Ghiberti and Lorenzo Monaco is also apparent. Looking at the elongation of the *St. Luke* (especially from the side), or the looping, heavy fold patterns, or the elegant, somewhat frosty face, one is reminded of works like Ghiberti's *St. John the Baptist* on Or San Michele or the scores of elegant saints by Lorenzo Monaco and his circle.

But what separates Nanni from more eclectic artists (Ciuffagni or Lamberti, for example) are his skill, inventiveness, and ability to develop rapidly. He was, after Donatello and Ghiberti, the most talented sculptor of the early fifteenth century. But like Ciuffagni, he occupies a middle ground between the older idiom of the late Trecento and the stylistic leaps of Donatello.

Nanni's strong personal idiom is well illustrated by the *Quattro Santi Coronati* (Plate 63), a group he carved for the Stone and Wood Carvers guild (the Arte dei Maestri di Pietra e Legname, to which he belonged) for their niche on the north side of Or San Michele. This commission (c.1413, almost exactly contemporary with Donatello's neighboring *St. George*) called for the representation of four ancient Roman sculptors martyred for refusing to make pagan idols for Emperor Diocletian.[23]

The fitting of four nearly life-sized figures into a rather shallow niche was the most immediate problem facing Nanni. He resolved it most satisfactorily by grouping them into a semi-circular arrangement, by overlapping the back figures with those farther forward, and by varying the postures from profile to frontal, thus creating enough room for them all. Each figure is linked to the others by the conversation in which they take part, not only with their imagined voices but also with their postures and gestures. The man on the far right opens his mouth in speech while holding out his hand to make a point (perhaps a sad one for the man behind has his hand on the speaker's shoulder in what looks like a gesture of consolation), while the others seem to listen intently as they await their turn to speak. There is a real sense of drama as each martyr participates in the animated but somber dialogue. It is always important to consider the location of these and all the other Or San Michele statues, for their niches are right above the spectator's head; and the feet of several of Nanni's saints protrude several inches beyond the base of the niche. Or San Michele has always been bounded by rather narrow streets, so it is impossible for the passerby not to notice the figures that flank its sides. All this is especially applicable to the *Quattro Santi Coronati*, as Nanni's four martyrs are often called, for their closeness to the observer soon draws one into their mute conversation.

But it is not an easy dialogue. Although their poses, gestures, and facial expressions are very human, the saints belong to a grave, dignified, and singularly serious race. Their ponderous toga-clad bodies stand firmly on the ground; their actions are charged with intense meaning. They are blood relatives of Nanni's *St. Luke* and the earliest works by Donatello.

In his Or San Michele group Nanni was extremely interested in the delineation of robes and hair. Each garment is folded in deeply cut patterns whose rhythms break up the surface by catching the light and direct the spectator's gaze from figure to figure. The shaggy beards and hair, perhaps inspired by Roman sculpture, add a strong abstract pattern. The group is a solid, quiet testimony to determination inspired by faith.

63. Nanni di Banco, *Quattro Santi Coronati*. Florence, Or San
Michele.

There existed in Florence during the first decades of the Quattrocento two
different ways of interpreting religious drama. The first, exemplified by Lorenzo Monaco and Ghiberti, makes religious imagery exist within a highly refined, often exotic milieu. Beautiful actors clothed in fashionable dress participate in the holy scenes with self-conscious style. Donatello and Nanni are the
major exponents of the second type of interpretation, which is concerned with
the immediacy of the sacred images. Their figures are monumental and heroic
in their dignity, purpose, and seemingly unshakeable resolve, yet they are closer
to the observer (both physically and psychologically) than the more mannered
actors of Lorenzo Monaco or Ghiberti.

Of course, there are a number of overlaps between the two ways of perceiving
drama. We have already seen the influence of the more gentle style in Nanni's
St. Luke and Donatello's marble *David*; and in chapter 7 the sway of the sterner
idiom on men such as Bicci di Lorenzo and Gentile da Fabriano will be demonstrated. In actuality, the artists of the early Quattrocento often moved back
and forth between the two styles, and it is a mistake to believe that Florentine
art of the period c.1400 –1420 was divided into two separate, irreconcilable
camps, or into factions that historians have erroneously labeled *progressive* and
regressive. Such distinctions are fabrications and have little relation to the very
fluid artistic interchange that always took place in Florence.

A good case in point is Nanni's last work, carved between 1414 and the
artist's death in 1421, placed above one of the Duomo's north doors. At the
center of the composition the *Madonna della Cintola* (the Madonna of the Assumption giving her belt to St. Thomas; Plate 64) is enclosed in a *mandorla*
supported by angels. Thomas kneels at the lower left, extending his hands to
receive the *cintola* (now lost, it must have been made of tin or some other pliable
metal). In the lower right are a bear and a tree, forms that help to counterbal-
ance Thomas's bulk on the other side of the composition.

The dynamic figure of the Madonna owes much to Donatello's *St John*. Her
torso and head turn sideways and downward (her right foot and hand extending
just over the edge of the *mandorla*) as her legs move in the opposite direction.
Not only has the shifted axis of the *St. John* aided Nanni in his search for
movement, but the angels — especially the one with the bagpipe — are carved
with a vigor and abstraction that recall Donatello's Evangelist and several other
of his early sculptures. But Nanni's figures also contain echoes of an earlier
style. The grace and fluidity of the attenuated Virgin, the self-contained energy
of her robes, and the sweetness of her face are surely indebted to contact with
the work of Ghiberti, Lorenzo Monaco, and their immediate followers.

The abstraction of monumental form and the suavity of figure may have been
derived from several sources, but Nanni has welded them perfectly. The easy

64. Nanni di Banco, *Madonna della Cintola*. Florence, Duomo.

carving of the shapes, most noticeably those of the flanking angels, and the
unity of the composition are Nanni's. With the extremely beautiful St. Thomas
the sculptor has demonstrated his skill at integrating a figure into its stone
environment. The saint's body and head are carefully articulated, and sensi-
tively constructed cupped hands express Thomas's restrained longing. In the
Madonna della Cintola, for the first time, Nanni is working in a more emotional
and stylistically complicated manner. His inspiration and execution are the
equal of those of any of his contemporaries, and one wonders what paths his art
would have followed had he lived longer.

In both sculpture and painting the first two decades of the Quattrocento witnessed a number of crosscurrents. On the whole, stylistic development formed
by the cooperative workshop system went on as it had before with the gradual
merging of one style into another in a slow, orderly succession. The idiom of

Gaddi, Spinello, and Antonio Veneziano gave way to the exotic, radiant style of Lorenzo Monaco, Rossello di Jacopo Franchi, the Master of the Bambino Vispo, Ghiberti, and others belonging to the same circle. That they represent the mainstream of Florentine taste is evident from their numerous important commissions, including, most prominently, Ghiberti's doors. But in the very first years of the Quattrocento the remarkably vivid images of Donatello pointed toward a new interpretation of style and content destined to have a great effect on several artists of utmost importance.

It is against this background that one should see Masaccio's pictures. His stylistic origins and evolution are made more understandable and somewhat less mysterious by a knowledge of his heritage, for he was, like all great artists, a child of his age. From his humble rural birth in the Valdarno through his years in Florence, he was continually affected by the stylistic character of the paintings and sculptures that surrounded his brief but brilliant artist's life.

IV.

Masaccio: Origins and the Early Panels

SAN GIOVANNI VALDARNO is situated in the Arno valley about forty miles upstream from Florence. The small Tuscan town was founded in 1296 by the Florentines to check the expansion of the powerful Ubertini family of Arezzo. In the early years of the Quattrocento San Giovanni Valdarno was a thriving, if rather provincial, place dependent on the great city of Florence.[1] Today it is an important industrial center.

On 21 December 1401 Tommaso (later to be called Masaccio) was born in Castel San Giovanni (as the city was then called) to Ser Giovanni di Mone Cassai and Monna Iacopa di Martinozzo.[2] Ser Giovanni was the son of Mone di Andreuccio, a maker of *cassoni* (marriage chests) and other boxes for domestic use. At the time of Masaccio's birth Giovanni was 20 and was still living with his father. Monna Iacopa was the daughter of an innkeeper named Martinozzo from Barberino di Mugello, a town not far from Giotto's birthplace.

Masaccio had a younger brother named Giovanni — nicknamed Lo Scheggia, "the splinter" — who was born in 1406. He followed Masaccio's footsteps, became an artist, and in 1430 matriculated in the Florentine Arte dei Medici e Speziali.[3] A fresco (seemingly dated 1457) in the church of San Lorenzo in San Giovanni Valdarno shows him to have been a painter of extreme crudity.

Very little is known about Masaccio's childhood. In all likelihood his family was not poor; his father was a notary, a respected if not always well-paid profession. What his family life was like, what he thought and did during his youth, and to what influences he was subjected remain a mystery. However, something can be said about the artistic milieu of San Giovanni Valdarno during the years Masaccio was growing up, and that may help one understand some of the later development of his style.

Not surprisingly, San Giovanni Valdarno never developed its own visual culture or stylistic idiom. The city was small and commissions for major works of art were relatively scarce. Like almost all other provincial centers, it imported art and artists (see the discussion of Bicci di Lorenzo in chapter 2). Art in San Giovanni Valdarno, like trade and politics, was under the influence of Florence, just as farther to the south small towns were tied to Siena's power and swayed by the Sienese idiom.

The first stylistic wave that swept through Masaccio's home town was set in motion by Giotto, an artist whose influence cut across all national boundaries. While no Giottesque painting survives in San Giovanni Valdarno — surely there must have been some — a picture by an artist dependent on Giotto is still to be seen in the Collegiata at Figline Valdarno, a neighboring town. The large altarpiece (Plate 65) by a painter known as the Master of Figline[4] shows the strong impact of Giotto's clear and monumental composition. Within an ordered universe, religious drama unfolds with great simplicity and decorum. The volume created by the rounded throne and its protruding footrest serve to fix the weighty central figures of Virgin and Child in space, while from the sides, static rows of saints look on. The directness of the figures reveals that the artist has closely studied and understood paintings by Giotto and his shop.

Certainly Masaccio must have seen many pictures stylistically akin to the one in Figline Valdarno, for the first part of the Trecento witnessed the painting of Giottesque works everywhere. By the time Masaccio was growing up, some of them were especially prized, and by the early Quattrocento they were already considered part of a revolutionary new style introduced into Florence by Giotto. Because they were old, such works must have been considered extremely holy: in a society that valued tradition they were highly venerated.[5]

Another painting possibly familiar to the young Masaccio is the large polyptych (Plate 66) by Giovanni del Biondo now in Santa Maria delle Grazie, San Giovanni Valdarno (formerly on the high altar of the Oratorio of San Lorenzo in the same city). This *Coronation of the Virgin* surrounded by saints is a good example of Giovanni's style (see chapter 1) from the mid-1370s. His Cionesque heritage is expressed in the uncertain space of the central panel, which is packed to overflowing by the large Christ and the Virgin. They sit suspended in space, surrounded by a *mandorla* of cherubim and fronted by music-making angels. Some of the figures have wide, staring eyes set in masklike faces, which are also reminders of Giovanni's first training with Nardo. However, in this same panel there is a new emphasis on bulk and volume and a new directness of gesture. These innovations mark the beginnings of Giovanni's departure from the Cionesque style toward that more monumental, less introverted idiom of the last years of the Trecento, Giovanni's *Coronation* altarpiece (and other works by his

65. Master of Figline, Altarpiece.
Figline Valdarno, Collegiata.

contemporaries) would have shown Masaccio the style of the painters active just before Lorenzo Monaco and other modern artists of Masaccio's early days.

There is no record of painting in San Giovanni Valdarno by Lorenzo Monaco, but two works in the town are attributed to Mariotto di Nardo (see chapter 2), an artist who came under the influence of Monaco and his circle: a *Pietà* with symbols of the Passion, and a Saint, both in the Oratorio of San Lorenzo. Men like Mariotto di Nardo, Lorenzo di Niccolò, and other middling painters working in Florence during the first decades of the Quattrocento often received commissions for many of the small Tuscan towns. The idiom of these men, as we have seen in chapter 2, slowly evolved out of the Trecento and then, under the sway of Lorenzo Monaco, developed into an elegant, fashionable style. Very probably a painting like Mariotto's *Pietà* in San Giovanni Valdarno was Masaccio's first introduction to the contemporary art of his time.

One of the crucial unanswered questions about Masaccio concerns his training: With whom and where did he receive his artistic education? Lacking documentation, we can only speculate. There is a possibility that he was apprenticed to a local artist, perhaps one of the men who decorated his grandfather's *cassoni*,

66. Giovanni del Biondo, Altarpiece. San Giovanni Valdarno,
Santa Maria delle Grazie.

which were often painted. If that were indeed the case, the boy's first introduction to the practice of painting would have been the direct, often crude, but always vigorous scenes that ornamented the marriage chests; and if his apprenticeship were typical, it would have lasted many years.

If Masaccio first studied in San Giovanni Valdarno, the roots of his style would probably have been conservative, a bit out of date, and of a nature pleasing to a provincial, rather rural taste. If, on the other hand, the boy was sent to Florence to study, his teacher's idiom would probably have been more urban, more up to date, and less conservative. We do not know if the normal practice was to send promising painters to the big city for training.

There is one tenuous connection between Masaccio's family and Florence. His stepsister Caterina (Masaccio's father died in 1406, and his mother remarried) was married to the painter Mariotto di Cristofano,[6] who was also born in San Giovanni Valdarno. He was eight years older than Masaccio, and by 1419 he is documented working in Florence. It is possible, but not provable, that Masaccio may have been sent to Florence to study with his brother-in-law. In any case, he probably had some contact with Mariotto there.

67. Mariotto di Cristofano, Altarpiece. Carda, Parrocchiale.

An altarpiece in Carda (Plate 67; originally painted for the Benedictine Ab-
bey of Santa Trinità in Alpe near Talla, a town close to San Giovanni Valdarno)
has been convincingly attributed to Mariotto di Cristofano and dated around
1420. This picture reveals that he was a discreet, derivative artist of rather high
quality who was influenced by contemporary Florentine style, which he grafted
onto his basically old-fashioned idiom. The blond tonality of his faces reminds
one of Masolino, while the combinations of colors (pink, blue, red, brown,
gray) recall Monaco's palette. From the little evidence available, it appears that
Mariotto's unadventuresome work had small impact on the young Masaccio.

Aside from his birth date, the first certain documentation on Masaccio is 7
January 1422 (1421 Florentine style), the date he matriculated in the Arte dei
Medici e Speziali of Florence, the guild to which the painters belonged. This is
the first evidence of Masaccio's presence in Florence; at the time he was living
in the popular San Niccolò district. His matriculation indicates that he was
working in the city, for it was probably necessary for an artist to join a guild
before he could begin all but the most minor commissions, but it does not
necessarily mean that Masaccio had been trained in Florence.[7]

68. Masaccio, San Giovenale Triptych. Florence, Uffizi.

The date of the earliest known work by Masaccio, the San Giovenale triptych (Plate 68), is also 1422. The inscription on the frame reads ANNO DO/MINI MCCCCXII A DI VENTITRE D'AP[RILE]. The painting was found only in the early 1960s, and its discovery enables us to judge what Masaccio's early style was like.

The triptych, which is now in the Uffizi, was found in its original location in the Church of San Giovenale in Cascia,[8] a tiny town in the Valdarno about ten miles from Masaccio's birthplace. This raises a question: Was the commission for the triptych given to Masaccio before he moved to Florence? The very fact that it was done for such a small place may indicate that it was commissioned locally for a modest sum and that the church authorities looked for an artist in nearby San Giovanni Valdarno. On the other hand, it is possible that someone who knew Masaccio from San Giovanni Valdarno recommended him as a good, but fledgling (and not too expensive), artist working in Florence. In any case, the painting's date proves that it was finished about three months after Masaccio's matriculation in the Florentine Arte dei Medici e Speziali.

The triptych is rather small (maximum height about one meter) and is composed of three separate panels, each ending in a pointed arch. It is a modest work of simple design; *predella* scenes, finials, or pilaster panels seem not to have been attached. Triptychs with pointed arches were introduced into Tuscan painting in considerable numbers during the first half of the Trecento, but they were mainly small portable altarpieces intended for domestic worship. Larger triptychs with the Madonna and Child in the center panel and flanking saints in the wings came into fashion during the second half of the Trecento. The available evidence (which is far from complete) suggests that by 1422 such triptychs were no longer in favor in Florence. So, while the San Giovenale painting was not really archaic in 1422, neither was it innovative. In fact, it seems to have been just the type (not too modern) that a provincial artist might paint for a provincial church.[9]

The center panel depicts the enthroned Madonna and Child fronted by two kneeling angels. In the left wing are SS. Bartholomew and Blaise; in the right SS. Giovenale and Anthony Abbot. The Madonna and Child with angels is the most common subject for the center of triptychs, so it is of no help in particularizing the circumstances under which the work was conceived. Aside from St. Giovenale, the patron saint of the church for which the altarpiece was made, and St. Blaise, who is often represented in the first half of the Quattrocento, iconography is of little aid in localizing the triptych's origins.

The center panel is spatially more active than the side wings. Filling the middle of the composition is the great body of the Madonna, which forms a triangular shape extending from the smooth, plastic oval of her face to the flared hem of her robe. The rhythm of this descending triangle is continued and then amplified by the bodies of the kneeling angels, whose outstretched hands lead the eye back toward the Madonna.

The quick up-and-down movement of the triangle is counterbalanced by the throne, before which all the figures exist. Its convex backrest, the sweep of the arms, and the forward flight of the footrest make this a dynamic, space-creating architectural structure whose precise geometric surfaces and units contrast strongly with the figures' crinkled and folded robes. There is a highly sophisticated interlocking of solid and void as Masaccio plays the bulky, frontal form of the Virgin against the well of space created by the curving throne, or makes the angels' bodies stop the outward rush of the foreshortened armrests. Such careful, successful composing suggests that this picture is not Masaccio's first and that a period of experimentation lies behind it.

While the spatial arrangement of the center panel is extremely inventive, some of its individual elements are quite traditional. A similar, but certainly not identical, throne appears in the Giottesque altarpiece from Figline Valdarno discussed earlier. Strongly curving backs and protruding, semi-circular foot-rests are seen in both paintings. Because such throne types are not common, it is possible that in his search for a monumental, space-forming structure Masaccio remembered the panel near his native town. And, in fact, the Figline Valdarno picture (and others like it by followers of Giotto) may have helped Masaccio with certain spatial problems — the positioning of bodies, the gravity of heavy figures—whose solutions he could not satisfactorily find in the paintings of his close contemporaries.

A comparison of the San Giovenale triptych with Spinello Aretino's *Madonna and Child* (Plate 14) in the St. Louis Museum of Art (completed c.1410) will elucidate Masaccio's stylistic relation with a nearly contemporary painter. It is possible that Masaccio received his earliest education from an artist who either was trained by or was deeply under the sway of someone from Spinello's generation — the generation that set the course for Florentine painting from the 1370s until the first years of the Quottrocento. Spinello's and Masaccio's compositions contain the same elements: the triangle formed by the Madonna, the kneeling angels at the lower left and right, and the large throne. But the resemblance does not extend much further than the sharing of elements and types.

Masaccio's already consummate mastery of foreshortening is seen in the two angels, whose bodies direct our attention into the picture's space. Their heads are in lost profile so that no facial features are visible; the faces appear as smooth, bulbous, geometric shapes. The emotional state of the figures is expressed solely by their fervent, adoring body gestures. How different this is from Spinello's carefully delineated profiles! There are, to my knowledge, no examples of lost profiles in Tuscan painting before Masaccio. His sacrifice of expressive facial features for the much more formally exciting and abstracted lost profile heads is an early indication of his daring disregard of certain ancient conventions.

This is equally true of the forms and the handling of the triptych's surface. With the possible exception of Giotto, no one had ever painted body and drapery planes of such breadth. The shapes that subtly form themselves into high-lighted plateaus or shadowed troughs are set down with an amazing freedom. Masaccio has abandoned the tight control of the surface of most previous painting and has replaced it with a new energy that perfectly matches the formal and emotional amplitude of the triptych's figures. The palpability of both the bodies and the space in which they exist is much greater than in Spinello's work or in any other late-Trecento picture.

The substantial figures move through an almost visible atmosphere, and the naturalistic light falls on the weighty material in a most convincing fashion. It is as though actual daylight has permeated the surface of the painting. One feels in close proximity to the bulky bodies. A similar destruction of the old iconic barrier between the spectator's world and the realm of the image has already been noted in Donatello's early sculpture. The San Giovenale triptych is one of its earliest manifestations in paint.

The strong presence of the figures is aided (and to some extent forged) by the perspective of the triptych's various parts. The ground plane is made of wide dark boards (a feature unique to this painting). They all converge in a location on the horizon behind the Madonna, thus imparting a tight spatial unity to the altarpiece. The three separate panels are composed as though they were one. In a sense, the San Giovenale triptych is the logical conclusion of the movement toward the spatial unification of altarpieces attempted — but not fully achieved — by Agnolo Gaddi, Spinello Aretino, Antonio Veneziano, and others working during the last quarter of the Trecento.

Perhaps the most striking thing about the palette of the San Giovenale triptych is its simplicity. The center panel has only a very limited range of colors: the blue of the Madonna's mantle (now damaged and oxidized to a black), the green of its lining, the rose of her tunic, the very similar red-rose of the angels' robes, and the gray of the throne. These large areas of color are employed not as decorative elements but to enhance the overall composition and to delineate the separate masses. Small notes of green, red, and yellow (all the hair is blond) appear on the throne and the angels' wings. But the palette is generally restricted, somber, and controlled. The young artist already demonstrates that his use of color, like his handling of space and form, is economical, simple, and sober.

The restrained palette of the San Giovenale triptych has its origins in the late Trecento; although in the right wing the clash of St. Giovenale's rose robe with the greenish gray of St. Anthony's cloak is reminiscent of the harsh contrasts of the mid-Trecento. But Masaccio's choice and use of color seem to be highly personal and not strongly indebted to any particular artist.

Neither the palette nor the form of the triptych suggests that Masaccio had been captivated by the style or spirit of Lorenzo Monaco, Ghiberti, or Gentile da Fabriano — all highly influential artists at work in Florence around 1422. There is none of their lightness, grace, or elegance. The stolid Madonna and saints are serious, purposeful, and earthbound, unlike the more wistful figures by Ghiberti or Lorenzo Monaco. In the formidable San Giovenale triptych the hems of the saints' garments are kept under tight control. Never are the folds of their robes allowed to form the rhythmic, calligraphic patterns that were fashionable in the first decade of the Quattrocento. Nor is there the range of lively color so often found in the works of Lorenzo Monaco and his followers.

Does this indicate that the young Masaccio (he was twenty-one when he dated the triptych) had only a minimal acquaintance with works by the most up-to-date Florentine artists, or, conversely, that he knew their pictures but was not influenced by them? There is a strong possibility that Masaccio had seen works by Monaco and his circle but consciously ignored them; in which case, as early as 1422 he would have been striving for an idiom very different from the one then in vogue — an unusual tack for a young artist from the provinces.

What, then, can be said about the stylistic makeup of Masaccio in 1422? First, the triptych seems to owe a great debt to his study of Giottesque paintings like the one in Figline Valdarno, which appear to have helped him solve very basic compositional problems. His triptych also reveals a rather diluted influence from the mid-Trecento. The smoky faces of SS. Bartholomew and Giovenale with their impassive features and wide eyes recall visages painted by members of Orcagna's circle: the Santa Maria Maggiore altarpiece (see chapter 1), or the early work of Giovanni del Biondo. As we have seen, certain color passages are also reminiscent of painting around 1350.

The serious, weighty figural types and the simple compositional elements of the San Giovenale triptych are, not surprisingly, like those of Agnolo Gaddi and Antonio Veneziano. They are particularly close to an artist like Spinello. But they also recall the modified survival of this late-Trecento idiom in the painting of some of the masters of Masaccio's youth: among others, the early works of Mariotto di Nardo, Lorenzo di Niccolò, and Bicci di Lorenzo. The *Annunciation* at Stia of 1414 by Bicci (see chapter 2) may have been the sort of painting Masaccio was then studying, either in San Giovanni Valdarno or in Florence. The imitable, unadventuresome style of Bicci; his stern, but not frightening, quasi-majestical figures; and his formulaic repetition of motifs probably interested the young, provincial Masaccio. (Bicci's accessible art, it will be remembered, seems to have attracted many commissions from the small towns of Tuscany.) I do not mean to suggest that Bicci had a specific, direct influence on Masaccio; but one should recognize that the San Giovenale triptych and works by artists like Bicci di Lorenzo and Mariotto di Nardo belong to similar generic types.

The revolutionary space, form, and surface of the San Giovenale triptych, however, have few recognizable prototypes in previous Tuscan painting. What was it that allowed Masaccio to paint such a bold, convincing work? Giottesque painting and Donatello's sculpture may provide a clue, but not the answer.

Whatever the reason, there can be little doubt that the San Giovenale triptych is one of the first painted events of the new relation then forming between worshipper and sacred image.

By April 1422 Masaccio had completed the San Giovenale triptych and was already matriculated in the Florentine Arte dei Medici e Speziali. Shortly afterward he probably began work on another altarpiece, the *Madonna with Child, St. Anne and Angels* (Plate 69; originally in Sant'Ambrogio, Florence, now in the Uffizi). This painting seems to mark Masaccio's establishment in the art world of Florence, for while it was not a very important commission, it was, after all, an altarpiece for a Florentine church.[10]

The Sant'Ambrogio panel is a medium-sized altarpiece (1.75m high). In all likelihood, it never had side wings. It is not in good condition, having been badly abraded in several places (including the face of St. Anne), retouched, and overcleaned. Luckily, enough of the paint surface remains to reveal much about the picture's original state.

Iconographically the altarpiece is quite unusual. There are very few representations of the Madonna, Child, and St. Anne in Florentine art, and none that I know before the Sant'Ambrogio picture. Thus Masaccio probably did not have a fund of older images to draw upon (as he did for the San Giovenale triptych) in solving the very difficult compositional problem. His solution (which is comfortable, but not totally convincing and perhaps symptomatic of his inexperience with the problem) was to seat St. Anne in a high backless throne. The Madonna is below her, holding the Child. While the posture of the Madonna is understandable, one is not sure exactly where she sits: on the edge of the throne, or on a stool covered by her robes?

The geometry of the Sant'Ambrogio altarpiece is similar to that of the San Giovenale triptych, although the subjects are quite different. In essence, there are three rough triangles in the center of the Sant'Ambrogio painting. From top to bottom they are: the blunted triangle formed by the cloth of honor held by the angels; the triangular shape of St. Anne; and the pyramid of the seated Virgin. These three geometric figures echo one another, creating an integrated, stabilized network of shape. As in the San Giovenale triptych, large areas of form exist in a harmonious balance.

The sloping, expanding shapes of the triangles are checked and counterbalanced by the two angels at the sides of the throne, who act as stabilizing vertical elements. All three of the upper angels echo the top of the arched panel (originally some type of framing was placed around the gold circles behind them). The boldly shaped elements and the way they articulate the composition remind one of the San Giovenale triptych, in which both figures and space work within broad, interrelated geometric forms.

69. Masaccio, Sant'Ambrogio Altarpiece. Florence, Uffizi.

But the Sant'Ambrogio altarpiece is more spatially advanced. Masaccio has pushed his figures closer to the picture plane and, consequently, closer to the viewer. Rather than recede in space, the figures seem to come forward. St. Anne's right knee and hands move toward the picture plane, while the Virgin's knees almost seem to touch it. In fact, the center of the picture is filled with groping hands, outward-looking faces, and protruding kneees, all very near the viewer's own space. It is an aggressive composition.

Also new is the handling of the figure, which reveals Masaccio's increasing economy. The Sant'Ambrogio figures are bigger, more schematic, and blunter than those in the San Giovenale triptych. The robes and their bulky folds are expansive, the closed silhouettes are monumental, and the large areas of skin are subtly modeled. Only a few artists in the entire history of Florentine art could paint so simply and directly. Giotto was one of them, and his pictures seem to have had a considerable influence on Masaccio by the time he painted the Sant'Ambrogio altarpiece. Certainly Masaccio must have heard of Giotto (who by the early Quattrocento was one of Florence's most famous historical figures) while he was still in San Giovanni Valdarno; but not until he arrived in Florence could he have seen some of Giotto's greatest works, those in the churches of Santa Maria Novella, Ognissanti, and Santa Croce.[11] We can well imagine that Masaccio was overwhelmed by these sublimely economical masterpieces, and suppose that he remembered their direct form and spirit as he designed the Sant'Ambrogio altarpiece.

Masaccio knew Giotto's famous Madonna (Plate 70), now in the Uffizi, while it still stood in the church of Ognissanti, in Florence. The triangle of Giotto's Madonna is echoed by the ponderous Virgin in Masaccio's Sant'Ambrogio altarpiece, and in both paintings the heavy woolen mantles hang across the protruding knees in large, soft folds. But the similarity of these two pictures is stronger than the simple sharing of motifs. Both have a corporeal presence that draws the observer close to the monumental but approachable figures, and both manifest a vibrating human sense seldom found in the art of Florence. But it is in spirit that Masaccio is closest to Giotto. Each was heavily influenced by his own immediate past and by the contemporary art that surrounded him; nevertheless, a community of feeling links their work across the century that separated them.

A more detailed comparison of the Sant'Ambrogio altarpiece and the San Giovenale triptych confirms that the two paintings are the work of the same artist. The heads of the Madonnas are nearly identical. Both exhibit a strong feeling for the underlying bony structure, and the facial planes in each are joined by the same subtle highlight. Other shared features are specific eye shape, the

70. Giotto, Ognissanti Altarpiece.
Florence, Uffizi.

treatment of the lips, the way the drapery folds, and the broad chest of Christ (who seems more Hercules than baby).

Although the light in the San Giovenale triptych seems to come from only one source, it is actually a diffused and generalized illumination with no recognizable origin. In the Sant'Ambrogio altarpiece, however, Masaccio has used a consistent light source coming from the left. Masaccio's lighting is now more sophisticated. By making all the panel's elements receive light in the same way, he unifies the picture and emphasizes the three-dimensional quality of the faces and the nude body of Christ. At the same time, he creates a strong relief by making areas of shadow appear darker and deeper. The consistent illumination also corresponds to our own experience: the painting appears lit by the actual light around it.

Certain areas of the Sant'Ambrogio altarpiece (usually the St. Anne and several angels) have long been attributed to Masolino da Panicale, and that, of course, raises a major problem.[12] It has been suggested that Masolino and Masaccio had some sort of close professional relation. While there is no documentation to prove this connection, there is stylistic evidence that the two artists

had a share in at least two works: the Sant'Ambrogio altarpiece and the Brancacci Chapel in Santa Maria del Carmine.

Recent research has confirmed that Masolino came from the small town of
Panicale near San Giovanni Valdarno, so it is possible that Masaccio and Masolino were drawn together because they were natives of the same region.[13] It
is often postulated that Masolino was older than Masaccio and was his teacher;
but this theory is, to say the least, shaky. Masolino's first documented work is
of 1424, and he entered the Florentine Arte dei Medici e Speziali only in 1423,
a year after Masaccio. There is nothing about Masolino's painting to indicate
that he was a great deal older than Masaccio; stylistically he appears to be an
artist trained with the first followers of Lorenzo Monaco.

The discovery of the San Giovenale triptych shed much light on the Masolino–Masaccio question. The painting is one of Masaccio's first works (and his
earliest extant one); it shows no trace of the fluid style of Masolino's Bremen
Madonna of 1423 (Plate 42). The earliest known panels of Masolino clearly
document his love of the idiom of Lorenzo Monaco and his circle. Yet the first
works by Masaccio, which are contemporary with Masolino's earliest surviving
paintings, reveal none of this; so it seems illogical to suggest — on the basis of
both their hands on several works — that Masolino was Masaccio's teacher.

However, the problem of their sharing of the Sant'Ambrogio altarpiece still
remains. The Madonna and the Child are attributed to Masaccio by almost all
the critics. The question really centers around the St. Anne and the angels,
which have repeatedly been given to Masolino.

Attribution is not a science; without exact documentation of authorship there
is bound to be controversy over who did what, where, and when. I think that
the hand of Masolino is absent from the St. Anne. The broad, bold conception
of the figure, its great girth and huge lap do not resemble anything by him.
Instead, I find the figure's design and the handling of its broadly painted, heavy,
voluminous robes extremely close both to the Madonna from the same panel
and to the figures of the San Giovenale triptych. One has only to look at the
hands of St. Anne: the right is inelegant, with stubby, almost misshapen fingers;
the strongly foreshortened left advances, as though pushing against the picture
plane. Such hands, characteristic of Masaccio's work, are almost completely
alien to Masolino's much more delicate sensitivity.

To my mind it is not the St. Anne that is in question, but the angels. Their
bodies are more springy, elongated, and lithe than those of the central figures.
Their faces — with bright, alert eyes and blond curly hair — are slightly more
rounded, just a bit puffier than those of the Madonna and St. Anne or the
figures from the San Giovenale triptych. All the small bodies are articulated

with a gentle angularity (vaguely reminiscent of Lorenzo Monaco) that sets them apart from the blunter forms of the figures from Masaccio's hand. The angels are painted with a palette — again recalling Monaco — that is slightly lighter and gayer than those of the large figures of the Sant'Ambrogio altarpiece or the San Giovenale triptych. Color combinations like the yellow and pink of the lower-left angel and the orange-yellow of the angel in the upper left are not typical of Masaccio. The appearance of red shadows on the green-robed angel in the upper right corner is also uncharacteristic of Masaccio, who never uses such shot colors to indicate shadow and highlight; instead, he simply creates shadows by making them a more deeply saturated area of the same color. Equally unlike Masaccio's work is the big, extremely active pattern on the cloth of honor.

Many of the stylistic properties of the angels — proportion, color, use of pattern — have a specific relation to all of Masolino's work. There is, moreover, a strong generic resemblance between the Sant'Ambrogio angels and the blond Madonnas (the Bremen Madonna of 1423, for example) and angels found in several paintings by Masolino. Consequently there is good reason to attribute the Sant'Ambrogio angels to him.

How was it possible for two artists to work on a panel and for the finished picture to show a clear stylistic disparity between them? We know, of course, that almost any work from the Trecento and Quattrocento is not the product of a single hand. Painting and sculpture were made in cooperative shops directed by a single master. Apprentices did much of the preparatory labor (for example, grinding colors and putting gesso on the panels) before the painting could begin. It was the master who made the design, which then served as a stylistic map for the helpers.[14] So while the planning and design of an altarpiece was an individual action, the physical act of its painting, by master and pupils alike, was not. In fact, most of the training apprentices received was aimed at making the final picture homogeneous: a surface where various areas painted by different hands was stylistically uniform.

Very seldom do several clearly recognizable hands appear. The unusual disparity of style of the Sant'Ambrogio altarpiece seems to suggest that Masolino and Masaccio did *not* work on it at the same time. The differences in proportion, articulation, and color between the angels and the central figures are fundamental and imply that the designs of two artists are present. Since the location and actions of the surrounding angels are determined by the central figures, it would seem that Masaccio designed and painted them first. The panel was then completed by Masolino, who planned and put in the five surrounding angels.

How and why this happened is not known. Perhaps Masaccio was given the commission for the Sant'Ambrogio altarpiece but could not finish it within the stipulated time. Maybe he left the altarpiece to work on a larger, more important project. Or maybe he fell ill and was unable to paint. There are scores of possible reasons, but without documentation they must remain mere conjectures.

Although it seems most unlikely that Masaccio and Masolino worked on the altarpiece together, it is of interest that they shared in its completion. Several years later both men painted in the Brancacci Chapel. This second appearance of the two artists' hands on a single work may mean that Masaccio and Masolino had more than a casual, temporary acquaintance.

Several key points can be drawn from the visual evidence of the Sant'Ambrogio altarpiece. The most important is the glimpse it affords of Masaccio's style just a few years after the San Giovenale triptych of 1422. The style of the altarpiece is even more vigorous and powerful and is now firmly directed toward the unification of sacred image and spectator.

The young Masaccio, probably only recently established in Florence, certainly must have been influenced by the contemporary stylistic events of this, the most artistically active city of the Italian peninsula. He had already left the conservative style of Bicci di Lorenzo, Mariotto di Nardo, Lorenzo di Niccolò, and their circles far behind. Clearly he was not interested in duplicating the effects of Lorenzo Ghiberti, Lorenzo Monaco, or Gentile da Fabriano, all of whom were near the peaks of their careers in the mid-1420s. Instead, most of his attention — it seems to me — was turned to the sculptors of the period, whose free-standing statues were the three-dimensional embodiment of his painterly ideals and from which he learned much about representing solids in space. One can imagine the youthful Masaccio standing in awe before the recently completed statues by Donatello and Nanni on the Duomo and Or San Michele. The volume-defining, sculptural forms and the convincing space of his Sant'Ambrogio altarpiece must stem from his understanding of contemporary sculpture. The Sant'Ambrogio Madonna derives much of its spatial existence from Donatello's wondrous *St. John the Evangelist* (Plate 58) in the Museo dell'Opera del Duomo. Just as Masaccio had turned to earlier painting — to Giotto — for help, so must he have spent long hours looking at the tremendously exciting works of the Florentine sculptors that were just then beginning to grace the city's buildings.

We do not know how the Sant'Ambrogio altarpiece, one of Masaccio's first Florentine panels, was accepted by the artist's contemporaries. Were they aware of its explosive potentials for the depiction of the figure in space? Did they recognize that it — like the San Giovenale triptych — marked a departure from the much more contained, isolated, iconic world of previous Florentine painting? One wonders. But Masaccio's style was evolving rapidly. In 1426 he was to begin the great altarpiece for the church of the Carmine in Pisa, a work that would make the Sant'Ambrogio painting seem almost timid.

V.

Masaccio: The Pisa Altarpiece

IN 1424 MASACCIO joined the Compagnia di San Luca, the painters' company of Florence. This is the first record we have of him since his matriculation in the Arte dei Medici e Speziali in 1422. It appears, from other cases, that it was customary to join the Company of St. Luke only after the matriculation.[1]

Two years after Masaccio enrolled in the Company he began work on the Pisa altarpiece. This partially destroyed and dispersed painting was commissioned by Ser Giuliano di Colino degli Scarsi da San Giusto for his chapel in the church of the Carmine in Pisa.[2] Construction on the chapel (which was probably dedicated to Julian, the donor's patron saint) had started at the end of November of the previous year. The altarpiece, begun on 19 February 1426, was to cost 80 florins, a considerable but not huge sum for a sizeable painting. The records of the payments — which went on during almost all of 1426, the final payment being made on 26 December — contain some fascinating information.[3] On 24 July, 10 florins were set aside for Donatello, "marble worker from Florence." Whether this proportionally large sum was for a debt owed the sculptor or covered some artistic matter is not known. It does, however, indicate that Donatello and Masaccio must have known each other before 1426. On 15 October Masaccio promised not to begin other work until the Pisa altarpiece was finished. Such a promise is not an uncommon clause in artistic contracts; but its presence in the payment documents may indicate that Masaccio was spending too much time on other things and that Ser Giuliano was trying to get him to finish the altarpiece.[4]

The payments reveal that Masaccio had an assistant named Andrea di Giusto. Andrea is a recognizable artistic personality who was active from 1426 to 1455, but where and when he met Masaccio is not known. A number of his works are in the Valdarno, and he may have been a native of that region.[5]

The records also state that Antonio di Biagio of Siena made the frame for the painting.

The sixteenth-century painter and biographer of artists, Giorgio Vasari, described the Pisa altarpiece before it was dismantled, perhaps in the late 1500s:

> In a picture of one of the chapels in the screen [Vasari must mean the choir screen] of the Carmine at Pisa he [Masaccio] did our Lady and Child, with some small angels playing music at her feet; one playing the lute and listening with his ear down to the harmony he has produced. The Madonna is placed between St. Peter, St. John the Baptist, St. Julian and St. Nicholas, all figures of great vigor and life. In the predella beneath are scenes from the lives of those saints in small figures, the middle being occupied by the three Magi offering their gifts to Christ. In this part there are some very fine horses drawn from life — one could not wish for better — and the men of the suite are dressed in the various costumes in use at the time. Above, to complete the picture, there are saints arranged in panels about a crucifix.[6]

Vasari's description of the main part of the altarpiece recalls a number of works from the early Quattrocento. We have already seen one in Würzburg, by the Master of the Bambino Vispo, depicting the enthroned Madonna with Child and small music-making angels at the foot of the throne (Plate 31). There are also four flanking saints, as there once were on the Pisa painting. This altarpiece type, which first appeared around 1330, reached the height of its popularity in the late Trecento and early Quattrocento.

From Vasari's description we learn that the Pisa altarpiece had a *predella* and some scenes above its main panels. The large panels of a work by Bicci di Lorenzo at Bibbiena, dated 1435, represent the Madonna (although here without angels) and four flanking saints (Plate 71). Below is a *predella* divided into three major sections, each one with iconographic reference to the main figures. Above the central scenes are smaller painted pinnacles; the *Crucifixion* is placed over the Madonna panel. Altarpiece types changed slowly in the early Quattrocento, so one can assume that Masaccio's Pisa painting must originally have looked like the nearly contemporary works in Würzburg and Bibbiena.

The records and description of the Pisa altarpiece are of the greatest importance, for they can be used to identify Masaccio's only documented picture. It is strange, but true, that of the handful of paintings by Masaccio that remain, only the Pisa altarpiece can be documented. It thus becomes the key for the identification of the other pictures attributed to Masaccio on the basis of style alone.

Until relatively recently, none of the pieces of the Pisa altarpiece were known, but from the late nineteenth century onward various parts began to surface.

71. Bicci di Lorenzo, Altarpiece. Bibbiena, Santi Ippolito e Donato.

The largest (135 x 73 cm) and most important for the understanding of Masaccio's style is the Madonna and Child with music-making angels (Plate 72) in the National Gallery, London. Although its provenance cannot be continuously traced to Pisa, there seems little doubt that this is the panel that Vasari describes as "our Lady and Child, with some small angels playing music at her feet; one playing the lute and listening with his ear down to the harmony he has produced."

The *predella* described by Vasari as scenes from the lives of the saints represented above (Peter, John the Baptist, Julian, and Nicholas), with the "middle being occupied by the three Magi offering their gifts to Christ," may be identified in three panels now in the Staatliche Museen, Berlin (each measures about 61 x 22 cm). According to Vasari, the *Adoration of the Magi* (Plate 73) was placed under the Madonna panel in the middle of the altarpiece. When some type of framing is imagined, the measurements of the Berlin *Adoration* make it just about the right size to fit under the London Madonna: it is 61 cm wide, while the Madonna is 73 cm wide. From the two other *predelle* one can assume that the still-missing large side panels (each with two saints) were also about

72. Masaccio, *Madonna and Child*. London, National Gallery.

73. Masaccio, *Adoration of the Magi*. Berlin, Staatliche Museen.

70 cm wide; so the total width of the painting would have been around 210 cm. It appears to have been a large but not gigantic altarpiece of a type popular during the teens and twenties of the Quattrocento.

The two other Berlin *predelle* are devoted to stories of the saints originally shown on the large panels of the Pisa altarpiece. The *Martyrdom of St. Peter*

74. Masaccio, *Martyrdom of St. Peter*. Berlin, Staatliche Museen.

75. Masaccio, *Martyrdom of St. John the Baptist.* Berlin, Staatliche
Museen.

and the *Martyrdom of St. John the Baptist* occupy one (Plates 74 and 75); the
other depicts *St. Julian Mistakenly Killing His Parents* and *St. Nicholas Rescuing Three Maidens from Poverty and Prostitution by Throwing Gold Balls into
Their Rooms* (Plate 76).[7]

The original arrangement of the central saints can be inferred from the com-

76. Masaccio, *St. Julian Mistakenly Killing His Parents* and *St.
Nicholas Rescuing Three Maidens.* Berlin, Staatliche Museen.

position of the *predelle*. The figure of St. Julian begins a diagonal left-to-right
direction intensified by the diagonal upward movement of the room occupied
by the three maidens. The vigorous gesture of the man holding the hair of St.
John sets up a counter right-to-left movement, which is then carried into the
scene of St. Peter's Crucifixion by the executioner's upraised sword.

The inward movement from left to right in the Julian and Nicholas panel
and the opposite compositional direction of the Peter and John the Baptist
predella seem to indicate that the former would have been to the left of the
Madonna and the latter to her right. If the reverse placement were true, the
diagonal recession would not move the viewer's eye toward the center of
the altarpiece, but away from it, leaving a vacuum of space at the outside ends
of the *predelle*.[8]

Referring to the upper part of the altarpiece, Vasari says: "Above to complete
the picture, there are saints arranged in panels about a crucifix." Three panels
have been identified as these parts: a *Crucifixion* (Plate 77) with the Virgin,
Mary Magdalen, and St. John the Evangelist in the Capodimonte Museum,
Naples; a *St. Paul* (Plate 78) in the Museo Nazionale, Pisa; and a *St. Andrew*
(Plate 79) in the Lanckoronski Collection, Vienna. The *Crucifixion* measures
83 x 63 cm; the two other panels are c.50 x 30 cm each.

Now there can be little doubt that these three pictures are by Masaccio; and
it is this very secure attribution that may have led to some confusion about their
provenance. Though the St. Paul is in Pisa, its history can be traced back no
further than the eighteenth century. Neither of the other two panels was known
before the late nineteenth century.[9] There is, therefore, no documented link
between these three paintings and the Pisa altarpiece; nor is the identification
of the saints originally placed on top of the altarpiece certain. In spite of all this,
most critics have assumed that the Vienna, Pisa, and Naples panels must be
those to which Vasari refers. But the matter is not quite that simple.

The *Crucifixion* is nearly as wide as the London Madonna and almost three
quarters of its present height. While there are many altarpieces of the first decades of the Quattrocento crowned by sizeable panels, never are the upper pictures quite so large in relation to the lower ones. In any of the proposed reconstructions of the Pisa altarpiece, the sheer size of the Naples *Crucifixion* always
seems to overpower the London Madonna. It is true that the latter has been cut
down, but even with another 25 cm added to its height, it would still be overwhelmed by the *Crucifixion*. The same proportional relation exists when one
imagines the panels in Vienna and Pisa above the saints who originally flanked
the Madonna. Although there were no firm rules governing the proportional
relationship of panels, the relation of the saints and *Crucifixion* panels to the

77. Masaccio, *Crucifixion*. Naples, Museo di Capodimonte.

78. Masaccio, *St. Paul*. Pisa, Museo Nazionale di San Matteo.

79. Masaccio, *St. Andrew.* Vienna, Lanckoronski Collection.

London Madonna and missing side saints does not seem comfortable or correct. The top is simply too heavy for the main part of the altarpiece.

But if the Naples *Crucifixion* and the Pisa and Vienna saints did not originally belong to the Pisa altarpiece, where did they come from? Did they all form part of a single work of art? The three panels seem proportionally compatible and are of the same shape, so they probably belonged together. Perhaps they were part of a triptych or small polyptych made up of the *Crucifixion* and two or more half-length figures. Such small polyptychs were quite common in the first half of the Trecento, but less popular during the period c.1350–1430. And there exists at least one complete altarpiece in Pisa of the type with a *Crucifixion* at its center.[10]

In summary, the Pisa and Vienna saints and the Naples *Crucifixion* do not seem to fit comfortably with the London Madonna, but there is no easy or sure way to explain the incompatibility of the panels, nor is there a real expectancy that the problem will be solved with the evidence in hand.

Four small panels (Plates 80 and 81) in the Berlin Staatliche Museen (representing St. Augustine, St. Jerome, and two unidentified saints, each 38 x 12 cm) have also been connected with the Pisa altarpiece. The narrow rectangular shape of these panels suggests that they formed part of the side pilasters of some large altarpiece. It has been hypothesized that the two unidentified figures wearing white habits are Carmelites.[11] If so, they may come from a work intended for a Carmelite church such as the Carmine in Pisa, the original location of Masaccio's altarpiece. The Berlin panels, as we shall see, are certainly by Masaccio, and their style is close to that of the London Madonna, so there is good reason to suspect that they were done at about the same time. It is therefore quite possible (although not provable) that the Berlin saints were once part of the Pisa altarpiece.

The extant fragments from the Pisa painting indicate that it was once a splendid ensemble. Its destruction has robbed us of Masaccio's most important work on panel; however, the surviving pieces still reveal a great deal about the artist's stylistic development up to 1427.

80. Masaccio, *St. Augustine and an Unidentified Saint.* Berlin, Staatliche Museen.

81. Masaccio, *St. Jerome and an Unidentified Saint.* Berlin, Staatliche Museen.

There are a number of clear ties between the London Madonna (which is badly rubbed in places) and the Madonnas from the San Giovenale triptych and the Sant'Ambrogio altarpiece. In all the pictures the massive shapes form great triangles as the bodies fill out the expanse of the seats. Also similar is the slow folding of the heavy, wool-like robes. The heads, composed of smooth, highly plastic planes united by transitional passages of subtle shading, are all from the same mold. The face of the London Madonna is overcleaned, but one can still make out the formal geomtery it shares with the other Madonnas.

The resemblance between the babies is startling. Each little Hercules is engaged in some quick, childlike motion. One senses that these poses and gestures are the result of the acute observation of real children: a feeling that one does not get from Florentine painting before Masaccio, although Sienese pictures of the first half of the Trecento often contain a number of remarkably lively infants.[12] The great barrel-chested child in the London panel eagerly grasps the grapes (symbols of Eucharistic wine) from his mother's hand. Instead of making a symbolic gesture of blessing, he sticks two fingers squarely in his mouth, while regarding the spectator with a look of innocent curiosity. His expression is very different from his mother's; she gazes thoughtfully toward the lower right. One feels that she, like the Virgin in the San Giovenale triptych, is concerned about the fate of her divine, but very robust, son.

The bodies of the foreshortened angels at the foot of the throne recall the angels of the San Giovenale triptych: in their shaggy hair and round faces there is a strong family resemblance. In the London panel Masaccio has also placed two angels behind the throne, where they are unable to see either the Madonna or the Child. Their appearance in the picture has more to do with Masaccio's quest for deep space than with their role as adoring beings; this is a daring break with tradition.

It is in the panel's space that Masaccio's ever-increasing power is most apparent. In the two earlier pictures there is a dichotomy between the bulky, foreshortened figures, whose weight and volume are placed close to the picture plane, and the surrounding limited space, which ends abruptly at the gold background. Certainly the thrones and figures have some extension into space in these two works; but there exists, nevertheless, a marked separation between the volume of the solids and the inherent flatness of the shallow space. Such a separation was present in all previous Florentine paintings, but the presence of Masaccio's ponderous figures strongly emphasized it, making the picture seem to contain two different spatial realities.

By the time of the London Madonna all this has been changed; the tension was broken, the problem resolved. One no longer feels that there is a shallow space between picture plane and the gold background, for the throne is so convincingly placed and foreshortened that it appears set in a deep, highly realistic space. The ancient convention of figures existing before a space-denying background of flat gold has been nearly destroyed, and light, volume, and atmosphere can be sensed in the area behind the picture plane. The bulky figures and the massive throne (as much architecture as furniture) now stand in a world very like our own.

All this is done by firmly fixing the spectator's viewpoint and making the elements of the picture conform to it rigidly. The spectator is clearly below the throne and is looking up at the Madonna and her baby. The relentless recession of the orthogonals toward a single vanishing point (at the level of the Child's head), in combination with the sharp foreshortening of the sides of the throne, pulls the viewer into space and holds him there with a constant logical, clear force.

Space has been formed into compartments: the music-making angels sit before the throne; the throne itself encloses the Madonna like a protective niche; and behind — in yet a third unit — are the standing angels. One feels that it would be easy to enter this space, to grasp the engaged colonette firmly while looking at the standing angels. But Masaccio has not been content to limit the space to just the area one can see: he has suggested movement beyond by making the upper corners of the throne and the standing angels' bodies move outside the picture's limits. An implied space exists outside the panel, just as our space exists outside the limits of our own vision. Once again, the picture seems to stand within our world, its figures sharing our time and environment.

Also highly realistic is the lighting of the London Madonna. It falls from a single source in the upper left, creating subtle gradations of tone. The left side of the picture is generally lighter than the right, which, near the Madonna's knee, is cast into rather deep shadow. This imbalance enlivens the picture, makes its relief stronger, and distracts us from the overall symmetry of the composition. Yet, light does more than that, for in Masaccio's hands it acts in harmony with the forms to forge objects of an extremely palpable nature. The light falling on the smooth ovals of the lutes, the round colonettes of the throne, and the rosettes above the head of the seated angel to the left energizes these objects by giving them relief, solidity, and texture. The geometric quality of much of the artist's composing is made sharper by the glorious light.

The use of cast shadows (seen next to the small rosettes and at the right, where the Madonna blocks the light, throwing almost the entire right side and front edge of the throne into darkness) is extremely unusual in early Quattrocento painting. By comparison, the upper part of the throne seems all the more luminescent. Such careful manipulation of light and shadow is almost entirely without precedent, and its appearance in the London Madonna marks Masaccio as one of the most innovative of all Florentine artists.

Masaccio's use of correct one-point perspective and his careful, unified observation of light indicate his growing interest in the so-called scientific aspects of picture-making. In fact, the whole development of one-point perspective in the early Quattrocento is frequently discussed as though it were the most — and, sometimes, only — important aspect of the painting of the time. I think that it is a mistake to consider one-point perspective as some isolated and self-sufficient force in Florentine art. Rather it should be seen for what it was to the artists of the early fifteenth century — not a toy or a scientific discovery but an aid in the convincing representation of form in space and a device that allowed the many supernatural events of the Christian drama to be portrayed in a highly realistic fashion.

Almost perfect one-point perspective had been known since the first half of the Trecento. In his *Annunciation* of 1344 Ambrogio Lorenzetti created an interior in which the orthogonals of the floor seem to recede to a central, unique vanishing point on the horizon.[13] Actually, they do not meet in one precise location; they all converge in several spots in one area in the background. But the point is that the *Annunciation*, like several other contemporary Sienese pictures, appears to have a measured, coherent perspective. For some unknown reason the Sienese abandoned this type of construction after c.1350; perhaps they felt that it was too real, that its clearly definable space brought sacred images too near the spectator, making them not icons but graspable, down-to-earth images. It is also possible they felt that pictures like Ambrogio's *Annunciation* had lost some of their holiness, a holiness synonymous with the less-approachable painting of the past, where religious drama was set in a space far removed from the worshipper's own. The abandoned experiment of the early fourteenth century suggests one thing: it was not the representational technique (a perspective system, for example) that dictated how things were painted; rather, it was the need for a certain type of image that determined the technique to be used.

By the beginning of the Quattrocento the spiritual climate had changed. That a desire for more immediate religious images was felt is clear from the early works of Donatello and Masaccio; something in society had suddenly created a need for more realistic, accessible representation. Perhaps this need arose from the new-found attitude toward man discussed in chapter 3; but whatever the cause, the way several important artists conceived religious art was fundamentally affected. The first painter to respond to this changing demand was Ma-

saccio, who, especially in the London Madonna, constructed a new, more immediate relation between observer and painting. He was not, however, the earliest to make such images, for Donatello's heroic, vivid, almost alive statues date
from a decade earlier. It is worth repeating that there is little doubt that Donatello (who, the Pisa altarpiece payments suggest, knew Masaccio) was an inspiration to the brilliant young painter fresh from San Giovanni Valdarno. The
play of light on simple, solid, monumental form would have been carefully
noted by Masaccio as he stood before Donatello's newly created *St. John the
Evangelist* or the figures on Or San Michele.

One wonders what effect the startling, realistically direct images of the Pisa
altarpiece had on Masaccio's contemporaries. If we contrast the London Madonna with an important contemporary Madonna by Gentile da Fabriano, we
can perhaps discover some differences that would also have been apparent to
the Florentines of the early Quattrocento. Gentile's *Madonna and Child* (Plate
82) in the Collection of H.M. the Queen, Hampton Court, originally formed
the center of the now dispersed Quaratesi altarpiece (finished in 1425, one year
before the Pisa altarpiece) painted for the church of San Niccolò in Florence.[14]
(It is interesting to note that the area of San Niccolò was Masaccio's neighbor-
hood when he matriculated in the *Arte dei Medici e Speziale* in 1422.)

Everywhere Masaccio's Madonna is starkly formal, while the Quaratesi Madonna is decorative. The most fundamental difference between the paintings
stems from the two artists' attitudes toward fashioning images. Gentile conceived of the Quaratesi Madonna as both a holy being and a sumptuous, elegant
woman. The intersections of her body, the sinuous path of her golden hems, the
outward-turning movement of the baby, and the surfaces with embroidered rosettes and leaf patterns are decorative devices totally alien to Masaccio's aims.
The graceful sweetness of the Quaratesi picture finds no place in Masacccio's
art: compare its angels with the rugged urchins at the foot of Masaccio's Madonna's throne. The spirit of Gentile's splendid style is much closer to that of
Lorenzo Monaco and Ghiberti than to Masaccio's leaner, less-adorned vision.

In their mind's eye, Masaccio's contemporaries must certainly have contrasted
his London Madonna with works like the new Quaratesi altarpiece, or pictures
by Monaco or the Master of the Bambino Vispo, which adorned numerous
chapels in the Florentine churches. Eyes used to the glory of the gleaming gold,
rainbow palettes, and sumptuous rhythmic altarpieces by these painters must
have been shocked by the compositionally sober, elemental Madonna and her
lively son. This distilled, direct treatment of holy figures (which we value so
much today) may even have seemed vulgar. The very treatment of the surface — the vigorous, unpolished way the paint was applied — was probably

82. Gentile da Fabriano, *Madonna and Child*. Hampton Court,
Collection of H.M. the Queen.

grating to the sensibilities of men accustomed to the easy elegance of much contemporary painting. Perhaps it was at this time that the suffix *accio* (meaning sloppy or ugly) was attached to the name Maso (the shortened form of Tommaso), by which the artist had sometimes been called.

Fundamental differences between Masaccio and Gentile can also be seen by comparing the 1423 Strozzi *Adoration of the Magi* (Plate 41) and Masaccio's *predella* of the same subject (now in Berlin) painted three years later. Again, the surface of the latter is calmer and simpler. The exciting visual clutter of the earlier panel is suppressed; in its stead is a scene of quiet, unornamented grandeur. The story unfolds before a range of low, rolling hills, not unlike those of the Valdarno. Beyond, the vision fades into the blue haze of the far distance. How different this is from Gentile's fantastic world, or the bizarre landscapes of Lorenzo Monaco with their twisting mountains topped by tiny toy castles. The background of brown hills in the Berlin panel is one of the first instances of an accurate topographical portrait in Florentine painting. Masaccio differed from most of his contemporaries in that he placed his action in a locale that the worshipper would recognize. Now onlooker and holy legend seem to exist within the same definable, earthly space. Once again, however, a precedent is found in Donatello's sculpture. The *predella* of the Or San Michele St. George shows a similar concern for the correct and convincing representation of the environment, even though there still remains a trace of the fantasy usually associated with Lorenzo Monaco, a fantasy noticeably absent in Masaccio's *Adoration*.

The Berlin *Adoration* is the earliest surviving narrative painting by Masaccio and contains his first known thoughts on the physical and psychological interaction of holy figures. Here he is not only painting the images of Madonna, Child, and angels but also grappling with an historical scene demanding interpretation. He chose to make the story as simple as possible. There are only about a dozen figures, and each one moves toward a single object: the infant seated on the Virgin's lap. This intense concentration differs strikingly from Gentile's unfocused Strozzi *Adoration*, where the members of the Magi's train look and gesture nearly everywhere except toward the Madonna and Child. Masaccio's actors move with purpose and dignity; their slow, measured gestures are like those of some race of heroes. The formal and emotional confusion of Gentile's altarpiece has been replaced by serenity.

Masaccio's stable, monumental figures are enveloped in heavy cloaks, which ripple across the surface of their substantial bodies. Masaccio does not use Gentile's gorgeous, gold-encrusted costumes; instead his protagonists are clothed in robes similar to those worn in fifteenth-century Florence.

The palette of the Berlin *Adoration* is limited. As in Masaccio's previous works, the colors are not the shot pastels so often used by contemporaries; rather they are simple clear reds, blues, golds, and browns. The entire composition is enlivened and tied together by the notes of red and blue that march across the center of the picture. Red appears in the stockings of some of the standing men, in the tunic of the figure holding the crown, and in the cloth around Christ; blue is seen in a saddle cover, on the tunic of the standing figure with upraised hands, and on the Virgin's cloak. Red is really the only very bright note in the entire *predella*. Color does not exist as an independent force as it did in the panels of Gentile or Lorenzo Monaco; here it is an aid in the construction of form and the creation of the serious mood of the grave figures set before the undulating landscape.

Masaccio is extremely aware of the geometry of his pictures. The smooth planes of the horses' bodies, the stylized curves of their necks, the shapes of the animals and of the men's legs, and the configurations described by the bodies of the principal actors are carefully adjusted to one another and to the overall composition. Such geometric abstraction is not new in Florentine art (it was brilliantly utilized by Giotto); but its role in early Quattrocento painting is nowhere as strong as it is here. There is, in fact, an almost overwhelming interest in the movements of the figures through space and in the rhythmic sequence of their bodies. The participants in the *Adoration* seem to exist in a still, unchanging world, a world not to be seen again for several decades, when Piero della Francesca began to paint.

The Berlin Peter and John the Baptist *predella* scenes contain the same bold, formally exciting landscapes and figure types found in the *Adoration*. Lit from the left (like all the images associated with the Pisa altarpiece), they depict bulky actors moving with great purpose before somber, simple backgrounds: a building in the Peter scene, a little prison and some sharply folded mountains behind the execution of John the Baptist. Coloristically, these scenes are close to the *Adoration*; the same notes of red and blue and nearly the same range of hue are seen. Also very like the *Adoration* are the basically geometric compositions of the scenes. The diagonal rhythms established by the triangle of Peter's upside-down body and the surrounding stone pyramids are countered by the verticals of the figures standing in the background. The sharply foreshortened, bending men in the foreground create another series of dynamic spatial movements. In the *Execution of John the Baptist* the figures form a loose semicircle around the kneeling saint; everyone's attention is concentrated on the event taking place before them.

But even with all those resemblances, something about these scenes sets them apart from the Berlin *Adoration*. Perhaps it is the more particularized handling of the surface, which lacks the *Adoration*'s boldness and vigor. There is also a timidity in some of the figures, especially those in the background of the *Crucifixion of Peter*, who appear just a bit too brittle and small in comparison to the actors of the *Adoration*. Furthermore, certain minor proportional differences hint at an eye lacking Masaccio's understanding. For instance, the kneeling men with hammers, while brilliantly designed, seem a bit too large in comparison with the rest of the figures.

These slight discrepancies in style between the SS. John and Peter stories and the Berlin *Adoration* may be explained by assuming that Masaccio executed the general design of the *predella* scenes and then let an assistant do the actual painting, according to the custom of the Trecento and Quattrocentro. Perhaps the assistant was Andrea di Giusto, who is named in the documents. Such a hypothesis may account for the close proximity to Masaccio in type and color and the slight variations in handling, proportion, and execution.

This does not seem to be true for the Berlin *predella* of the scenes of SS. Julian and Nicholas. Here the weak dramatic and formal concentration and the figures, who are much spindlier and more elongated than any ever painted by Masaccio, clearly indicate that this panel is from the hand of another artist, perhaps that of Andrea di Giusto. The overall compositional rhythm is coordinated with the Peter and John the Evangelist panel; and, like the other pictures from the Pisa altarpiece, the light falls from the left. Yet there are in the SS. Julian and Nicholas scenes almost no other design or surface qualities that would lead one to believe that it was once a part of the Pisa altarpiece. The three maidens' bodies and the vigorous figure of St. Julian killing his parents are reminiscent of Masaccio; but much the same can be said for other figures executed by artists under his sway. So while the SS. Julian and Nicholas stories certainly seem to have been part of the Pisa altarpiece, their style indicates that they were not designed by Masaccio.

The three Berlin panels, with their range from Masaccio's autograph in the *Adoration* to the total absence of his hand in the SS. Julian and Nicholas stories, demonstrate that Masaccio was not actively involved in the entire *predella*. Maybe he was anxious to finish the work and so delegated parts of it to helpers. Or it is possible that the commissioner forced him to use an assistant in order to meet a deadline. It is even plausible that Masaccio may have left the work for some time (we do not know whether it was painted in Pisa or Florence) and entrusted its supervision to an assistant. There are many answers, but none of them can be proved.

There can be no doubt, however, that Masaccio was responsible for three panels associated with the upper level of the Pisa altarpiece: a *Crucifixion* in the Capodimonte Museum, Naples; and the saints in the Museo Nazionale, Pisa, and the Lanckoronski Collection, Vienna. The *Crucifixion* is a moving, powerful work. The crucified Christ is flanked by the Virgin and St. John the Evangelist. Mary Magdalen kneels at the foot of the cross. Christ is a mighty figure with a huge chest, wide hips, and bowed legs: the child from the London panel grown up. There is a rare awkwardness about this stout, twisted figure. The crucified Christ is usually represented as a much more graceful, smoothly articulated being; for example, compare the Naples picture with Lorenzo Monaco's Crucifix discussed in chapter 2. It is as though Masaccio consciously wished to make the figure clumsy and rude. Part of this impression is conveyed by the head, which does not seem to be attached to the body by the neck but appears fixed behind the shoulders. It has been suggested that this rather bizarre head is the result of Masaccio's attempt to make the figure seem convincing when seen from below (the panel, it will be remembered, may have been one of the pinnacles of the Pisa altarpiece).[15] Such a process, of course, must be likened to Donatello's proportional adjustments of the Duomo *St. John the Evangelist.* But when one looks up at the picture from floor level (which is five feet or so below the panel) the relation between the head and body still does not appear correct. Possibly Masaccio's study of full-round sculpture convinced him that its spatial effects could be reproduced in painting; and this, in turn, may have led to the unsuccessful attempt seen in the Naples *Crucifixion.* In any case, it is the only awkward note in an otherwise well-formed picture.

The bulky body of Christ is not echoed in the figures of Mary and St. John, which are the most elongated and graceful ever painted by Masaccio. The elegant silhouette of John's body and the elaborate pattern traced by the hem of his robe are complemented by his frail, finely drawn face and flowing hair. There is a beautiful fluidity in the way he holds his body and hands. Mary is slightly sturdier, but her shape against the gold background forms a complicated, slow-moving outline unusual in Masaccio's work. The prominent bright blue of her robe and the fine gradations that mark its folds are also uncharacteristic. One wonders if here, and here only, Masaccio fell for a moment under the spell of Lorenzo Monaco. The two standing saints and the space in which they exist recall the atmosphere, grace, and suavity of Monaco's nearly contemporary Uffizi *Adoration.* Perhaps this is a mistaken idea; but the proportions of the figures and their articulation are strange. There is also the remote possibility that Masaccio was harkening back to an even older style. Little *Crucifixions* with flanking figures of Mary and John appear on Quattrocento altarpieces with some frequency, and in several cases these scenes seem to copy the idiom of the early Trecento.[16] It may be that these fifteenth-century *Crucifixions* were meant to replicate ancient, venerated images. The conscious imitation of old pictures in order to obtain some of the holiness traditionally associated with them is an important factor in early Italian painting. Perhaps, then, the Naples *Crucifixion* is an archaizing work; but, once again, no definitive statement can be made.

Kneeling at the foot of the cross is the Magdalene, one of Masaccio's most supreme creations. She is among those marvelously articulated figures (similar to those who kneel around Christ in Giotto's Arena Chapel *Lamentation*) who express the deepest emotions by bodily gesture alone. With her arms flung out and her body bent in a spasm of grief, the Magdalene is an unforgettable, haunting image. The bright orange-red of her voluminous robe and the flowing strands of her golden hair draw the eye to the foot of the cross. The physicality of her unmeasurable sorrow and the scream she surely must be sounding reverberate through the picture. With her gigantic winglike sleeves she resembles some great bird struggling to be free of the ground.[17]

The two saints in Vienna and Pisa are close in style to the other fragments identified as probably belonging to the Pisa altarpiece. They exhibit the same monumental body and sweeping treatment of surface as the London Madonna and angels, but they are more abstracted. The head of St. Paul in Pisa is extremely foreshortened; the facial features and beard are rendered with a breadth more characteristic of fresco than of tempera. While in Pisa it is very likely that Masaccio was influenced by the sculptor Giovanni Pisano (c.1250–c.1314), who executed a series of monumental half-length statues and a large pulpit for the Pisa cathedral complex.[18] The angular articulation of the St. Paul and the dynamic energy of his body are reminiscent of a number of similarly expressive works by Giovanni. The blocklike St. Andrew in Vienna also seems to owe a great deal to Masaccio's careful observation of Giovanni's exciting work. Once again, sculpture may have been an aid in the creation of the three-dimensional form clearly desired by Masaccio. But Giovanni's influence is restricted to the more formal properties, for Masaccio's figures are not the tense, tormented beings created by the sculptor's chisel.

The Pisa St. Paul is one of Masaccio's most beautifully colored works despite the fact that only a few colors are used on the entire panel: The mantle is an almost indescribable rose-violet, and the tunic is golden yellow. Darker violets appear in the shadows of the robe, and white is used for highlights. The simplicity of the slightly disparate colors is pleasing, and each is foiled by the black sword, which creates a diagonal at the left. In all of Masaccio's work, color is used in the service of form, to help create believable substances before the viewer's eye. It does not assume the more independent decorative existence seen in Lorenzo Monaco's paintings, or the sumptuous role it plays in Gentile da Fabriano's Strozzi altarpiece (although by the time of the 1425 Quaratesi altarpiece Gentile's palette had changed). This does not mean that Masaccio was insensitive to color and its combinations, for he clearly was capable of creating marvelous and original colors (witness the robes of St. Paul) and color combinations; but he saw color primarily as a handmaiden to form.

The small saints in Berlin (which seem to have come from the sides of the Pisa altarpiece) are very like the two larger panels in Vienna and Pisa. The purposeful stances of the Berlin saints, their large foreshortened heads, and their voluminous robes all mark them as the same type of direct, simple, monumental figure seen in every panel associated with the Pisa altarpiece, except for the Berlin SS. Julian and Nicholas *predella*. The palette of each of these small saints is restrained and restricted. The brightest color belongs to the robe of St. Jerome, and it may be that this was just one of a series of strong red notes seen over the entire altarpiece; one has only to remember the use of red in the Berlin *Adoration*. The other saints are dressed in white, brick-red, and pinkish robes. No shot colors are introduced, and the coloristic simplicity and sobriety are in strong contrast to many contemporary panels: for instance, Lorenzo Monaco's Uffizi *Adoration*.

The scattered pieces identified as parts of the Pisa altarpiece are landmarks; they are the first paintings of a revolutionary Florentine style. Without doubt, Masaccio was deeply indebted to his artistic ancestors and contemporaries for the formal and iconographic components of his idiom. Yet with these he created something never before seen in painting: vivid, immediate, direct images of religious drama in an environment very much like that of the spectator's. The old visual rhetorical devices that had traditionally separated object from observer are done away with. Never in Florentine painting had such monumental, almost breathing, heroic figures stood so near to earth. Nearly overnight the worshipper's space had become intermingled with the realm of the Virgin, Christ, and the saints. Holy drama was secularized, and the secular world made holy.

The steps leading to the creation of these events are partially discernible in Masaccio's earlier pictures. In turn, the splendid fragments connected with the Pisa altarpiece give some hint as to what is yet to come. But nothing can prepare one for the stunning images of the Brancacci Chapel, Masaccio's greatest surviving work.

VI.

Masaccio: The Frescoes

AFTER WALKING DOWN the Borgo San Frediano, one turns left into the bustling, spacious Piazza del Carmine. Surrounded by low ochre and white buildings, the unfinished thirteenth-century church of Santa Maria del Carmine looms over the square. Upon entering the building one is surprised to see that it is decorated in the sober Florentine style of the late eighteenth century. Like most ancient structures of the city, it has been remodeled several times to accommodate changing tastes, and the present interior was commissioned after a disastrous fire ruined almost the entire church.[1]

Pausing at the end of the long nave, one looks across to the right transept, which ends in a rather small vaulted chapel lit from a tall window on the altar wall (Plate 83). This chapel — named the Brancacci after its patrons — houses several of the world's best-known paintings: the frescoes of the legend of St. Peter by Masaccio, the object of the stare of thousands of awed tourists and the subject of scores of critics' pens.

The Brancacci Chapel presents many problems, and no survey of its frescoes can be complete without a consideration of at least the most important of them.[2] There are no documents giving the date of the frescoes, the names of their patrons (who must have been members of the Brancacci family), or the identity of the artists responsible for their execution. Any conclusions about the dates of the paintings and their attributions must therefore be based on style.

But a stylistic examination is complicated by the fact that the chapel is not in its original condition. In the Quattrocento a tall lancet window occupied the center of the altar wall. This wall is now partially covered by an ugly Baroque altar, behind which is a new, much wider window. The vault and lunettes (covered by highly illusionistic and crowded eighteenth-century paintings) once formed part of the fifteenth-century fresco cycle. The marble wainscot with inscriptions is also a later addition. To visualize how the chapel appeared in Masaccio's day it is necessary to remove, in the mind's eye, the later accretions of the ceiling, Baroque altar, and marble wainscoting, and to imagine the entire chapel painted with frescoes of a single period, the whole lit by the tall window that used to be in the middle of the altar wall.

The destroyed Quattrocento decoration of the vault and lunettes formed part of the St. Peter cycle. The four Evangelists seem to have been in the vaults (as was common in the late Trecento and early Quattrocento), while the lunettes were probably given over to the *Calling of SS. Peter and Andrew* and the *Navicella*. There may have been two more frescoes on either side of the top of the window; according to Vasari, one was *St. Peter Weeping* (after his third denial?), but the other remains a mystery. All eight paintings were probably by Masolino, the author of several other frescoes in the Brancacci Chapel.[3]

Masolino covered the chapel's upper right wall with two frescoes: the *Temptation of Adam and Eve* (Plate 84), on the entrance pilaster, and *St. Peter Raising Tabitha and the Healing of the Lame Man by SS. Peter and John* (Plate 85). The upper half of the window wall also contains two frescoes: to the right, *St. Peter Baptizing* (Plate 86), and to the left, *St. Peter Preaching* (Plate 87), both by Masolino.

Below these pictures are, to the left, *St. Peter Healing with His Shadow* (Plate 88) and, at the right, the *Distribution of Communal Goods and the Death of Ananias* (Plate 89). These frescoes are by Masaccio, who was also the author of the three scenes on the chapel's left wall: the *Expulsion of Adam and Eve from Paradise* (Plate 90), on the entrance pilaster across from Masolino's *Temptation*; the *Tribute Money* (Plate 91); and part of the *Resurrection of the Son of Theophilus and St. Peter Enthroned* (Plate 92).

The remainder of the chapel was completed in the late 1400s by the Florentine painter Filippino Lippi, who finished the fresco of the *Resurrection of the Son of Theophilus and St. Peter Enthroned* (Plate 93) and did the *St. Paul Visiting St. Peter in Prison*. He also covered the lower right wall with *St. Peter Freed from Prison*; *St. Peter, Paul and Simon the Magician Before Nero*; and the *Crucifixion of St. Peter*.[4]

At least three hands were active in the fifteenth-century frescoes in the Brancacci Chapel. Filippino Lippi simply completed the unfinished parts of the fresco cycle, but the relative roles of Masaccio and Masolino are not so clear. It is sometimes stated that the two men were commissioned to paint together,[5] but this theory is based on a number of rather fragile assumptions.

Perhaps the primary reason for assuming that Masolino and Masaccio worked together in the Brancacci Chapel has been the belief that Masolino was Masaccio's teacher. There is absolutely no proof for this; and, as a survey of the Brancacci frescoes will show, it was Masaccio who exerted an overwhelming force on Masolino's artistic thought.

83. Brancacci Chapel. Florence, Santa Maria del Carmine.

84. Masolino, *Temptation of Adam and Eve*.
Florence, Santa Maria del Carmine.

85. Masolino, *St. Peter Raising Tabitha and the Healing of the Lame
Man by SS. Peter and John*. Florence, Santa Maria del Carmine.

86. Masolino, *St. Peter Baptizing*.
Florence, Santa Maria del Carmine.

87. Masolino. *St. Peter Preaching*.
Florence, Santa Maria del Carmine.

88. Masaccio, *St. Peter Healing with His Shadow.* Florence, Santa
Maria del Carmine.

89. Masaccio, *Distribution of Communal Goods and the Death of Ananias*. Florence, Santa Maria del Carmine.

A second common assumption is also questionable. This is the notion that
the two independent artists were commissioned to do the chapel together. In
the entire history of Florentine painting up to the time of Brancacci Chapel, we
have no evidence of a dual commission for a fresco cycle. In fact, the very idea
of a dual commission seems to run contrary to the nature of the Florentine
artists' shops, where a single master was responsible for signing the contract,
designing the work, and supervising the execution. To postulate that two masters were commissioned to design part of a chapel decoration to be painted by
both at the same time, is to ignore not only contemporary shop practice but also
the visual evidence of every other Florentine fresco cycle, all begun by a single
artist and his shop. There is no doubt that there are areas in the Brancacci
Chapel done exclusively by Masaccio and by Masolino. However, to believe
that they were painted simultaneously is risky, to say the least.

A much more logical explanation for the different hands in the Brancacci
Chapel is that the cycle was begun by Masolino, who started in the vaults.
(Almost all fresco cycles were painted from the top down to avoid the damage
done by the running of wet plaster.) He left the work unfinished, and painting
was then resumed by Masaccio, whom Masolino may have recommended for
the job. They had both worked on a single panel (the Uffizi *Madonna and St.
Anne*), so there is an earlier situation analogous to the Brancacci frescoes. In
fact, the two artists may have had some sort of casual working relation, but
certainly not that of master and teacher.

Another problem crucial to the student of the Brancacci Chapel involves iconography. While single scenes from the life of St. Peter are not rare in Florence,
no other Florentine work contains such a full, detailed treatment of his legend.
It has long been assumed — perhaps rightly, but without any proof — that the
unusual subject must have had a connection with contemporary Florentine
events; more specifically, that the scenes of the *Tribute Money* — in which Christ
commands Peter to pay a tax collected to support the temple — has some reference to the *Catasto*, the Florentine tax first imposed in 1427.[6] Since very little
is known about the political beliefs of the Brancacci, it would be rash to do
more than suggest a political meaning in the choice of the St. Peter legend,
particularly since references to contemporary events are exceedingly rare in previous Florentine fresco cycles.

To understand the Brancacci frescoes it is necessary to know something
about their condition. The first reaction of visitors to the chapel is almost always
disappointment, for the surface of the paintings is covered with layers of grime
over which several coats of varnish and a waxy substance have been applied.
Underneath these disfiguring and dulling coats, the frescoes are only partially
intact. In 1771 a fire destroyed much of the church of the Carmine, and the

smoke, and perhaps also the heat, damaged the paintings. Recently a small piece of the molding from the Baroque altar was removed, exposing a portion of two heads at the far left of *St. Peter Baptizing*. This section seems to have been covered during the fire and subsequent restoration, so its discovery reveals something about the original color of the paintings. The blues and whites are brilliant and fresh. The entire tonality of this small piece is totally different from anything else in the chapel. The browns, blacks, reds, and yellows that now appear dull and lifeless were probably crisp and vibrant. One must try to reconstruct in the mind's eye a fresco cycle in which lighter greens, pinks, yellows, and violets played an important enlivening role.

During repainting campaigns (perhaps many) parts of figures have been reworked and details were touched up or added. Much of the background on the altar wall is repaint, and everywhere lines have been reworked, made bolder and harsher. The exact dimensions of the retouching cannot be determined until a restoration has been carried out. Thus the condition of the frescoes presents yet another barrier to our understanding of the Brancacci paintings. One has constantly to remember that the works have been damaged and to imagine their original appearance.

In Masaccio's *Expulsion* (Plate 90), on the chapel's left-hand entrance pilaster, Adam and Eve are being driven from the gate of Paradise by a red angel hovering above their heads. One glance reveals both the fresco's kinship with Masaccio's earlier work and the increased artistic power of the Brancacci paintings. The *Expulsion* shows Masaccio to be a master of fresco technique, although we do not know what experience he had with it before the Brancacci paintings. It may well be that he had already executed works in that medium. However, Masaccio was a born painter, with a rare natural feeling for materials, an instinct shared by artists such as Donatello, Rembrandt, and Picasso. From the San Giovenale triptych, his earliest known work, he demonstrates an ease and a confidence in the handling of paint that belie his youth.

One of Masaccio's great contributions to the art of fresco painting was his shaping of form exclusively through the use of light and dark. Unlike his Florentine predecessors (with the exception of the late Giotto in the Peruzzi Chapel[7]), he does not use line to delineate figures; this is why the repainted reinforcement of the silhouette with line is so disfiguring to his frescoes. The light, which always comes from the direction of the window in the Brancacci Chapel, defines the massive shapes of Adam and Eve and gives their bodies palpable form. So solid are the sharply highlighted protruding planes, and so deep are the shaded hollows, that the figures remind one of free-standing sculpture. The sure, rapid brush has quickly and brilliantly formed the concavities

90. Masaccio, *Expulsion of Adam and Eve from Paradise*. Florence,
Santa Maria del Carmine.

and convexities of the bodies' surfaces in a manner akin to the cuts made by the sculptor's chisel.

These bold forms are a complement to the fresco medium, which must be executed quickly and surely before the plaster dries. We know from Masaccio's panels that he thought in broad compositional terms and avoided detail. These tendencies are amplified in the *Expulsion*, where the loaded brush slashes across the wall in wide, fast strokes, building up the bulk of the figure from light to dark, making the planes of the bodies turn into and out of space. Here a monumental vision is linked to a total disregard of irrelevant detail.

Monumental also is Masaccio's conception of the emotional states of Adam and Eve. Like several artists of great vision, he was able to make the very shapes of his figures expressive of their role in the religious drama. The solid, earthbound protagonists stride slowly and heavily, their backs turned on the paradise from which they have been banished by their own weakness. Adam's powerful body is bent forward, his massive head covered in shame, his grief graphic but mute. Totally dejected, he seems incapable of any feeling other than humiliation.

Eve also strides forward. The two figures' left-to-right movement away from the gate of Paradise is both the composition's dominant rhythm and the key to its subject of *Expulsion*. Eve covers her breasts and pubic area; for the first time she is aware of her nakedness. Masaccio may have been inspired by a Roman *Venus Pudica* type, where the hands are placed almost the same way, but he has transformed the classical gesture of modesty into one of shame.[8]

Adam's cries seem to be mute, but Eve's sorrow is loudly expressed. Her amazingly plastic head is tilted back, and a desperate wail sounds from the open mouth. In this foreshortened face Masaccio reveals his genius as a fresco painter. The sloping eyes and brows are formed with a few rapid strokes of a large brush; the mouth is a dark cavern bounded by abstracted red-pink lips. A distillation of form to its most expressive essential is the leitmotif of the fresco. The contrast between the man and the woman is wonderfully made: the quiet, withdrawn Adam hiding not his body but his face is opposed to the corpulent Eve, who covers herself while loudly vocalizing her grief and shame.

Hovering above the two figures is an angel holding a large sword. Although its robes lack clarity (almost certainly because of repainting) and its face is retouched, this menacing red presence is an integral part of the composition, for it stands guard over the gate of Paradise while, with its left hand, it directs the sinners into the world of work. The landscape that Adam and Eve enter is as bleak as the life facing them. Bare low hills appear in the background; there is not a plant, flower, or tree to relieve the stony monotony. Here Masaccio has found a visual equivalent of the scene's psychological core.

91. Masaccio. *The Tribute Money.* Florence, Santa Maria del Carmine.

The textual source of the *Tribute Money* (Plate 91; the fresco to the right of the *Expulsion*) — the most famous painting in the Brancacci Chapel and perhaps the best-known work from the first half of the Florentine Quattrocento — comes from Matthew 17:24–27:

> On their arrival at Capernaum the collectors of the temple-tax came up to Peter and asked, "Does your master not pay temple-tax?" "He does," said Peter. When he went indoors Jesus forestalled him by asking, "What do you think about this, Simon? From whom do earthly monarchs collect tax or toll? From their own people, or from aliens?" "From aliens," said Peter. "Why then," said Jesus, "their own people are exempt! But as we do not want to cause offense, go and cast a line in the lake; take the first fish that comes to the hook, open its mouth, and you will find a silver coin; take that and pay it in; it will meet the tax for us both."

Masaccio has divided the story into three separate but closely interrelated parts. In the center, surrounded by a semicircle of his followers, stands Christ confronted by the tax collector of Capernaum (here the fresco varies from Matthew, in which the money was demanded from Peter). This central area is the hub around which the two sides of the fresco revolve. As the tax collector holds out his hand for the tribute, Christ gestures to St. Peter at his right. Christ's movement is echoed and carried on by Peter's outstretched arm, which points to the left side, where the saint appears again, this time squatting by the lake and extracting a coin from a fish's mouth. The spectator's eye is also led from the middle of the painting to the right side by the pointing hand of the tax collector. It initiates a rightward movement that is then amplified by the mighty thrust of Peter's arm as he forcefully pays the tribute to the collector in the right-most part of the painting.

In the *Tribute Money*, a certain amount of tension is created by Masaccio's use of simultaneous narration, in which a single actor is seen more than once. In many earlier pictures, the absence of full spatial integration or rational composition prevents our being disturbed by repeated appearances of the same character. However, in the *Tribute Money*, all the action occurs within a single moment and in a convincing, contiguous atmosphere. There is no disjuncture in time or space. In fact, so seamless is the combination of events that it takes the spectator several minutes to realize that St. Peter appears three times and the tax collector twice. By the time Masaccio began the *Tribute Money* the use of simultaneous narrative was no longer popular. We do not know why he utilized this old-fashioned form of narrative in a fresco of such sophisticated spatial and temporal setting.

Masaccio has stopped the picture's rearward expansion by a large range of gray-green mountains (this part of the fresco is now in a very bad state of preservation). Like all noteworthy fresco painters, he knew that the success of his picture depended on his ability to harmonize its narrative and decorative functions. He had to make sure that his paintings never opened fictive holes that destroyed the structural function of the walls. Everywhere in Masaccio's Brancacci Chapel paintings, the development of background space is carefully controlled to achieve a balance between illusion and decoration.

The central group of the *Tribute Money* is a marvel of integration. Christ's followers form a semicircle that the spectator's own body helps to close. At first glance Christ seems to be in the middle of the fresco, but he is actually to the left of center, the center itself being occupied by the tax collector. By his fully frontal position and the force of his gesture, Christ forms the psychological heart of the composition, yet he does not stand at its physical hub. Possibly Masaccio needed to place the tax collector at the midpoint so his gestures would help move the spectator's eye between the two halves of the composition.

The apostles — serious, sturdy, and monumental — stand between the mountains in the background and the tax collector in the near foreground. The huge bodies — covered by broadly folded robes of weighty wool — overlap one another, as the sober faces turn left and right to create independent compositional rhythms. As he planned the *Tribute Money*, Masaccio must have looked long and hard at Nanni's *Four Crowned Saints* (Plate 63) on Or San Michele, for there is a physical and mental kinship between the two groups of heroic men. Certainly Masaccio understood the body better, and he has simplified and clarified the drapery, but his apostle group still owes a great deal to Nanni's saints. For the stern heads of the apostles Masaccio is surely indebted to Donatello, whose Duomo *St. John the Evangelist* is vividly recalled by the fierce, bearded faces scattered around Christ.

The air of moral purpose about these substantial beings is Masaccio's creation. The Brancacci Chapel types are seen in a less-developed state in the San Giovenale triptych, the Sant'Ambrogio panel, and the Pisa altarpiece, but these earlier examples of monumental scale and seriousness are surpassed by the figures in fresco. To compare personages from the *Tribute Money* with those on Ghiberti's first bronze doors or from Lorenzo Monaco's frescoes in the Bartolini Salimbeni Chapel is to move from one world to another. The attitudes toward the form and meaning of religious drama are so different that it is sometimes startling to realize that all three artists lived and worked in Florence at the same time.

At the left of the *Tribute Money* St. Peter, wearing a blue-green tunic, squats to remove the coin from the fish's mouth. The foreshortened posture, lack of detail, and placement of this figure so wonderfully integrate it into the fresco's space that it seems far from the group of apostles at the center of the composition. Such convincing illusionism may appear elementary to present-day eyes, but to Masaccio's generation it must have been shocking indeed. We sense the physical distance between us and the saint and almost feel the intervening light and atmosphere. Compared with the much more static and contrived figural placement of even the most sophisticated of Masaccio's immediate ancestors and contemporaries (with the exception of Donatello's treatment of the St. George relief), the St. Peter figure is amazing. The illusion of recession is remarkable despite the fact that Masaccio wished to preserve the fresco's function as wall decoration and did not let its space become too deep or vast.

The awkward, twisted shape, the sharply foreshortened head (which is almost a rectangle), and the broadly articulated robes of St. Peter find no counterpart in paintings by Masaccio's contemporaries. In truth, such a figure is nearly the opposite of any by Ghiberti, Lorenzo Monaco, or Masolino. Never would they purposely create so ungainly a figure in such a contorted, ugly pose. The squatting saint tells one much about Masaccio's aims. It reveals that he was not interested in the gracefulness of much contemporary art and that he strove to fashion figures that were totally expressive of the tasks in which they were engaged. Masaccio's personages demonstrate a single-mindedness that must certainly be reflective of his own personality. Perhaps because of his early training or his rural background he was simply not prepared to come to terms with the refined, elegant, and urbane art being produced in the Florence of the 1420s. None of his paintings show a concern for the more conventional aspects of beauty.

At right of the *Tribute Money*, St. Peter pays the tax collector, a powerfully built man with wide shoulders, a bull neck, and a craggy face, who reappears confronting Christ in the center of the fresco. There Masaccio has drawn a brilliant contrast by placing this tense, animallike creature next to the much calmer Christ. The two bodies symbolize two very different emotional and spiritual natures: the base and the divine. Again Masaccio has used the most fundamental elements of form to illustrate inherent psychological attitudes.

But in St. Peter the tax collector has found his match. The saint (who wears the same heavy gold robe and blue-green tunic seen in his previous appearances) is as imposing as any figure in the entire fresco cycle. He delivers the money with a mighty thrust of a huge arm attached to a body firmly fixed to the earth. His rigid vertical shape contrasts with that of the tax collector, who turns in space as he stands on muscular but slightly relaxed legs. Both men are set against a gray building whose arched porch echoes the position and shape of St. Peter's body, while directing the spectator's attention into the background.

The palette of the *Tribute Money* is like that of Masaccio's panels. The colors are usually quite saturated, and their range is restricted. Masaccio is interested in employing color in the service of form, and not as pure decoration. Red-violet, rust, dusty rose, gold, green, and a limited range of blues are about the only colors used for the figures. The very damaged landscape is a mixture of gray and green (some of the trees seem to be later additions). Although the color was originally lighter, it would not have been as bright, intricate, or varied as the more pastel palettes of Lorenzo Monaco and his followers. Masaccio's restraint and control work well with the dignity of the figures and the seriousness of the drama.

Masaccio was not very interested in using color to knit his frescoes together, although the central group of the *Tribute Money* has unifying patches of rose-violet to either side (on the robes of the end figures), and other passages of the same color are observed elsewhere. The green of the robe on the figure to the far left reappears in the squatting St. Peter's tunic, while the red of the central group is seen again in the tax collector's clothes. A loose overall unity is achieved by employing various reds (combined with orange and violet) throughout the fresco.

On the lower right of the window wall the *Distribution of the Communal*

Goods and the Death of Ananias (Plate 89) narrates a scene (from Acts of the Apostles 5:1–12) in which the citizens of a town decided to sell their goods and distribute the profits to the poor.

> But there was another man, called Ananias, with his wife Sapphira, who sold a property. With the full knowledge of his wife he kept back part of the purchase-money, and part he brought and laid at the apostles' feet. But Peter said, "Ananias, how was it that Satan so possessed your mind that you lied to the Holy Spirit, and kept back part of the price of the land? While it remained, did it not remain yours? When it was turned into money, was it not still at your own disposal? What made you think of doing this thing? You have lied not to men but to God." When Ananias heard these words he dropped dead; and all the others who heard were awe-struck. The younger men rose and covered his body, then carried him out and buried him.

We do not know why this rare and terrifying story (the wife of Ananias was later struck dead) is included in the Brancacci Chapel. It may also be a reference to the Florentine *Catasto* or to another tax.

The format of this fresco differs from the horizontal rectangle of the *Tribute Money* (it is also much smaller) and from the narrower rectangle of the *Expulsion*. Masaccio always demonstrates a great sensitivity to the space in which he composes, and the *Distribution* is no exception. The major orientation of the foreground group and the architecture behind is vertical. As in the *Tribute Money*, there is a semicircular movement (stronger on the right) as the figures recede toward the point where St. Peter touches the hand of the woman holding the baby.

Once again Masaccio has stopped recession by blocking a view of deep space with gray buildings and gray-green mountains (the tiny white town hall in the distance may be the invention of a repainter). One is allowed into the picture, but just so far. Figures, architecture, and landscape carefully control the space. Masaccio's art shows an almost overwhelming concern for design. In the *Tribute Money* the organization of figures, architecture, and landscape is calculated to produce effects of great dignity and stability. Each unit in the picture is a monumental entity forming part of a cunningly constructed grid of spatial intervals alternating with large solids. The artist has confronted his pictorial problems with remarkable understanding, economy, and brilliant simplicity.

The story of the *Distribution*, like that of the *Tribute Money*, is one of moral purpose. The old saint gives the money to a young woman carrying a sturdy infant. But he does not seem to acknowledge her, for he and St. John the Evangelist, next to him, are wrapped in their own holy thoughts. In the foreground

Ananias lies at Peter's feet. The message of the picture is simple and clear: those who have shared their money cluster around the holy figure, while the lifeless body in the area of the picture nearest the onlooker is an example of the fate awaiting whoever holds back.

Very little in Masaccio's painting is not clear-cut and straightforward. Thus it is rather puzzling to find in the *Distribution* an individual whose identity and purpose are not readily apparent. Who is the man kneeling behind the outstretched hands of St. Peter and the young woman, his face covered by the two arms in front of him? He wears a red garment and a red hat very like a cardinal's skullcap. Why does he kneel? Why is his face masked? The text of the story gives no clue to his identity. Is he the chapel's patron? Kneeling figures with hands outstretched in supplication were a stock type of donor figure long before Masaccio's time. Perhaps a member of the Brancacci family wished to have himself represented in the fresco cycle in a semianonymous manner; semianonymous because, although his face is covered, his cardinal's robes (if that is what they are) would have revealed his identity to contemporary Florentines. That he is a puzzling figure alone seems to indicate that he has some special significance in the fresco.[9]

The *Distribution of the Communal Goods* has reference outside itself, for its composition is mirrored by *St. Peter Healing with His Shadow* (Plate 88), the fresco across from it on the lower left of the window wall. The story of *St. Peter Healing* is described in the Acts of the Apostles 5, 14–16:

> In the end the sick were actually carried out into the streets and laid there on beds and stretchers, so that even the shadow of Peter might fall on one or another as he passed by; and the people from the towns round Jerusalem flocked in, bringing those who were ill or harassed by unclean spirits, and all of them were cured.

In the fresco the orthogonal lines of the city buildings converge toward the right, that is, toward the window. This rightward movement is mirrored by the leftward recession of the large palace and the brown-gray tower in the background of the *Distribution of Communal Goods*. Now, the spectator standing in front of the window wall will notice that the two compositions share the same horizon line and that they both recede toward a central point in space located somewhere in the window. This device holds the two compositions together, while unifying the design of the altar wall. It also creates a strong illusion by connecting the paintings with the real world, where orthogonal lines do appear to converge on a central vanishing point on the horizon.

The lighting in these two paintings, and, in fact, in all those by Masaccio in the Brancacci Chapel, also helps create unity and illusion. In the *Distribution* the light comes from the left, illuminating the left sides of the buildings and figures. Light in *St. Peter Healing* emanates from the right, as one can see by looking at St. Peter's robe or at the faces of the figures at the left. The painted illumination of these scenes thus derives from a central location between them, which is, of course, the window, the chapel's real light source. Such lighting ties the paintings to the spectator's world; they seem to get their internal illumination from the very daylight that allows the viewer to see them. In other words, they appear to be lit by real light instead of painted light. Similar illumination occurs in the *Tribute Money*, in which the robes of the figures in the central group are lit from the right, from the direction of the window in the altar wall.

Masaccio was not the first Florentine to illuminate his compositions from the direction of the real light source; this practice had been used in Florence for over a century. The earliest masterpiece of the Florentine fresco — Giotto's Arena chapel decoration — contains paintings consistently lit from the direction of the window on the entrance wall. And nearly every Florentine fresco cycle gets its illumination from the direction of the real light. But seldom had the illusion of the lighting been so convincing as in the Brancacci Chapel. The dark shadows, the areas of medium illumination, and the highlights are rendered with realistic consistency, to the point that the solemn figures seem to breathe the same air as the spectator.

Naturally, light is of the greatest importance in *St. Peter Healing*, for without it there can be no shadow. The body of St. Peter in the right foreground blocks the light (which seems to come from the window), thus creating the shadow that heals the imploring man. *St. Peter Healing* was the perfect vehicle for Masaccio's keen interest in illumination, for in this fresco real light, painted light, and magical light all converge.

Light for Masaccio served not only for the constant and coherent illumination of compositions but also for the creation of forms. He uses light in an extremely sculptural way. In the paintings of almost all Masaccio's predecessors and contemporaries, line is an important element in the separation of shape from shape and in the internal delineation of figures, architecture, and landscape. Masaccio hardly uses line, except for the necessary articulation of parts of buildings. Form emerges out of shadow into light, its relief created only by the admixture of light or dark. As in sculpture, the basic definition of shape is not linear but three-dimensional. Masaccio could have realized that only by the most diligent study of contemporary Florentine sculpture, especially that by Donatello.

Not only are the light and perspective of the *Distribution* echoed by *St. Peter*

Healing but also the basic units of the two scenes are strikingly similar. In the *Distribution* the semicircular composition is slightly offset by the large figures of SS. Peter and John, whose overlapping bodies set up a strong diagonal thrust (right to left) into the picture's space. In *St. Peter Healing* this movement is countered and mirrored by the advancing St. Peter and the group following him. As the figures of SS. Peter and John move inward in the *Distribution,* in *St. Peter Healing* the same group of saints and their disciples move outward. There is an implied semicircular movement by and between the two groups.

In comparison with *St. Peter Healing,* the *Distribution of Communal Goods* is open and airy. The distant glimpse of trees and mountains provides relief from the stony closeness of the town. In *St. Peter Healing* space is confined to the narrow canyon of the street; all action unfolds in the city's shadowy boundaries; all views of nature are excluded. The environment is entirely the work of man.

This cityscape is of considerable interest for several reasons. Along with the few buildings in the *Distribution,* it is among the earliest examples of painted architecture that are spatially and proportionally realistic. The environment is rendered in a manner that almost exactly duplicates the spectator's own image of the streets and buildings of Quattrocento Florence. The architecture is accurately scaled to the figures: one feels that the structures could be lived in. Here Masaccio has clearly sought, and found, pictorial devices that help the onlooker enter the picture. He has brought holy narrative down to earth, but, at the same time, he has elevated the earthly city of Florence to the realm of great religious miracles. No longer does sacred drama occur in some abstract, undefined locale. Instead, it now unfolds in the same streets where the spectator will walk after he leaves Santa Maria del Carmine and makes his way across the great piazza fronting the church. The city — man's home — had been sanctified.

St. Peter Healing is one of the most monumental, solemn scenes in the entire chapel, as well as one of the most dramatic and supernatural. St. Peter, with St. John close behind, moves slowly toward the onlooker; his face is rapt; he is immutable and full of purpose. One feels that the only sounds are the imploring cries of the suppliants and the heavy tread of the apostles' feet. There are two foci of attention: the figures of the saints' group, all gazing outward (toward the spectator); and the sick at their right, looking toward St. Peter (as does the spectator). The only exception is the man in the elaborate headdress, who stares in the direction of the figure with his hands in prayer.

The infirm are seen in three positions. The closest to the onlooker kneels, supporting himself on a kind of crutch, his withered, skeletal legs folded under him; the bald man with crossed arms appears to be rising from a kneeling position; while the figure behind him stands upright with his hands in a prayerful gesture. It is almost as though these actions are those of one man who has lifted himself from a nearly prone position to a fully upright one. Perhaps this cinematic progression is meant to represent the upward movements of one miraculously healed by the saint's shadow.

In *St. Peter Healing* Masaccio's style is at its boldest and most abstract. The shapes of the figures, the delineation of their robes, and the formation of their heads and facial features are all starkly direct. For instance, the huge faces of the two standing men in the group of suppliants protrude and recede in large, strongly foreshortened planes. All these features of *St. Peter Healing* are closely paralleled in the *Distribution of the Communal Goods*. In the *Tribute Money* and *Expulsion*, however, the forms appear slightly less abstracted and bold. In these two frescoes (especially in the *Tribute Money*) there is slightly more delineation in the faces and more spring to the bodies. But that is really a matter of degree, for the *Tribute Money* and the *Expulsion* cannot, in any way, be considered as other than monumental paintings. The economy and distillation of these works are surprising for an artist still in his twenties.

Could the variation in style exhibited in the *Distribution* and *St. Peter Healing* be the result of Masaccio's growing confidence in the handling of fresco? We have already seen in the *Expulsion* and the *Tribute Money* that the large forms, tight control of space, and broad, quick brushstrokes are all suited to the fresco technique, which demands speed and bold, clearly readable compositions. In the *Distribution* and *St. Peter Healing* these tendencies are increased. As the differences between his panels reveal, Masaccio's style evolved quickly. Perhaps the same speedy development was responsible for the changes in the Brancacci pictures. In other words, what one may see on the walls of the chapel is the rapid maturation of Masaccio as a fresco painter.

Masaccio's last Brancacci fresco — which appears very close in style to his *Distribution* and *St. Peter Healing* — was begun on the lower left wall. He completed only part of the right side, with the scene of *St. Peter Enthroned* (Plate 92). The other three-quarters of the wall (the *Resurrection of the Son of Theophilus*; Plate 93) remained unpainted until the end of the Quattrocento, when Filippino Lippi was commissioned to finish it and the blank lower right wall. There is some doubt as to the exact area painted by Masaccio in *St. Peter Enthroned*, and it may well be that some of the figures were begun by Masaccio and finished by Lippi.

Clearly the composition was Masaccio's. St. Peter is the center of attention, as he sits high on his throne above a semicircle of figures who kneel before him in prayerful attendance. The scene is backed by a tall building slightly more

92. Masaccio, *St. Peter Enthroned*. Florence, Santa Maria del Carmine.

93. Masaccio and Filippino Lippi, *Resurrection of the Son of Theophilus and St. Peter Enthroned*. Florence, Santa Maria del Carmine.

elaborate than Masaccio's other Brancacci structures. To either side groups of standing men enclose the scene like brackets. Once again Masaccio has fashioned his composition through a series of geometric forms that give order and stability to his narratives.

As in most of Masaccio's Brancacci frescoes, physical movement is held to a minimum. The artist is much more interested in the nearly static than in the transitory. He has endowed his personages with an almost overwhelming gravity. His paintings are much more about a type of spiritual faith and permanence than about the physical actions that make up the holy narratives. This is especially true of *St. Peter Enthroned*, where the saint is worshipped like some great living icon. Such a treatment is particularly appropriate to this story.

St. Peter is the only seated figure by Masaccio in the Brancacci Chapel. In structure, he is remarkably like the Madonnas from the artist's three panels. The figure forms a triangle: its wide base is amplified by the bodies of the kneeling men, and its apex is the saint's large, abstracted, foreshortened head. The basic techniques for setting a seated figure firmly in space, which Masaccio learned while doing the tempera Madonnas, have been used successfully. In fact, the entire structure of *St. Peter Enthroned*, with its seated central actor fronted by kneeling figures and flanked by standing men, reminds one of the simple geometric construction used by Masaccio as early as the 1422 San Giovenale triptych.

Interestingly enough, this last fresco scene shows a small shift in palette. The range of color is still restricted (white, red, pink, and dark green), but the juxtaposition of color is more striking than in any other fresco by Masaccio. The light pink cloak worn by the kneeling man in the center is placed between the light gray habit of the Carmelite to the left and the red robe of the kneeling figure at the right. Such shifts in value from dark to light are not common in Masaccio's other Brancacci frescoes, and their appearance might signal a change toward a slightly lighter, more varied palette, like that used by Masolino in the Brancacci *Raising of Tabitha and the Healing of the Lame Man*. The bright yellow of St. Peter's robe seems to lend weight to this idea.

While it is certainly clear that Masaccio exerted a strong influence on Masolino, there is no reason not to believe that Masolino could also sway Masaccio. Perhaps as he worked on the walls of the Brancacci Chapel, he began to feel that Masolino's palette was more suitable for frescoes. This is speculation, but painters of the Trecento and Quattrocento were ever alert to works of art around them, for copying was the normal way to learn. The young Masaccio, whose style was still evolving, must have been susceptible to numerous idioms. Of course, the fact that he was not influenced by Lorenzo Monaco demonstrates that he did not accept them all indiscriminately.

Before turning to the other paintings in the Brancacci Chapel, let us consider the artistic and historical position of Masaccio's frescoes. They are, above all, innovative. They are the first Florentine compositions that set the holy stories in a rational and totally believable space, where figures stand firmly on the ground enveloped in light and atmosphere.

Only once before, in the work of Giotto, had Florence seen narratives so clearly composed, in which men of great character and seriousness acted with such purpose. Between that earlier artist and Masaccio there is a kinship. Their weighty, forceful actors move with dignity in compositions of distilled simplicity. The two painters express similar attitudes toward sacred subjects, but Giotto was not interested in depicting a highly illusionistic atmosphere. Rather, he often expends considerable effort to let the spectator know that he is looking at a painted picture of events that took place in a distant, removed past. For Masaccio almost the opposite is true. In his Brancacci frescoes he has forged a realistic atmosphere meant to include the spectator and his contemporary world, a world that has now become the locale for religious drama.

Masaccio's highly illusionistic portrayal of sacred stories placed in a recognizable and contemporary milieu was one of the key events in the history of the Florentine Quattrocento. It put religious painting on a new plane, giving the artist's contemporaries a different relation with holy art. The figures of the Brancacci frescoes are the painted counterparts of the images carved by the young Donatello.

But Masaccio was not the only artist to paint in the Brancacci Chapel, nor does he appear to have been the earliest to work there. Masolino was responsible for the frescoes of the *Temptation*, *St. Peter Raising Tabitha and the Healing of the Lame Man*, *St. Peter Baptizing*, and *St. Peter Preaching*; and there is good reason to suspect that he alone was commissioned to execute the cycle. A key to understanding the chronological sequence of the painting lies in a brief comparison of the frescoes of the two men.

The most obvious contrast is between Masaccio's *Expulsion* (Plate 90) and Masolino's *Temptation* (Plate 84), which contain the same protagonists in similar formats. Masolino's fresco has lost much of its detail, but it is obvious at once that his conception of the figure in space is very different from Masaccio's. The Adam and Eve by Masolino are not clearly placed on the ground, nor do their bodies exhibit the sculptural understanding of form common to Masaccio's figures.

The diffused light falling on the *Temptation* does not pick out broad, volume-defining planes, but casts a blondish radiance over the bodies. The painting's smoothness and softness are totally alien to Masaccio's *Expulsion*. Neither light nor shadow delineates the structure of the body or makes it palpable. The degree of detail in the *Temptation* is also foreign to Masaccio's style. The carefully rendered leaves and fruit of the serpent's tree represent a transferral of the small features of panel painting to fresco. Masaccio understood, in a way that Masolino did not, that the large scale of the wall demanded a firm, broad approach, which Masaccio — unlike other early Quattrocento artists — used on his panels as well.

The self-conscious feeling for style and beauty in the *Temptation* shows Masolino's strong debt to contemporary painting. The graceful elongation of the bodies and their delicate, mannered gestures reflect Lorenzo Monaco's art. The curvilinear emphasis — note the twisting of the elegant blond snake, or the way Eve's arm intertwines with the tree — demonstrates Masolino's love of sensuous form. How different from the much more direct, monumental, and, by comparison, wonderfully clumsy forms fashioned by Masaccio in the *Expulsion*! It was not within Masaccio to search for such obvious grace and beauty, and this aspect of his style sets him apart from other Florentine painters. A remarkable contrast between the spirits of the two men is afforded by Masolino's slender, dainty Adam and Eve and Masaccio's thick, ponderous figures.

Masolino's largest fresco in the Brancacci Chapel, the *St. Peter Raising Tabitha and the Healing of the Lame Man* (Plate 85), is on the wall directly across from the *Tribute Money*. The *Raising* appears in the right half, where Tabitha and the semicircular crowd surrounding her are enclosed within a porch on columns. To the left, the cripple is healed by SS. Peter and John; this also takes place before a gray-white porch, supported here on arches. A link between the miracles is formed by the two young men in the center of the composition, who saunter from right to left. These fashionable figures make the pivot that allows the spectator to move easily from one side of the painting to the other; such transitional figures were used repeatedly in Florentine painting of the late Trecento. In a way, the two men are the exact opposite of the central group in the *Tribute Money*, right across from them. Here the knot of apostles is the most important focus. At the sides, other groups are seen, but the spectator's attention always returns to the center. The middle of Masolino's picture, however, is occupied solely by the transitional group: its center, in other words, is inhabited by the personages with the least formal or iconographic interest.

Behind the two dandies there unfolds a passage of considerable importance. They stand in front of a large piazza bordered by Florentine palaces. From the windows of the homes lines hang, baskets dangle, and a monkey walks across a ledge. At the corners of the piazza the spectator is afforded a remarkable view down the streets leading into the square. All this anecdotal detail — which furnishes an interesting glimpse of Florence in the first half of the Quattrocento — is highly unusual; in fact, there is nothing quite like it in previous Florentine painting. Here, as in the *St. Peter Healing* and the *Distribution of Communal Goods*, miraculous scenes are placed in contemporary settings. But in Masolino's fresco the illusion is heightened, for the two men in the center wear fifteenth-century dress: the turban and long cloaks then so fashionable.

In Florence during the late fourteenth and early fifteenth centuries there was a growing tendency to open up the backgrounds of frescoes with either landscapes or townscapes, or the two in combination. Agnolo Gaddi and Lorenzo Monaco, among others, began to place their dramas before deep space. But there is little precedent for the rationally developed piazza of Masolino's fresco. Here the eye is carefully led back from either figure of Peter, through the two young men, to the woman holding the child by the hand, on to the *palazzi*, and finally down the streets flanking the buildings. Although the locations of the figures are not nearly as certain as those in Masaccio's Brancacci paintings, they are, nevertheless, believably placed in the picture's open space.

Given the conservative nature of Masolino, what is one to make of the background to *St. Peter Raising Tabitha and the Healing of the Lame Man*? His previous panels give no indication that he was capable of creating such a background, and so it has been claimed that Masaccio painted it. Since that seems almost impossible — the cityscape is much too crystalline and fussy both in design and in execution — it would appear that Masolino had more original pictorial thought than his earliest surviving works reveal.

While it is true that the figures of the central actors are still svelte and gracious, some modification in proportion and stance is apparent in the flanking groups, where the bodies are more dynamic, more foreshortened, and slightly more monumental. The form of the man with the gray beard to the right of Tabitha and the bearded actor wearing the turban suggest that Masolino is now interested in the creation of space by the recession of solids back from the picture plane. The wide, broadly modeled drapery worn by these men and the robes of the two St. Peters are simpler and more schematic than in any earlier work by Masolino. Much the same is true of their facial features and gestures. There seems little doubt that as he painted this fresco, Masolino was falling under Masaccio's sway, for the actors in *St. Peter Raising Tabitha and the Healing of the Lame Man* already resemble — albeit on a lesser scale — the monumental beings of Masaccio's panels, paintings with which Masolino must have been well acquainted before he began to work in the Brancacci Chapel.

If the form of Masolino's fresco resembles Masaccio's altarpieces, its spirit is quite different, for it lacks the seriousness of Masaccio's work. Masolino's divided, loosely knit composition does not have a powerful central focus. Here, as in the *Tribute Money*, there is a simultaneous narrative with St. Peter appearing twice, but because Masolino's composition is not strongly unified, the dual portrayal appears awkward. The two St. Peters are painted back to back, without a firm separating element between them. The rather weak, diffused mode of such composing precludes the possibility of the concentrated, heroic action seen time and again in Masaccio's works.

An unflinchingly serious narrative was not Masolino's goal. In *St. Peter Raising Tabitha and the Healing of the Lame Man* the figures manifest a variety of gesture and expression quite foreign to Masaccio's work. The visual rhetoric in Masolino's fresco gives it a charming animation and specificity quite distant from the much more abstracted, stoic, ordered *Tribute Money*. Masolino's work is simply not invested with the moral fervor found in Masaccio's painting, nor is it so intended. It is much more a product of its time, and it is really Masaccio's *Tribute Money* that varies from the norm.

The differing attitudes of the two painters are clearly reflected by their use of color. Even through its darkened and damaged condition, the palette of Masolino's picture is lighter, gayer, and more varied than that of any of Masaccio's panels or frescoes. The figures are pink, light green, rust, and gold, while the background buildings are brown, pink, and brown-gray. Masaccio's colors seem duller and more limited, while Masolino's spread out across the fresco's surface in a series of notes. Masolino is more interested in combinations of colors (often of different value): pink against green, gold next to pink, and green beside red. These pleasing, and sometimes beautiful, contrasts remind one of Lorenzo Monaco's use of color; the fashionable robes, hose, and headdresses worn by a number of the figures are also reminiscent of that artist. In general, Masolino's palette is closer to that of his contemporaries than is Masaccio's.

One sees more of Masaccio's influence in Masolino's other two Brancacci frescoes — *St. Peter Preaching* and *St. Peter Baptizing*. That style must have been progressively more compelling as Masolino painted on the chapel's walls.

St. Peter Preaching (Plate 87) is painted on the upper left of the window wall. Here Masolino works within the same upright rectangular format used by Masaccio for the lower scenes of the same wall: the *Distribution of Communal Goods* and *St. Peter Healing*. In Masolino's tightly packed fresco, St. Peter preaches in the left foreground, facing a group of reverent followers. Their bodies create a semicircular recession as they move back from the saint and from the monk in the right foreground. The badly damaged background appears to have contained a range of tall mountains that stopped the picture's space behind the kneeling group.

What strikes one as most unusual, when one recalls the other frescoes by Masolino, is the compactness of the composition and the rather massive, space-creating bodies set into it. There is a careful (if rigid) distribution of figures to create an illusion of a large, tightly knit group. Robes overlap, the foreground heads cover those farther back, faces look out in many directions. Further variety and increased spatial recession are created by the strongly foreshortened heads in the group of kneeling figures: those at the extreme right are surprisingly bold. There is also a slight simplification of drapery. The wide expanse of the monks' gray-white habits on the right side is handled with an economy and directness not seen in Masolino's other frescoes. The kneeling people in the foreground are enveloped in weighty robes that lend a solidity and presence to St. Peter's audience.

A further simplification appears in Masolino's *St. Peter Baptizing* (Plate 86), which is across the window from his *St. Peter Preaching*. Masolino has once again used a semicircular arrangement, which recedes from St. Peter on the left, through the background group, and is brought near the foreground by the shivering man at the right side. As in *St. Peter Preaching*, recession is stopped by a tall range of mountains (very repainted) rising in the background just behind the figures.

The bodies in *St. Peter Baptizing* demonstrate the greatest change in Masolino's style. The kneeling man in the foreground and the shivering man to the right are monumental figures formed by large planes boldly lit from the left (all Masolino's Brancacci paintings receive light from the direction of the window). The sharp foreshortening of heads and hands and the directness of pose come straight from Masaccio. This same influence is seen in many of the personages in the back, whose varied, upturned heads are rendered with a freedom unknown in Masolino's work before this fresco. Even the basic motions of body and hand have undergone substantial modification. The energy of St. Peter's gesture and the fervent pose of the kneeling man are quite distant from the much more elegant, self-conscious movements found in *St. Peter Raising Tabitha and the Healing of the Lame Man*. There is a tension here that is not present in other works by Masolino.

Also modified is his approach to the fresco medium. No longer does he render forms in detail. The figures are broadly modeled with light and shade, eliminating almost all line. The faces are created by a series of quick slashing strokes of a loaded brush. There is more feeling for the stylistic possibilities inherent in the fresco technique. There also seems to be some change in color in *St. Peter Baptizing*. No longer do the pinks, greens, and blues form individual color notes. Instead, the palette is more restricted, has fewer shifts in value, and is slightly more sober — again, possibly because of the influence of Masaccio.

St. Peter Baptizing is an exciting painting done in a mode quite different from that of Masolino's other works in the Brancacci Chapel. The suggestion that it is a work by Masaccio is understandable: it is close to his style indeed.[10] But I think this attribution is incorrect; the fresco does not exhibit Masaccio's brilliant ability to forge compositions of great economy containing a minimum of figures and architectural and landscape props. Even the briefest comparison with the *Distribution of Communal Goods* or *St. Peter Healing* will reveal how much more inherently monumental, unified, and distilled they are. Instead of hypothesizing that *St. Peter Baptizing* is a work by Masaccio, it seems more logical to believe that its Masaccio-like characteristics are the result of the artist's influence on Masolino. This influence seems to have been progressively stronger from the *Temptation* onward, until in the window-wall frescoes it nearly submerged Masolino's earlier style. *St. Peter Baptizing* is a very fine translation of Masaccio's idiom. Masolino (as we shall see in chapter 7) was quick to adopt idioms that exerted powerful influences on him and just as ready to abandon them for yet another style. In his *St. Peter Baptizing* one finds the peak of Masaccio's sway.

Near the middle of the left aisle wall of the Dominican church of Santa Maria Novella, Florence, is Masaccio's *Trinity with Donors and Skeleton* (Plate 94), the artist's most enigmatic work.[11] Like all his frescoes, it has suffered from the hands of restorers. It was painted for the location it now occupies but was covered by a sixteenth-century altar until its rediscovery in 1861. It was then detached from its setting and moved to the church's inside entrance wall. In 1952, when it was cleaned and moved back to its original location, the skeleton was found below the *Trinity*.

94. Masaccio, *Trinity.* Florence, Santa Maria Novella.

To the casual observer, the *Trinity* looks whole and relatively well-preserved, but this is not really the case. Great areas of loss have only recently been re-painted; among them are several small parts of the vault, about half of the kneeling male donor's robes, and much of the fresco's lower left section, including the bunched columns. The new step on which the donors kneel is based only on several small paint fragments. The restoration is very deceiving, for it forms a large area that looks original, yet is not. Consequently one must speak with considerable caution about what is the only surviving fresco by Masaccio outside of the Brancacci Chapel.

The fresco is not the model of rationality and clarity it appears to be on first sight. Above the skeleton are six figures: two unidentified kneeling donors, Mary, St. John the Evangelist, God the Father, and the crucified Christ. Christ, God the Father, and the dove (seen around the latter's neck) form the Trinity.

Fictive architecture, of a type inspired by the contemporary architect Filippo Brunelleschi, frames the scene. (Originally there may have been a painted border enclosing the entire fresco.) Two elegant fluted pilasters topped by Corinthian capitals hold an entablature marking the architecture's upper limit. Behind the pilasters are four Tuscan Doric columns supporting a coffered barrel vault that covers a room, apparently of considerable size. Because this room seems quite deep, the spectator's eye is drawn backward by the rushing orthogonal lines of the architecture; they punch a deep hole into the wall, negating its stony surface. Thus the basic concept of this fresco is very different from that of Masaccio's more spatially restricted Brancacci paintings.

The Virgin, St. John, Christ, and God the Father are inside the room. Nearest the spectator are St. John and the Virgin, who seem to be just behind the two foremost columns. God the Father, standing on a ledge, is in back of Christ — he holds the cross — but his position in space is not at all clear. One cannot tell precisely where the ledge is or how it is supported, or if God the Father is as far forward as the two standing figures or near the back of the room.

These questions lead to others: Just how big is the room? Is it really as large as it seems at first glance? What happens on the sides? Does the room extend laterally? While Masaccio's Brancacci frescoes were direct, coherent, and rational, the space and the location of the figures within the *Trinity* are not.

The relation of the donor figures to the vaulted room is also perplexing. Obviously they are outside it, but their psychological reference to it is not entirely clear. Do they actually observe the holy figures, do they worship a large painting, or do they see a vision? Are we looking at several levels of reality; and are the donors, like us, existing in a spatial and temporal realm different from that inside the room?

There are precedents for such enigmatic composing. Various levels of reality appear in several other Trecento and Quattrocento pictures. One has only to think of Giotto's Arena chapel, where the Virtues and Vices clearly belong to a sphere different from that of the frescoes above, or of a painting like Bernardo Daddi's in the Museo dell'Opera del Duomo, Florence, where two donors are placed before the image of a Miraculous Madonna panel.[12]

In the areas below the donor figures, more problems arise. In the first place, why is the skeleton placed there? The inscription on the sarcophagus, ONCE I WAS THAT WHICH YOU ARE AND WHAT I AM YOU ALSO WILL BE, indicates that the bones are a *memento mori* meant to remind the onlookers of their own mortality, yet that does not explain the appearance of the bones. There are very few *memento mori* in all of Florentine painting (the subject seems not to have fascinated Florentines), and none of them are seen in connection with a Trinity.[13] Perhaps the bunched columns were meant to support a painted altar table (or, possibly, to appear to hold an actual stone table set in front of the fresco). Nothing like this is known in Florence; the entire composition, from its figural arrangement to its architectural function, is unprecedented.

There seems to be little doubt that the skeleton has reference to a tomb (perhaps the donor's) placed in Santa Maria Novella. Much of the painted and carved decoration of the Trecento and Quattrocento is related to burial. The chapels containing frescoes and altarpieces were repositories for the bones of countless donors and their families. And, on occasion, even the bodies of saints were buried under altar tables, much like the skeleton in Masaccio's *Trinity*.[14]

The lighting of the fresco presents yet another problem. At first the images appear lit by natural illumination flooding into the room, but closer inspection reveals that the light source — which is difficult to find — is located around the body of Christ. Thus, the painting's light, like its space, is irrational.

A survey of the *Trinity* ends with confusion: What is it? What was its function? How was it to be understood? Almost all other Florentine paintings of the period can be classified according to type. There is no doubt, for instance, that Masaccio's panel in London was part of a traditional altarpiece, or that the Brancacci frescoes are narratives forming part of a fresco program that, in format at least, is like a number of other Florentine cycles. These works are well within the traditional types (forged in the Duecento and Trecento) that were carried out in a modified, but unbroken, succession for centuries. So, the *Trinity* is indeed unique; seldom, if ever, has there been a Florentine painting so unprecedented, so hard to classify, and so untraditional.

The enigmatic quality of the *Trinity* fresco brings several other questions to mind: How was it inspired? How was it possible for Masaccio, who fashioned some of the most direct and comprehensible works in the history of Italian art, to create such a strange and puzzling picture?

One can only guess at the first question. Obviously Masaccio was commissioned to paint the *Trinity*, and if the identities of the kneeling donors were known, perhaps they would provide some clue to its genesis. In any case, it appears unlikely that Masaccio himself picked the subject of the fresco. Many precedents point to the strong possibility that it was chosen by someone else, the donor or one of the Dominican friars of Santa Maria Novella. The latter seems especially probable, for this church was the home of a highly doctrinal and symbolic art. Nardo di Cione's frescoes in the Strozzi Chapel and Andrea da Firenze's paintings in the Spanish Chapel treat both subject and space in an iconic, complicated, arcane, and often confusing manner.[15] In these mid-Trecento frescoes one feels strongly the supernatural and unfathomable mysteries of Christian doctrine. They leave the spectator outside the realm of their existence: he is an observer, not a participant.

The interpretation of the *Trinity's* composition is as difficult as its functional and iconographic meanings. Most perplexing is how Masaccio — who in the Brancacci Chapel was an apostle of ordered formal clarity — could have painted a picture where so little is clear. His mastery of one-point perspective allowed the construction of rational, measurable environments where the relation of figure to figure, figure to landscape, and narrative to spectator were unambiguous. But Masaccio (and Donatello, as well) knew that one-point perspective could also be effectively utilized to place irrational and mysterious stories in convincing settings. Because of his complete mastery of perspective, many of Donatello's works after c.1430 are terrifyingly real. In the *Trinity* Masaccio uses a variety of illusionistic tools (space, perspective, light) to make a mystery more mysterious.

Of course Masaccio could have designed a more fathomable composition for the *Trinity*, but he consciously chose not to do so. Perhaps he felt that the very subject of the fresco was a highly symbolic, irrational concept, and that to render it as clear and comprehensible would have been contrary to its nature. Maybe this is the reason the spectator is confused not only by the iconography of the work but also by the very core of its composition. One may ask, how it is possible to conceive of and then paint three beings that merge into one?

Equally puzzling is the date of the *Trinity*. Certainly it is close to that of Masaccio's Brancacci Chapel frescoes, but whether it was painted before or after them is unknown. Its restricted palette is reminiscent of the *Tribute Money*. Several different pinks appear in the *Trinity*: on the architecture, where they create a disquieting visual static; on the tunic of God the Father; and in the mantle of St. John the Evangelist. The only other color notes are formed by the blues of the robes worn by God the Father, the Virgin, and the female donor, and the red of the kneeling man. These limited colors are set against an architectural framework of cool gray. The *Trinity* is slightly brighter than the Brancacci Chapel paintings, perhaps because of a different state of preservation. Because of the brevity of the artist's career, it is difficult to date Masaccio's paintings on the basis of their color alone; but even with this in mind, the palette of the *Trinity* is quite close to that of the Brancacci frescoes. In any case, it can date no later than 1428, the year in which the twenty-seven-year-old Masaccio died.[16]

A comparison of the *Trinity*'s Christ and the same figure from Masaccio's Naples *Crucifixion* reveals something else about the dating of the fresco. The awkward and angular Naples Christ has been suppressed in favor of the more monumental and unified figure seen in the *Trinity*. Increased confidence in both design and handling suggests that the Christ of the fresco is later than the one in the Naples panel, which may date from 1426.

For the *Trinity* Masaccio has, of course, borrowed from past crucifix types. The Christ with the elongated torso, bowed legs, and broad chest, like the Naples Christ, has its origins in conservative late Trecento works, such as the Crucifix by Niccolò di Pietro Gerini (Plate 23) discussed in chapter 2. Masaccio has also borrowed the pose and gesture of Mary from earlier Crucifixion scenes. But these two traditional types have been so completely integrated into the composition that their origin is not apparent. The same process of borrowing and adapting is seen in the kneeling donors, whose pose is taken from a type common to many late Trecento panels.[17]

The figures, however, are solely Masaccio's and extremely close to the *Tribute Money*: their articulation through space, their gestures, robes, and faces are very like those of the group that surrounds Christ in that fresco's center. On the whole, the bodies and faces in the *Trinity* appear a little more particularized than those of the Brancacci Chapel. This may suggest that the *Trinity* is slightly older than these paintings, but this is just speculation, since the stylistic difference between it and the Brancacci frescoes is minimal. It seems most sensible to date them both at about the same time.

Perhaps the most striking aspect of the *Trinity* is its originality. Although Masaccio certainly borrowed from older images for his figures, he probably had no prototype or iconographic tradition for the *Trinity with Donors*.[18] The interior space of the vaulted room and the contrast between it and the spaces where the donors kneel and the skeleton lies are unlike anything else from the first half of the Quattrocento. It is true that Masaccio has consciously excluded the spectator, making him once more the observer instead of the participant he is in the Brancacci Chapel, but this too is a sign of creativity and intelligence. The ability to change formal structure from work to work and context to context in order to create different psychological states in the onlooker's mind is found exclusively in artists of the highest talent. In the early fifteenth century it is seen only in the works of Masaccio and Donatello. The *Trinity*, then, is all the more fascinating because it affords a glimpse into the flexibility of Masaccio's pictorial thought and a hint of what he might have done had he lived beyond his twenty-eighth year.

VII.

Florentine Art around 1430: New Directions

ABOUT THE TIME of Masaccio's death, the art of Florence once again began to show signs of change. This modification is most apparent in the work of Donatello, the period's greatest sculptor, but it is also evident in the lesser and more derivative artists.

The first signs of a substantial reorientation of Donatello's art are seen around 1425, in his *Feast of Herod* bronze relief (Plate 95) for the font of the Siena Baptistery.[1] The space is carefully arranged into three separate compartments: in the foreground is the feast itself; the middle ground — glimpsed through the first range of arcades — is occupied by several people; while in the background the head of St. John the Baptist is held up to three men. This arrangement is not the well-ordered, rational sort traditionally associated with the first half of the Quattrocento. The Siena relief is crowded, compressed, and confused. The arcades seem to be placed at different levels, and the spectator cannot be sure of the size of each spatial unit. The arches are not allowed to line up with one another, so there is a jumble of arches, columns, and voussoirs across the top of the relief. In fact, space recedes upward as strongly as it does backward. Clarity has been sacrificed for a tumult of spatial energy.

In the foreground the severed head of St. John is presented to Herod. In Donatello's version of the story, the head is the fulcrum of a physical and emotional terror taking place before the viewer's eyes; all the protagonists (the spectator as well) are shocked and horrified. Herod throws up his hands in stunned surprise as the grisly head is proffered. At his feet children scramble out of the space, while the man next to him makes an accusatory gesture. At the right, a figure covers his face as he recoils in terror. Before a knot of onlookers Salome stops her dance, frozen by the terrible sight. The exact center of the composition is vacant, as though emptied by an explosion of fear.

95. Donatello. *Feast of Herod*. Siena, Baptistery.

Donatello has set the story within a complex and disorienting spatial framework fronted by a writhing, rhythmically entwined clump of figures. Moreover, he has carefully articulated the surface, making it nearly impossible for the spectator's eye to rest. Each part of the bronze is given a particular texture, which changes almost from inch to inch: the sharp lines of the various sized bricks, the close fluting of the columns, the rough surfaces of the pavement, the tousled hair, the wrinkled tablecloth, and the swirling robes. Everywhere there is a relentless, restless movement. Further visual excitement is created by the beams projecting toward the spectator. These sharply foreshortened objects — along with the rapidly receding holes made by leaving bricks out of the arcade wall — are agents of compositional disquiet. They serve the same purpose as the convulsed, erratic space.

Donatello has quite consciously made the spatial and figurative elements emphasize and amplify the dizzying horror of the Herod story. His primary aim seems to have been to fashion a narrative expression of the overwhelming revulsion caused by the presentation of the head of St. John the Baptist. Differing from all earlier Florentine artists who depicted it, Donatello has not been content to place the story in a calm context; instead, he has made the stylistic building blocks of his composition reel with the ghastly reality of the scene. And, unlike almost all of Donatello's previous sculpture, the relief portrays an unheroic narrative into which many strongly irrational elements are interjected.

In many ways the Siena *Feast of Herod* is a prophetic work. It contains the germ of much of Donatello's later development, a development that can be briefly illustrated by a survey of one of the rectangular bronze reliefs done for the altar of the Santo in Padua in the 1440s. During this decade all the artist's known work was commissioned and executed outside Florence.

The *Miracle of the Repentant Son* (Plate 96) shows St. Anthony replacing a leg severed from the body of a boy.[2] The event takes place in the near central foreground. The boy's hand, placed through the picture plane, seems to be entering the spectator's world. An irregular frieze of onlookers and passers-by meanders across the relief, creating a broken pattern along the lower half of its surface. Suddenly the rhythm of the composition is broken as the spectator looks beyond the foreground figures to an enormous, nearly empty arena. The sides of the arena move quickly and deeply into space, where they are stopped by a back wall and strongly countered by the sharp corner of another large building rushing toward the spectator. Further confusing and distracting movements are created by the arena's rails and benches, by the wide flights of steps, and by the foreshortened buildings to either side of the relief. Adding to the general sense of disorientation is Donatello's repeated use of line and texture to

96. Donatello, *Miracle of the Repentant Son*. Padua, Santo.

break up any smooth surface upon which the eye might rest. This technique is used here to even greater effect than in the Siena *Feast of Herod*.

What is one to make of this extremely odd narrative, with a sky occupied by a strange sun with starlike rays? How does one account for the empty arena, the flight into deep space, and the twisting, agitated, wraithlike foreground figures? Donatello, I believe, understood the nature of a miracle, and he knew that such an event is not to be viewed rationally. Like Masaccio's *Trinity*, the real power of the scene comes from its irrational (and here almost hallucinatory) quality. The replacement of the youth's leg is no ordinary act. Donatello realized that it must take place not in an understandable environment, but in a setting that is as illogical as the miracle itself. In each of the Padua bronzes Donatello demonstrates that miracles demand a special milieu. This environment is made highly plausible by the rational construction of one-point perspective, which allows for the convincing placement of objects in space. Donatello has taken this system and used it to make the miraculous seem real.

The remainder of Donatello's career is filled with works that, in many ways, amplify the emotional, disjointed, and supernatural qualities of the Siena *Feast of Herod* and the Padua *Miracle of the Repentant Son*.[3] This development is significant because it represents both a turning point in the history of Florentine sculpture and a departure from (and, in a very real sense, a repudiation of) Donatello's earlier works, which are monuments of solidity, balance, and heroism. Maybe by the late 1430s or early 1440s Donatello felt that the stylistic and psychological possibilities of his early sculpture had been exhausted. Perhaps he had experienced a profound spiritual crisis, which altered his conception of the sacred legends and their meaning.

97. Lorenzo Ghiberti, *Meeting of Solomon and Sheba*. Florence, Baptistery.

A major stylistic change also appears in the work of one of Donatello's most important contemporaries, Lorenzo Ghiberti. As we have seen in chapter 3, Ghiberti was among the most prominent practitioners of the gracious, melodious idiom best expressèd in paint by Lorenzo Monaco. A landmark of this style is found in Ghiberti's first bronze doors, completed in 1424. Yet, in the sculptor's second set of doors for the Florentine Baptistery (commissioned in 1425, finished in 1452) one sees a substantial modification in the construction of narratives.[4] The exact dates of the individual reliefs are not certain, but one example, the *Meeting of Solomon and Sheba* (Plate 97), may document Ghiberti's new approach.

Because there are only eight panels on the new doors, each narrative is considerably larger than those on the first set of doors. Ghiberti has done away with the old quatrefoil frame, replacing it with a square format surrounded by a simple molding. This shape harmonizes well with his rather expansive treatment of narrative on the second doors.

The meeting of Solomon and Sheba takes place in the center of a composition filled almost to overflowing with architecture, people, and animals. The royal couple is nearly lost in the clutter. How different this is from the ordered, balanced treatment in the quatrefoils of the first doors! The older idea of tightly controlling narrative space to emphasize the function of the doors as solid objects meant to close a building has been abandoned. In its stead there is nearly unlimited lateral and backward spatial expansion.

Obviously Ghiberti was fascinated by his ability to depict space and architecture in a highly convincing manner; but he is caught up in his own visual rhetoric. He fashions narratives that have little integration or focus. The complexity and chaotic diffusion in these reliefs, while differing in underlying motivation, are not unlike Donatello's. The diversity and measured disorder in the work of both artists are indicative of a new direction in Florentine sculpture.

In painting there were also a number of basic modifications taking place in the mid-1420s. Two groups of painters were at work in the city. The first was made up of artists who were already well known: they were, broadly speaking, Masaccio's contemporaries, and their number included Gentile da Fabriano, Masolino, Bicci di Lorenzo, and Lorenzo Monaco. The second group was composed of somewhat younger painters whose active, independent careers were not yet firmly established: to this group belonged Fra Filippo Lippi, Andrea di Giusto (Masaccio's assistant in Pisa in 1426), Fra Angelico (who seems, however, to have been about Masaccio's age), and several other noteworthy artists. The work of all these men, which is often indebted to Masaccio, indicates both Masaccio's historical importance and the direction Florentine art was to take.

Gentile da Fabriano's *Madonna and Child with Two Saints* (Plate 98; Frick Collection, New York) is an excellent example of a painting by a member of the first group of artists. Up to his years in Florence, Gentile's art (see chapter 2) was strongly influenced by the idioms of the several areas in which he had worked. The particularized richness of his style, which endeared him to the Florentines, resulted in expensive commissions for the Strozzi and Quaratesi altarpieces. Nevertheless, in both paintings one sees the nascent effect of Masaccio. By the time of the Frick picture, this influence had become almost the dominant note in Gentile's work.[5] Of course, some of the older stylistic motifs remain — the Madonna's elaborate, convoluted hem, the sumptuous use of gold, and the careful rendering of detail — but the basic compositional concepts are now heavily influenced by Masaccio. The triangular arrangement of the Madonna and the two kneeling saints reminds one of the San Giovenale triptych and the London Madonna. Never before in Gentile's work had there been so much insistence on the adjustment of the figures to make such stable compositional units.

That Gentile has paid much attention to Masaccio's use of foreshortening is

98. Gentile da Fabriano, *Madonna and Child*. New York, Frick
Collection.

99. Gentile da Fabriano, *Madonna
and Child*. Orvieto, Duomo.

especially evident in the two saints, who move easily into and out of the picture's
space. Here one recalls the marvelous angels of the San Giovenale painting or
the kneeling figures in the Brancacci *St. Peter Enthroned*. The compressed fervor of Gentile's saints and the chubby, broad-faced baby are also reminiscent of
Masaccio.

Compared with Gentile's earlier work, the entire structure of the Frick panel
is simpler, more clear-cut, more abstract. It shows a new interest in the broad
flow of robes over the bodies, and the bodies themselves now appear to have
weight and volume. The palette is soberer, and large areas of color are allowed
to exist unbroken.

In the Frick panel we see how the impressionable Gentile has carefully employed fundamental properties of Masaccio's idiom; but his interest in Masaccio, noticeable as early as the Strozzi altarpiece, finds its fruition and conclusion
in a badly damaged fresco he painted for the Duomo of Orvieto in 1425. The
remains of this picture — a monumental Madonna and her playful son (Plate
99) — demonstrate clearly that Gentile had arrived at a full understanding of
Masaccio's stylistic aims. In several ways Gentile's artistic development exemplifies how Masaccio's style affected artists of considerable talent. Aside from

100. Masolino, Scenes from the Legend of St. Catherine. Rome, San
Clemente.

Masaccio's ability to make his figures palpable and believable, it was the directness and the telling simplicity of his images that Gentile most admired in the
younger painter's work.

Gentile died in Rome in 1428. Had he lived longer, would he have developed
some of Masaccio's ideas further, or would he have veered off in yet another
stylistic direction? Gentile's career furnishes no answers, but the later development of Masolino provides an example of what an artist almost entirely under
Masaccio's sway did after leaving the realm of the painter's influence.

As we have seen, in the Brancacci Chapel Masolino fell increasingly under
the spell of Masaccio. His frescoes became clearer and more unified, his figures
more and more heroic. In fact, in his last paintings in the Carmine, Masolino
seemed to be losing his artistic personality. However, in the remainder of his
work his style changed, and within a short time he was once again moving in
new directions.

A glance at scenes from the legend of St. Catherine (Plate 100) from the
fresco cycle in San Clemente, Rome (c.1430), alerts one to several developments in Masolino's art.[6] They must have been painted just a few years after the

Brancacci stories, yet they document the lessening of Masaccio's influence. Most striking is their lack of narrative unification; in fact, they are even more loosely composed than any of Masolino's early Brancacci paintings. On the left Catherine stands before the emperor, at the center she converts the empress, while at the right the empress is beheaded. Far from being demarcated by any sophisticated compositional division, the three episodes seem to be taking place at the same time and in the same space. The principles of organization are much more like those of *St. Peter Raising Tabitha and the Healing of the Lame Man* than of the *Tribute Money*.

No attempt has been made to give the narrative an overall balance. A rotunda (perhaps based on the Pantheon) encloses the space in the scene at the left. A very insignificant, narrow painted column separates it from a strongly fore-shortened street that drives a wedge of space into the background of the adjoining scene, which contains the arcaded building before which the saint is executed. At the far right side the headless body of the empress concludes the story. Such rapid shifts between architecture and landscape, and between solid and void, without any clearly definable organizing principle, mark a new stage in Masolino's conception of the fresco: a stage in which the careful geometric planning of Masaccio plays a diminished role.

Also new is the treatment of figures in the San Clemente frescoes. Although still under the sway of Masaccio's types, the actors are slightly more graceful, undulating, and self-consciously posed. The blond tonality of hair and skin so common to Masolino's panels — and to the Adam and Eve scene — has returned; in fact, the entire palette is quite bright. Badly damaged but still readable, a number of yellows, pinks, whites, and blues appear throughout the fresco, giving the scene a light, almost joyous feeling. This is a far cry from Masolino's two paintings on the upper window wall of the Brancacci Chapel. The Masaccio-inspired gravity of Masolino's last Brancacci frescoes does not appear in most of the San Clemente pictures. Instead, one sees an enervated, almost fantastic world where all action seems suspended.

Some time after his work in Rome, Masolino went to the north of Italy to paint in the Baptistery of the Collegiata at Castiglione Olona, a town not far from Milan.[7] The dates of the frescoes are uncertain, but Masolino probably worked in the Collegiata during the mid 1430s. Most likely these extraordinary pictures are his last extant work, and in them his sense of fantasy — suppressed in the later Brancacci paintings and seen reemerging in the San Clemente cycle — is given full vent.

The lunette *Feast of Herod and the Presentation of the Head of St. John the Baptist to Herodias* (Plate 101) is a prime example of Masolino's work at Castiglione Olona. As in the San Clemente *St. Catherine* lunette, the narrative action

101. Masolino, *Feast of Herod and the Presentation of the Head of St. John the Baptist to Herodias*. Castiglione Olona, Collegiata Baptistery.

is drawn across the entire fresco. Once again, the various episodes of the story are not clearly demarcated, and the center of the composition is punctured by a vast spatial wedge pushed to the far background. Here the figures seem less significant than they do in the San Clemente fresco. It is as though the real interest is now centered on the elaborate architecture and the range of steep mountains rising in the background. The spectator's attention focuses on the flight of smooth pink columns and regular arches moving swiftly into space or on the cool green and yellow crags. The costumed figures do not seem terribly purposeful, and their poses and expressions are not compelling. These blond, svelte people appear to belong to some aristocratic race. Their restrained feelings are expressed only through a series of mannered, rather unconvincing gestures, such as those made by the two women near Herodias. In conceptualizing and setting down religious drama, the gap between these figures and those from Donatello's *Feast of Herod* is unbridgeable.

Another comparison between Donatello and Masolino is suggested by a superficial similarity between the great void in the middle of the St. John the Baptist fresco and the empty center of the wildly foreshortened arena in the

Padua *Miracle of the Repentant Son*. In Donatello's bronze the composition is
carefully calculated to make the spectator lose his balance, to let him sense the
spatial and emotional tumult caused by the supernatural event unfolding in the
foreground. Masolino's space does not have the same purpose or the same elec-
trical charge. It creates not drama but distraction. It ruptures the environment,
sending the onlooker's glance careening into the distance. Though different in
intent, the spatial constructions of the fresco and the bronze have something in
common: both lack the concentrated drama so characteristic of the early Donatello and of the Masolino of the Brancacci Chapel. The disjointed, out-of-kilter
feeling of the Padua and Castiglione Olona works is shared with many panels
from Ghiberti's *Gates of Paradise* and a number of other works from the 1430s
and 1440s; fantasy, multiplicity, and confusion have become important pictorial
elements.

Throughout his career Masolino was easily influenced by numerous stylistic
trends; witness his early adaption of Monaco's idiom. Undoubtedly, the most
powerful influence was Masaccio's, but it did not last much beyond 1430. In
the San Clemente cycle its effects are rapidly diminishing, and by the time of
the Castiglione Olona frescoes Masaccio's art seems very far away indeed. In
these last paintings Masolino's style has developed into a brightly mannered,
fantastic idiom quite distant from his Brancacci *St. Peter Preaching* and *St. Peter
Baptizing*.

A lesser artist than Masolino, Bicci di Lorenzo, also fell under the sway of
Masaccio, and his works help to furnish a picture of the state of Florentine
painting around 1430.[8] The *Madonna, Child and St. Anne* (Plate 102) in
Greenville, South Carolina, probably dates from the late 1420s or early 1430s,
and is obviously based on Masaccio's Sant'Ambrogio altarpiece of the same
subject. From Masaccio, Bicci has borrowed the main compositional elements:
the positions and locations of the two central figures, the brocaded cloth of
honor, and the sharply foreshortened throne. He has heavily modified a number
of them, but it is clear that he was impressed by the centralized, stable composition of Masaccio's picture. Bicci probably did not try to form figures of such
weight and breadth again. His timid, halting style was not capable of duplicating the properties of his model, and the fragility of his picture sets it far apart
from Masaccio's design. The dramatic interlocking of the parts of the
Sant'Ambrogio altarpiece has escaped transfer to Bicci's work.

However, Bicci's Greenville panel affords a fascinating glimpse into the way
an artist trained in an older tradition understood and interpreted Masaccio's
stunning innovations. Bicci made the design of his rather austere prototype
both more intimate and more complex. The tiny nursing baby is unlike the

102. Bicci di Lorenzo, *Madonna,*
Child and St. Anne. Greenville,
Bob Jones University Collection.

rugged child of Masaccio's painting. Suppressed is the groping rhythm of the outstretched hands; added is the intertwined and moving pattern on the carpet, haloes, and hems. The spatially aggressive forms of the Sant'Ambrogio altarpiece have given way to Bicci's self-contained, weak figures. Masaccio's painting has been domesticized, made homey. Thus, while Bicci has borrowed Masaccio's composition and several of his shapes, he has used them for different purposes. He has lifted them out of their original context and placed them in a new setting of a diverse formal and psychological order. This is similar to what Masolino did in his San Clemente and Castiglione Olona frescoes, and to what Donatello did — although using his own earlier inventions — after the 1430s.

By 1435 Bicci's style had undergone yet another change. The *Nativity* (Plate 103) in San Giovannino dei Cavalieri, Florence, of that year, contains a confused and confusing plethora of shapes. A multitude of angels hover at the top of the picture, while others fly above the principal foreground figures. Several walled towns appear in the background. Mountain ridges, the *Annunciation to the Shepherds*, a forest, a donor, and a dog are seen elsewhere. There is a feeling for the anecdotal and the particular, which are characteristic of Bicci's later work. If one compares Masaccio's heroic, lean *Nativity* from the Pisa altarpiece

103. Bicci di Lorenzo, *Nativity*. Florence, San Giovannino dei
Cavalieri.

of 1426 with Bicci's frivolous *Nativity*, one sees how little the spirit of Masaccio's work meant to Bicci nine years later.

Bicci's *Nativity* has the same disjointed, crowded feeling as several other works discussed in this chapter. In Ghiberti's *Meeting of Solomon and Sheba*, Donatello's *Miracle of the Repentant Son*, and Masolino's *Feast of Herod*, the drama is equalled or overpowered by the complexity of the setting. The drama takes place in a milieu outside our own experience, in some world we seem to recognize, yet where we feel strange and disoriented. Although these works are often very dissimilar in intent and quality, they all share, at least in part, this new vision of religious events, where things are a little out of joint and where the onlooker is made to feel slightly queasy. They are markedly different from the art of the first three decades of the Florentine Quattrocento, when several styles coexisted and intermingled, but none were employed to create narratives so deliberately disparate. Thinking back to the fluid, harmonious work of Lorenzo Monaco, or to the younger Ghiberti, or to the stable and earthbound style of the early Donatello, or to Massacio's Brancacci Chapel, one remembers a more optimistic, calmer world. By 1430 that world was disintegrating rapidly.

104. Fra Filippo Lippi, Tarquinia
Madonna. Rome, Galleria Nazionale.

Confidence and balance, suavity and lyricism were being replaced with a particularized, crowded, often homey, and sometimes unstable conception of religious drama. Although these changes are often apparent in the painters and sculptors who were Masaccio's contemporaries, they are seen most clearly in the works of the artists who began to paint around the time Masaccio disappeared from the Florentine scene.

One of them, Filippo Lippi (c.1403–1469), was a monk in the Carmine when Masaccio was painting there.[9] His first dated work is from 1432, although by that date Filippo probably had been an independent painter for some time. The Tarquinia *Madonna* (Plate 104; formerly at Corneto Tarquinia and now in the Galleria Nazionale, Palazzo Barberini, Rome), dated five years later (1437), reveals a good deal about the early formation of his style. One is immediately struck by the monumentality and seriousness of the mother and child in the small room. The shape of the Madonna's body, the space-defining fullness of her robes, and the way they pull across her solid body, all demonstrate how much Lippi owes to a work like Masaccio's London *Madonna*, painted only a decade earlier. The vigorous, broad-faced child clambering onto his dreamy-eyed mother is also a direct descendant of Masaccio's infants.

The muted gray and red, brown-yellow and white are reminiscent of Maaccio's restricted, sober palette. Lippi's color harmonizes well with the somber mood of the two central figures. That Lippi has studied Masaccio's use of form is apparent from the implied triangle of the two bodies. This geometric shape is countered by the strong semicircle of the throne's back, which in turn is opposed by the semi-circular step.

The background is fairly complex: to the right a bed, in the rear the carefully rendered outside wall of a *palazzo*, and at the left a window opening on a hillside occupied by a bridge and a castle. It is completely different from anything in Masaccio's Madonna panels, in which spatial recession is stopped by the gold background, although the increased spatial complexity of the London Madonna might indicate that Masaccio's thoughts were turning in the direction of a more complicated setting. But, fundamentally, the origins of Lippi's picture seem to lie in the Brancacci Chapel, in the work of both Masaccio and Masolino. Deep realistic landscapes alternating with massive figural units and architecture are found in several of Masaccio's frescoes; and the accurate topographical portrait of Quattrocento buildings first appears in Masolino's *St. Peter Raising Tabitha*.

There are two distinct parts to the Tarquinia *Madonna*: the foreground, which is occupied almost exclusively by the monumental, closed group of mother and child, and the background, which is open, sharply foreshortened, and slightly chaotic. In strong contrast to the spatial breadth of the rest of the picture is the weighty solidity of the two figures. The tension created by the opposition of these two areas does not stem from Masaccio, but from Lippi's own inventive mind. In this painting he leaves the world of Masaccio for a broader, less-concentrated treatment of religious imagery.

Several things in Lippi's picture are commonly found in works done after c.1430. One is the polarity between solid foreground figures and a dramatically receding background, which produces a slightly unstable composition that often blurs the story's dramatic focus. Another is a particularized feeling for peripheral, often quite homey, detail and accoutrements: note the book, the veined marble, the *palazzo*, the rings, and the jewels. Like work by Masolino, Ghiberti, or Bicci after the third decade of the Quattrocento, Lippi's painting manifests certain unmistakable modifications of the elevated sacred drama so characteristic of the early years of the Florentine Quattrocento.

The tendencies evident in the Tarquinia *Madonna* are carried to their conclusion in a late work by Lippi, the Uffizi *Nativity* (Plate 105), painted around 1450. Here the mystic and visionary play a role of primary importance. The center of the foreground is occupied by the Christ child and his parents, but the rest of the painting is filled with a myriad of images with only a tenuous relation to the central event of Nativity.[10] To the lower left a saint peeks out from behind

105. Fra Filippo Lippi, *Nativity.* Florence, Uffizi.

a rock. Farther back a kneeling St. Jerome contemplates the cross. Behind him is a range of folded mountains dotted with trees. Before the shed floats a group of angels just emerging from a cloud bank. In the distant background one sees a forest whose border is populated by shepherds and their flock. Near the right edge of the panel the penitent Magdalene props herself up on a crumbling wall.

The picture is disjointed, having neither a convincing physical unity nor a logical narrative progression. Seemingly unrelated images coexist loosely and episodically, like a series of apparitions, each occurring at nearly the same time and within roughly the same space.

Lippi's development (which is also apparent in a number of his other works) from an idiom heavily influenced by Masaccio to a more detailed, less organized, and less coherent composition and style, is paralleled by those of a number of other Florentine artists. We have already seen similar, but not identical, stylistic evolutions in the work of Ghiberti, Donatello, Masolino and Bicci, especially in Bicci's *Nativity*. It is not clear why this phenomenon occurred in the art of Florence. It does not appear to have been brought about by the influ-

106. Fra Angelico, Altarpiece. Florence, San Marco, Museo
dell'Angelico.

ence of a single individual. (For example, after the 1430s Donatello's idiom was
so personal that it seems not to have been artistically understood even in his
native city.) Nor was it precipitated by the predominance of a collective style.
In fact, from about the third decade of the Quattrocento it is almost impossible
to classify the artistic production of Florence into stylistic types. In the years
around Masaccio's death there emerged a number of strong individual idioms,
related only loosely by conventions of workshop practice and the shared religious vision of the time.

The style of Fra Angelico exemplifies one of these idioms.[11] One of his earliest
works (his painting career extended from c.1418 to 1455) is a small altarpiece
of around 1425 in the Angelico Museum at San Marco, Florence (Plate 106).
It is clear, especially from the center panel, that this work is heavily indebted to
Masaccio. There is a striking resemblance in type between Angelico's Madonna
and the Madonna from Masaccio's 1422 San Giovenale triptych. The pro-
nounced triangles of the bodies and the heavy, sweeping, treatment of the robes
are quite similar. Although the face of Angelico's Virgin is slightly sweeter, it

107. Fra Angelico, *Madonna
and Child*. Florence, San Marco,
Museo dell'Angelico.

is, nevertheless, a tactile, solid oval with strong ties to the same figure from the
San Giovenale picture. The stolid flanking saints, while perhaps of slightly
inferior quality, also show the influence of Masaccio in their serious counte-
nances and immobile stance. It is quite unlikely that Angelico saw the San
Giovenale picture *in situ*, but perhaps he knew others like it from Masaccio's
hand.

The Child, however, is of the type of elongated, graceful infant invented by
Lorenzo Monaco. And, indeed, the baby shows another of Angelico's interests.
He must have felt keenly the pull of the various styles then coexisting in Florence. A Madonna panel (Plate 107; also in the Angelico Museum, Florence,
and perhaps from the 1420s) shows him working in an idiom quite close to
Monaco's. Here, although better articulated, is the same type of Christ Child
seen in the altarpiece just discussed. The Madonna clearly owes much to Monaco, both in the studied grace of her robes and in the litheness and mobility of
her body. The regal sumptuousness of this picture reveals Angelico's complete
understanding of Lorenzo Monaco's spirit.

In Angelico's famous *Deposition* (Plate 108; Angelico Museum, Florence) of
about 1435 one still finds the influence of Masaccio (compare the kneeling man

108. Fra Angelico, *Deposition*. Florence, San Marco, Museo
dell'Angelico.

to the kneeling figure at the right in the Brancacci *St. Peter Enthroned*) and of
Lorenzo Monaco (Monaco-like greens and light grays appear throughout the
picture). But these influences are adapted to a new context and spirit that are
entirely Angelico's. One no longer feels the immediate sense of drama common
to the painting of Florence before c.1430. Instead, there is an emphasis on
meditation and contemplation. It is as though the physical deposition has been
made totally symbolic. The various figures serve as interlocutors between worshipper and event. There is no real action, no real sorrow. Hands are raised,
heads bowed, and knees bent, but this seems to be some ritual of contemplation
set in the glorious sun-filled Florentine countryside. Perhaps this treatment of
religious drama is the result of Fra Angelico's constant reading of devotional
literature, in which the faithful are always asked to contemplate the symbolic
import of the events of Christian history.[12] (It is interesting to note, in this
respect, that the *Deposition* was originally commissioned to the monk Lorenzo
Monaco, who completed only the pinnacles and the *predella*.)

Yet, the picture has much in common with other works from its time. It shares a particularized quality with the paintings by Masolino and Bicci discussed in this chapter, and the same isolated and disparate feeling found in Lippi's Uffizi *Nativity*. A proliferation of forms and a multiplicity of colors and textures link all these works and at the same time separate them from the much simpler, more restrained works of the first part of the century. The exception is Gentile's Strozzi *Adoration*, which is, in some ways, a prophetic picture. However, as we have seen, Gentile abandoned the style of this work for a less complex, more balanced vision of sacred imagery, a vision greatly indebted to Masaccio.

Most of Angelico's Florentine contemporaries also moved away from the art of the early Quattrocento toward more spatially complex, less dramatic styles. Their work emphasizes the visionary, supernatural quality of religious drama, while showing a concern for the careful, detailed rendering of the actors and atmosphere of the holy stories. On the whole, neither the broader, more heroic styles of Masaccio and the early Donatello nor the mellifluous idiom of the Monaco followers survived much beyond the 1430s.

An important exception to this general stylistic trend is found in the career of Piero della Francesca, a native of the small town of Sansepolcro, near Arezzo.[13] Piero was born around 1420 and is first recorded in Florence in 1439 as a pupil of Domenico Veneziano.[14] During the rest of his working life Piero executed a number of commissions for his native city and for the courts of Rimini and Urbino.

From his first independent paintings, which must date from the early 1440s, Piero painted in a style that in form and spirit was like the idioms of the first thirty years of the fifteenth century. He composed with a simple forthrightness and geometric rigor that was long out of fashion. Perhaps his early training in a small provincial town (a town similar to the one in which Masaccio grew up) was in some way responsible for this.

In Piero's *Resurrection* fresco (Plate 109) in Sansepolcro (c.1460), the triangular shape formed by the resurrected Christ, whose head is the apex and whose arms start the slow descent to the base found in the sleeping soldiers, is worthy of Masaccio. The steady diagonal rhythm of form is punctuated and relieved by the horizontal sarcophagus and the trees rising from the low, Tuscan hills. The gridlike composition reminds one of Masaccio's London *Madonna* or the Berlin *Adoration of the Magi*.

The severe and dramatic foreshortening of the figures, who appear to be made of some very hard stone, recalls sculpture in general and Donatello's works in particular. Close to Donatello is the way the skin seems to be stretched tightly over the flesh, revealing the various layers of skin and bone in the face.

109. Piero della Francesca, *Resurrection*. Sansepolcro, Pinacoteca
Comunale.

Muted and restricted, the palette of the *Resurrection* resembles, in type, the coloring of the Brancacci Chapel. Earth colors are used both to unify the composition and to help create a somber mood. But it is in spirit that Piero comes the closest to Masaccio. He imbues his picture with the dignified, holy, still quality that one senses in the Brancacci Chapel. Here is the same purposeful, heroic Christ, at once divine and mortal. The landscape seems permeated by a sacred presence. An almost undefinable primordial feeling links the work of Masaccio and Piero over the years. Perhaps it is the result of a similar rural childhood or some other shared experience. Piero must have looked long at Masaccio's pictures, but when he borrowed from them, he so transformed what he took that it became an integral part of his personal visual language. The relation between Titian and Rembrandt or between Mozart and Beethoven springs to mind.

The spirit and form of Piero's *Resurrection* were not to be echoed. Confined to several courts and the sleepy towns of Sansepolcro and Arezzo, Piero's notable style was taken up by only a few mediocre followers. In a sense he can be called Masaccio's only real pupil and heir, even though he began working over a decade after Masaccio's death. The stylistic world of Florence had already changed when Piero arrived as an apprentice in the late 1430s, and it was further transformed while he painted his magnificent, but by then old-fashioned, masterpieces.

To trace, even in the most summary way, the development of Florentine painting after mid-century is outside the scope and purpose of this chapter. Yet, several stylistic events took place at the end of the Quattrocento that brought the story of Masaccio's art to its conclusion. I refer to the revival of interest in his painting by a few artists of genius: Michelangelo, Raphael, and Leonardo da Vinci, men who understood better than Masaccio's contemporaries certain aspects of his style and who would make several of Masaccio's innovations the property of Western art.

Perhaps the most important of these artists was Michelangelo. According to Vasari, around 1490, at the start of his career, Michelangelo studied in the Brancacci Chapel for many months.[15] His pen and chalk drawing (Plate 110) of St. Peter before the tax collector in the *Tribute Money* is now in the Staatliche Graphische Sammlung, Munich. The young artist must have been very impressed by Masaccio's massive figure, for he has spent considerable effort trying to capture the girth and breadth of the saint's robes. The drawing is not a slavish copy, for Michelangelo has altered (perhaps *corrected* would be a better word) the position of the shoulder and made several modifications on the sleeve. Nonetheless, even in the tight and careful drawing, he has marvelously caught the form and spirit of the powerful image.

110. Michelangelo, *St. Peter*. Munich,
Staatliche Graphische Sammlung.

At exactly the same time, Michelangelo was making drawings after Giotto's frescoes in Santa Croce.[16] This is most interesting because it demonstrates that he was looking at the old masters in order to learn how to compose both figure and setting with an economy and gravity not found among the works of his teachers. Just as Masaccio had turned back to Giotto, so Michelangelo looked at Masaccio, who by the end of the Quattrocento already belonged to history.

Nearly twenty years after the Munich drawing Michelangelo painted his famous *Expulsion of Adam and Eve* (Plate 111) on the Sistine Chapel ceiling. It does not seem unreasonable to suggest that Adam, Eve, and the angel are influenced by the same figures by Masaccio in the Brancacci Chapel. But Michelangelo's indebtedness to Masaccio transcends the simple copying or modification of motifs and types. The space-defining, ponderous forms and serious, yet energetic, figures show his debt to the older master. The very conception of this scene would have been impossible without Masaccio's fresco.

The great narrative paintings in the Brancacci Chapel also served as a source of inspiration for Michelangelo's contemporary Raphael. In the second decade of the sixteenth century he designed cartoons (now at the Victoria and Albert

111. Michelangelo, *Expulsion of Adam and Eve from Paradise*. Rome, Vatican, Sistine Chapel.

Museum, London) for a series of tapestries to be placed in the Sistine Chapel.[17] There are several references to the *Tribute Money* in the cartoons, the most obvious being Raphael's design for the *Charge to Peter* (Plate 112). (The subject alone might have reminded him of the extensive Petrian iconography of the Brancacci Chapel.) Striking similarities between cartoon and fresco are found in the two Christs. Although Raphael's figure is of a very different type, its bearing and gesture are quite like the Brancacci Christ. The way in which the figure in the cartoon acts as a connection between the group of apostles to the right and the sheep at the left is not unlike the pivotal role played by the Christ of the *Tribute Money*.

The group of apostles can be compared with the men who surround Christ in the Brancacci Chapel fresco. The resemblance is deeper than the simple utilization of the same types by both artists. In the beautiful rhythmic intervals between the heads, in the construction and weight of the robes, and in the sobriety of expression, there are direct ties between Raphael and Masaccio. It is possible that the weighty kneeling figures in the *St. Peter Enthroned* might also

112. Raphael, *Charge to Peter*. London, Victoria and Albert Museum,
Lent by H.M. the Queen.

have served as one source of inspiration for the fervent St. Peter kneeling before
Christ in Raphael's cartoon.

Like Michelangelo, whom he admired and imitated, Raphael learned much
from the Brancacci Chapel frescoes and the other works by Masaccio he saw in
Florence. It is difficult to pin-point other influences from Masaccio in many of
Raphael's pictures, but surely the great figures and abundant, measured space
of the Stanza della Segnatura scenes have as part of their heritage the panels
and frescoes painted by Masaccio a century earlier.

Leonardo da Vinci, the third of the great trio of artists of the early Cinquecento, wrote that Masaccio's paintings demonstrated that to make perfect works
of art, painters had to take their inspiration only from nature.[18] Leonardo
viewed Masaccio historically as well as artistically, and he believed that Masaccio had introduced a new way of painting. To Leonardo's eyes, art before Masaccio must have seemed badly contrived, falsely fabricated, and far from nature.

It is extremely difficult to see any direct influence from Masaccio on the
works of Leonardo, but there can be little doubt that Leonardo, like many other
artists of his time, spent hours studying the frescoes in the Brancacci Chapel.[19]
Perhaps in the design of the unfinished Uffizi *Adoration of the Magi* (begun in
1481), with its semicircular arrangement around the Madonna, who forms the

113. Leonardo da Vinci, *Last Supper.* Milan, Santa Maria delle Grazie.

picture's focal point, Leonardo was recalling the central section of the *Tribute Money.* The wonderful figures, with their varied attitudes and poses, may also owe something to Masaccio, even though they do not exactly resemble specific types painted by him.

In a later work, the *Last Supper* (Plate 113; Santa Maria delle Grazie, Milan), painted in the 1490s, Leonardo may have remembered Masaccio once again. Although it cannot be proved, the arrangement of the Christ with outstretched hands, flanked by the skillfully spaced apostles, may owe something to the central group of Christ and his followers in the *Tribute Money.* As his words suggest, Leonardo thought this work and others by Masaccio nearly perfect.

Vasari, the biographer of Michelangelo, Raphael, and Leonardo, considered Masaccio one of the founders of the Florentine school of painting, a school that found its apex in Vasari's friend, idol, and teacher Michelangelo.[20] Certainly the early Cinquecento saw a new interest in Masaccio, and it is probably this interest that led to Vasari's elevated opinion of the artist. Yet, as we have seen, between the time of Masaccio's death in the late 1420s and the end of the·Quattrocento, Masaccio's painting was not very influential, nor did his artistic ideals find a large or sustained following, even in the years immediately following 1428. So, while art historians have usually accepted — following Vasari — the idea that Masaccio was an important artist, that does not seem to have been the case in his own time.[21]

The nature of the commissions received by Masaccio indicates something about his artistic reputation during the 1420s. Perhaps his most prestigious panel was the Carmine altarpiece for Pisa of 1426. The two other surviving panels — the San Giovenale triptych and the Sant'Ambrogio altarpiece — were certainly not very expensive, nor were they painted for very important institutions. Santa Maria del Carmine was one of Florence's poorest churches, and the Brancacci Chapel was just one of a number of private chapels in the church. Moreover, it is likely that Masaccio was not given the commission for the fresco cycle, but was called in to complete the job after Masolino left it. No doubt, the large painting of the *Trinity* in Santa Maria Novella was a significant work, and it is probably indicative of the type of commission Masaccio would have received had he lived longer. Yet it remains an exception, and the evidence of all Masaccio's paintings suggests that he was an artist given decent but not highly prestigious work.

There are other substantial reasons for questioning the traditional concept of Masaccio's importance in his own time. Since he had so few imitators, we may infer that Masaccio did not have many admirers in Florence. He is mentioned in some of the Quattrocento texts on art, but that shows only that he had attracted the attention of writers concerned with the theoretical aspects of painting.[22] His art did not attract the widespread and diverse clientele that Lorenzo Monaco, Bicci di Lorenzo, and Andrea di Giusto enjoyed. Masaccio, of course, painted on commission for only about a decade; yet even after allowances are made for his short career, in comparison with his contemporaries he seems to have been an unfashionable artist.

Fashionable Florentine taste of the first quarter of the Quattrocento was probably catered to by the paintings of Lorenzo Monaco and his followers. The more conservative patrons appear to have been interested in Mariotto di Nardo, Lorenzo di Niccolò, Bicci di Lorenzo, and the like, and their styles predominated. In sculpture the innovative works of Donatello found a wide audience, especially among patrons commissioning for communal buildings where heroic works of art would have inspired the citizen-spectator. Masaccio seems never to have received such major public commissions.

Another possible reason for the limited contemporary acceptance of Masaccio's art was the nature of its narrative message. Unlike Donatello (or Giotto before him), Masaccio did not emphasize the psychological complexity and emotional sublety of his texts. Instead, his painted stories are concerned with the straightforward, dignified actions of a small group of monumental people — a solemn race of giants come to earth to perform miracles. Masaccio's imagination revolved around the majesty of the legends he was painting; his single-minded effort produced the powerful presence of the figures standing before the onlooker.

Every element of his world — the protagonists, the landscape, the form, and the color — is focused on the expression of a stoic, unshakeable faith in the holy stories. Masaccio's relentless concentration, however, excludes much from the interpretation of the sacred stories. His work is devoid of anecdotal and peripheral distractions, and does not allow for accident — everything seems fixed, immutable, predestined. Nor is there room for humor. Above all, Masaccio's paintings are serious, unflinchingly serious.

Yet, it is the very lack of accident, humor, and fantasy that makes his pictures great, although at the same time limits their appeal. In a way, they are like Beethoven's Ninth Symphony, or Mozart's Requiem, or Rembrandt's *Return of the Prodigal Son*. One respects and loves them, but one also realizes that works of such grandeur and purpose demand an equally serious, unwavering response from the listener or viewer. Their special quality makes them impossible to imitate and even stops artists from daring to copy them; they belong to an elevated, transcendental realm.

Masaccio's contemporaries must have taken note of his paintings even if they did not understand or appreciate them. Their very impact may have kept artists from imitating them and patrons from commissioning them. It was only much later in the century, when several men of equal stature began to copy the work of Masaccio and to incorporate parts of it into their own paintings, that a permanent concern for his art arose. From the painters (often the makers of taste), the interest was taken up by the critics, who, in a line from Vasari onward, have considered Masaccio one of the geniuses of Western art.

APPENDIX

NOTES

BIBLIOGRAPHY

INDEX

APPENDIX

The Sagra *and Some Works Attributed to Masaccio*

THE *Sagra* or *Consecration of the Church of Santa Maria del Carmine*, an important painting by Masaccio, was destroyed around 1600. Mentioned by several early writers on Florentine art, this fresco of *terra verde* (an almost monochromatic palette of green and black often used in exterior decoration) was over a door in the cloister of Santa Maria del Carmine.[1] Vasari describes the scene, which must have been of considerable scope, depicting part of the Piazza del Carmine filled by a large crowd:

> Masaccio painted the scene as it occurred, in *verde terra* and chiaroscuro, in the cloister over the door leading to the convent. There he drew the portraits of a great number of citizens in mantle and hood, who are taking part in the procession . . . and not only did he draw all these notabilities from life, but also the door of the convent, and the porter with keys in his hand. The work possesses many perfections, for Masaccio's knowledge enabled him to put five or six people in a row upon the piazza, judiciously diminishing them in proportion as they recede, according to the point of view a truly marvelous feat, especially as he has used his discretion in making his figures, not all of one size, but of various stature, as in life. . . .[2]

Six Florentine drawings from the late fifteenth and early sixteenth centuries seem to be copies after various parts of the *Sagra*.[3] Four of them represent a group of turbaned, heavily robed men looking to the right; this group must have stood to the left of center. The most complete copy of this group from Masaccio's fresco is a drawing in the Folkestone Museum and Art Gallery. The upper left corner of the same sheet contains what appears to be part of a group (all looking to the left) found originally in the right side of the *Sagra*. Men from this group appear on two drawings by Michelangelo; one of these figures has keys and may be the porter Vasari mentions.

Of course, without a copy of the entire fresco, one cannot say for certain that these figures are after those of the *Sagra*. Yet, in their volume, gravity, and interval, many of the people in the drawings do seem to stem from Masaccio. This is especially true of Michelangelo's drawings, which remind one of his copy after the St. Peter in the *Tribute Money*.

Naturally the *Sagra* must have been painted after the Carmine's consecration in 1422, but its exact position in Masaccio's career is impossible to determine from the copies. Certainly the figural groups (which, judging from the evidence of the later drawings, must have been well studied by artists around 1500) appear close to the Berlin *predella* from the 1426 Pisa altarpiece and to the *Tribute Money*, but little more can be said about the chronological position of the lost fresco.

The fresco's contemporary subject and its rather panoramic view may have been novel. One wonders if there might exist some relation between it and Masolino's Brancacci *Healing of the Lame Man and the Raising of Tabitha*, which depicts an early Quattrocento street scene. A later fresco by Bicci di Lorenzo (c.1424), *Pope Martin V Consecrating the Church of St. Egidio in 1420*, may also owe something of its panoramic treatment to the lost *Sagra*.[4]

Throughout the centuries scores of works have been attributed to Masaccio. Many cited by the older sources are lost, and because there is usually no basis for judgment, the correctness of the attributions remains untested. Today a number of older attributions of extant works are no longer taken seriously. However, several paintings, aside from those mentioned in this book, still find a few proponents; but I believe that the design and the surface of these works indicate, beyond any doubt, that Masaccio had nothing to do with either their planning or their execution. The following list includes most of these pictures. After each work is another attribution which, to me, seems more reasonable.

Agony in the Garden and the Communion of St. Jerome, Staatliches Lindenau-Museum, Altenburg. Andrea di Giusto.

Nativity (Birth Platter), Staatliche Museen, Berlin. Florentine around 1435.

Legends of St. Julian, Museo Horne, Florence. Ruined almost beyond recognition. Follower of Masaccio(?).

Madonna and Child, Loeser Collection, Palazzo Vecchio, Florence. Florentine around 1430 (?).

God the Father, National Gallery, London. Quattrocento Florentine.

SS. John the Baptist and Jerome (wing from Masolino's Santa Maria Maggiore altarpiece), National Gallery, London. Florentine around 1440.

Madonna of Humility, National Gallery, Washington. Totally repainted. What remains under the modern repaint is unknown.

Half-length profile portraits in the National Gallery, Washington; Gardner Museum, Boston; Musée Benoit-Molin, Chambéry. Florentine artists active during the 1430s and 1440s.

Notes

Introduction

1. For an interesting survey of artists' personalities see R. and M. Wittkower, *Born under Saturn* (New York, 1963). See also E. Kris and O. Kurz, *Legend, Myth and Magic in the Image of the Artist* (New Haven, 1979).

2. Much research still remains to be done on the organization of artists' shops of the Trecento and Quattrocento. On the problem see M. Wackernagel, *Der Lebensraum des Künstlers in der florentinischen Renaissance* (Leipzig, 1938); U. Procacci, "Di Jacopo di Antonio e delle compagnie di pittori del Corso degli Adimari nel XV secolo," *Rivista d'arte* (1960):3–70; and J. Larner, *Culture and Society in Italy 1290–1420* (New York, 1971), pp. 285–348. See, above all, the work diary of the painter Neri di Bicci, which provides a fascinating glimpse into how an artist's shop was organized and run: B. Santi, ed., *Neri di Bicci, Le ricordanze* (Pisa, 1976).

3. On the reputation of Giotto in the Trecento see B. Cole, *Giotto and Fiorentine Painting: 1280–1375* (New York, 1976), pp. 161–65.

4. For the relation between artist and society in the fourteenth and early fifteenth centuries see Larner, pp. 265–348. On artists' shares in the *Monte* see M. Becker, "Notes on the *Monte* Holdings of Florentine Trecento Painters," *Art Bulletin* 46 (1964):376–77.

5. Artists were enrolled in the Arte dei Medici e Speziali (the guild of doctors and pharmacists) because they bought their ground colors from the latter. On the Arte dei Medici e speziali see R. Ciasca, ed., *Statuti dell'Arte dei Medici e Speziali* (Florence, 1922); Ciasca, ed., *L'arte dei Medici e Speziali* (Florence, 1927).

6. For apprentice contracts see V. Ottokar, "Pittori e contratti d'apprendimento presso pittori a Firenze alle fine del dugento," *Rivista d'arte* 19 (1937):55–57; Larner, pp. 285–303.

7. The shop manual *Il libro dell'arte*, written by the Florentine painter Cennino Cennini around 1400, remains the most important original document for the artistic practices of the *bottega*. See D. Thompson's edition of *Il libro dell'arte* (New Haven, 1932) and the same editor's translation of Cennini, *The Craftsman's Handbook* (*Il libro dell'arte*) (New Haven, 1933). The function of Cennini's book was to preserve and pass along, from generation to generation, the practices used in the Florentine *bottega*. For the inventory of a late Quattrocentro painter's estate see G. Coor, *Neroccio de'Landi, 1447–1500* (Princeton, 1961), pp. 152–59.

8. There is no comprehensive study of the altarpiece types for the period 1375–1430. For investigations in the shape and framing of older examples see E. Garrison, *Italian Romanesque Panel Painting. An Illustrated Index* (Florence, 1949); H. Hager, *Die*

Anfänge des italienischen Altarbildes (Munich, 1962); M. Cämmerer-George, *Die Rahmung der toskanischen Altarbilder im Trecento* (Strasbourg, 1966).

9. Some of these charcoal designs have been revealed by the removal of the paint film from the gesso. See, for example, U. Baldini and P. Dal Poggetto, *Firenze restaura* (Florence, 1972), figs. 103, 104.

10. On the art of fresco painting see, besides Cennini, E. Borsook, *The Mural Painters of Tuscany* (London, 1960); and *The Great Age of Fresco: Giotto to Pontormo* (New York, 1968).

11. For the relation between *sinopia* and fresco on a Trecento painting by Taddeo Gaddi and an assistant see B. Cole, "Some Sinopie by Taddeo Gaddi Reconsidered," *Pantheon* 24 (1976):99–102. See also U. Procacci, *Sinopie e affreschi* (Milan, 1961).

12. On the changing methods of fresco painting see R. Oertel, "Wandmalerei und Zeichnung in Italien," *Mitteilungen des Kunsthistorischen Institutes in Florenz* 7 (1940):217–314; Procacci, *Sinopie*, passim.

13. For a good demonstration of this see U. Procacci and L. Guarnieri, *Come nasce un affresco* (Florence, 1975).

14. Cennini urges young artists to copy the works of their master to get "a grasp of his [the master's] style and spirit." See Cennini, *The Craftsman's Handbook*, p. 15; Cole, *Giotto*, pp. 7–10.

15. On the artistic collaboration in sculptors' shops see J. White, *Art and Architecture in Italy 1250–1400* (Harmondsworth, 1966), pp. 291–98; U. Middeldorf, "Some Florentine Painted Madonna Reliefs," in *Collaboration in Italian Renaissance Art* (New Haven, 1978), pp. 77–84.

16. On the various objects produced in painters' shops see Procacci, "Di Jacopo di Antonio"; Neri di Bicci, passim.

17. For an illustration (by Andrea Pisano) of a Trecento painter and sculptor at work see L. Becherucci, *Andrea Pisano nel campanile di Giotto* (Florence, 1965), plts. 27–30. On the location of painters' workshops see Procacci, "Di Jacopo di Antonio"; Neri di Bicci, passim.

18. On panels painted without commission see B. Cole, "The Interior Decoration of the Palazzo Datini in Prato," *Mitteilungen des Kunsthistorischen Institutes in Florenz* 13 (1967):61n2; Larner, pp. 310–15.

19. For a survey of artistic contracts see D. Chambers, *Patrons and Artists in the Italian Renaissance* (Columbia, S.C., 1971). For the commissioning of a Quattrocento artist see Neri di Bicci, passim. For a remarkable, but stingy, patron of the early fifteenth century see I. Origo, *The Merchant of Prato* (London, 1957).

20. For the strictly prescribed subjects to be painted see, for example, the contracts of Neri di Bicci, Alesso Baldovinetti, and Domenico and Davide Ghirlandaio in Chambers, pp. 11–15. See also Neri di Bicci, passim.

21. For miracle-working Madonnas see B. Cole, "On an Early Florentine Fresco," *Gazette des Beaux-Arts* 80 (1972):91–96; Cole, "A Popular Painting from the Early Trecento," *Apollo* 101 (1975):9–13. On the profaning of holy images see G. Brucker, *The Society of Renaissance Florence* (New York, 1971), pp. 150–53.

22. For a survey of early literature on early Italian art see J. Von Schlosser, *La letteratura artistica* (Florence, 1964).

I. The Last Quarter of the Trecento

1. On Giotto see B. Cole, *Giotto and Florentine Painting: 1280–1375* (New York, 1976). For Giovanni da Milano see A. Marabottini, *Giovanni da Milano* (Florence, 1950); M. Gregori, *Giovanni da Milano alla Cappella Rinuccini* (Milan, 1965).

2. For Giotto and his followers see Cole, *Giotto*, passim; R. Oertel, *Early Italian Painting to 1400* (New York, 1968); G. Sinibaldi and G. Brunetti, *Pittura italiana del Duecento e Trecento (Catalogo del Mostra Giottesca di Firenze del 1937)* (Florence, 1943); O Sirén, *Giotto and Some of His Followers*, 2 vols. (Cambridge, 1917); R. Offner, "Giotto, non-Giotto," *Burlington Magazine* 74 (1939):259–68; A. Martindale and E. Baccheschi, *The Complete Paintings of Giotto* (New York, 1966); G. Previtali, *Giotto e la sua bottega* (Milan, 1974).

3. On Florentine painting around the middle of the Trecento see W. Suida, *Florentinische Maler um die Mitte des XIV Jahrhunderts* (Strasbourg, 1905); K. Steinweg, *Andrea Orcagna* (Strasbourg, 1929); H. Gronau, *Andrea Orcagna und Nardo di Cione* (Berlin, 1937); M. Meiss, *Painting in Florence and Siena after the Black Death* (New York, 1973); Cole, *Giotto*, pp. 121–45.

4. For the theory that the Black Death of 1348 was responsible for a dramatic change in the painting style of Florence see Meiss, passim.

5. For Nardo di Cione see R. Offner, "Nardo di Cione," *Studies in Florentine Painting* (New York, 1927, 1972); Offner, *Nardo di Cione, Corpus of Florentine Painting*, IV, II (Glückstadt, 1960).

6. For Jacopo di Cione see R. Offner, *Jacopo di Cione, Corpus of Florentine Painting*, IV, III (Glückstadt, 1965).

7. On Daddi's San Pancrazio altarpiece see L. Marcucci, *Gallerie nazionali di Firenze. I dipinti toscani del secolo XIV* (Rome, 1965), pp. 33–37.

8. On Daddi's other works see R. Offner, *Bernardo Daddi, Corpus of Florentine Painting*, III, III (Berlin, 1930).

9. For the Bologna altarpiece see Martindale and Baccheschi, pp. 118–20; and Previtali, pp. 316–17.

10. For the SS. Annunziata altarpiece see R. Offner, *Andrea di Cione, Corpus of Florentine Painting*, IV, I (Glückstadt, 1962).

11. For some observations on the palettes of the late Giotto and his followers see Cole, *Giotto*, pp. 96–145.

12. See Meiss, passim, for some observations on color in Florentine painting around mid-century. See also Cole, *Giotto*, pp. 135–38.

13. For Taddeo see P. Donati, *Taddeo Gaddi* (Florence, 1966); Oertel, pp. 188–92; Cole, *Giotto*, pp. 128–34.

14. For Agnolo see R. Salvini, *L'arte di Agnolo Gaddi* (Florence, 1936); B. Cole, *Agnolo Gaddi* (Oxford, 1977).

15. For Andrea da Firenze see W. and E. Paatz, *Die Kirchen von Florenz* (Frankfurt am Main, 1952), vol. 3, pp. 720–22; and Meiss, pp. 94–104.

16. For a survey of the extensive documentation on this chapel see Cole, *Gaddi*, pp. 87–88.

17. See Cole, *Giotto*, pp. 96–120.

18. For a discussion of the relief see Meiss, pp. 27–28.

19. On Spinello see G. Gombosi, *Spinello Aretino* (Budapest, 1926); L. Bellosi, "Da Spinello Aretino a Lorenzo Monaco," *Paragone* 16 (1965):18–43; A. Masetti, *Spinello Aretino giovane* (Florence, 1973).

20. For a reconstruction of the Monteoliveto altarpiece see S. Fehm, "Notes on Spinello Aretino's So-Called Monte Oliveto Altarpiece," *Mitteilungen des Kunsthistorischen Institutes in Florenz* 17 (1973):257–72.

21. Around the end of the Trecento there appears to have been a rather widespread revival of Giotto's style. On this see M. Boskovits, "'Giotto Born Again,' Beiträge zu den Quellen Masaccios," *Zeitschrift für Kunstgeschichte* 29 (1966):51–66; D. Wilkins, "Maso di Banco and Cenni di Francesco: A Case of Late Trecento Revival," *Burlington Magazine* 111 (1969):83–84.

22. For examples of *mandorle* in painting from around the mid-Trecento see Meiss, plts. 1, 8, 50, 54, 87, 89.

23. For Antonio Veneziano see G. Fogolari, "Antonio Veneziano," U. Thieme and F. Becker, eds., *Allgemeines Lexikon der bildenden Künstler*, vol. 2 (Leipzig, 1908):13–15; R. Offner, "The Panels of Antonio Veneziano," *Studies in Florentine Painting* (New York, 1927; 1972), pp. 67–81; J. Czarnecki, "A New Panel by Antonio Veneziano," *Burlington Magazine* 119 (1977):188–91.

24. For a similar panel by Niccolò di Pietro Gerini, also made for a flagellant society, see L. Marcucci, *Gallerie nazionali di Firenze. I dipinti toscani del secolo XIV* (Rome, 1965), pp. 114–15. On the flagellants see N. Cohn, *The Pursuit of the Millennium* (New York, 1977), pp. 127–47.

25. For Taddeo see note 13. On Maso di Banco see R. Offner, "Four Panels, a Fresco and a Problem," *Burlington Magazine* 54 (1929):224–45; and M. Bianchini, *Maso di Banco* (Milan, 1966).

26. On the original appearance of Antonio's Altenburg panel see R. Oertel, *Frühe italienische Malerei in Altenburg* (Berlin, 1961), pp. 122–24.

27. On Giovanni del Biondo see R. Offner and K. Steinweg, *Giovanni del Biondo, Corpus of Florentine Painting*, IV, V (Glückstadt, 1967, 1969), parts 1, 2. See also the review of this book by B. Cole, *Art Bulletin* 52 (1970):200–202.

28. For Gerini see R. Offner, "Niccolò di Pietro Gerini," *Studies in Florentine Painting* (New York, 1927, 1972), pp. 83–95; U. Baldini, *La Cappella Migliorati nel San Francesco di Prato* (Florence, 1965).

29. On Gerini's collaboration with other artists see Marcucci, pp. 109–10; Offner, *Studies*, pp. 88–89.

30. See, for example, R. Oertel, *Early Italian Painting*, pp. 309–16.

II. The Beginnings of the New Century:
Painting c.1390–1420

1. There is no comprehensive history of Florentine painting of the late Trecento and early Quattrocento. R. Oertel's excellent *Early Italian Painting to 1400* (New York, 1968) slights the period after 1375, while P. Toesca's *Il Trecento* (Turin, 1951) is unjustly negative. M. Boskovits's *Pittura fiorentina alla vigilia del Rinascimento 1370–1400* (Florence, 1975) is a specialists' book that contains, in any case, a number of highly debatable attributions.

D. Colnaghi, *A Dictionary of Florentine Painting* (London, 1928) is a valuable source for the documentation on early Quattrocento Florentine artists. B. Berenson's *Italian Pictures of the Renaissance: Florentine School*, 2 vols. (London, 1963) is the most important source of attributions and illustrations. R. Fremantle, *Florentine Gothic Painters from Giotto to Masaccio* (London, 1975) is also helpful for its numerous bibliographical references and photographs. A brief survey of the period is contained in L. Bellosi's "Da Spinello Aretino a Lorenzo Monaco," *Paragone* 16 (1965):18–43.

2. O. Sirén's *Don Lorenzo Monaco* (Strasbourg, 1905), the only full-scale monograph on the artist, is now outdated. See also V. Golzio, *Lorenzo Monaco* (Rome, 1931); L. Bellosi, *Lorenzo Monaco* (Milan, 1965); the latter has several good color plates.

3. On the crucifix see M. Eisenberg, "A Crucifix and a Man of Sorrows," *Art Quarterly* 18 (1955):45–49.

4. On the ensemble of the Bartolini Salimbeni chapel see W. and E. Paatz, *Die Kirchen von Florenz* (Frankfurt am Main, 1953) vol. 5, p. 291.

5. For Taddeo's frescoes in the Baroncelli chapel see Berenson, vol. 1, plts. 118–24.

6. On Rossello di Jacopo Franchi see Berenson, vol. 1, pp. 192–94; Fremantle, pp. 461–70.

7. Recently an unconvincing attempt was made to identify this artist with Gherardo Starnina, a painter known only through several fragments of a documented fresco cycle; see J. Van Waddenoijen, "A Proposal for Starnina: Exit the Maestro del Bambino Vispo?" *Burlington Magazine* 116 (1974):82–91. For Starnina see U. Procacci, "Gherardo Starnina," *Rivista d'arte* 15 (1933):151–90; 17 (1935):333–84; 18 (1936):77–94.

For the Master of the Bambino Vispo see O. Sirén, "Di alcuni pittori fiorentini che subirono l'influenza di Lorenzo Monaco," *L'arte* 7 (1904):349–55; G. Pudelko, "The Master of the Bambino Vispo," *Art in America* 26 (1938):47–63; Fremantle, pp. 441–50.

8. On the influence of Giotto during the late Trecento see chapter 1, note 20.

9. For the Master of 1419 see P. Pouncey, "A New Panel by the Master of 1419," *Burlington Magazine* 96 (1954):291–92; H. Francis, "Master of 1419," *Bulletin of the Cleveland Museum of Art* 43 (1956):211–13; W. Cohn, "Notize storiche intorno ad alcune tavole fiorentine del '300 e '400," *Rivista d'arte* 31 (1956):49–52.

10. On Lorenzo di Niccolò see Berenson, pp. 121–24; B. Cole, "A New Work by the Young Lorenzo di Niccolò," *Art Quarterly* 33 (1970):114–19; R. Fremantle, pp. 391–400.

11. For Monaco's altarpiece see O. Sirén, *Lorenzo Monaco*, pp. 76–87.

12. On the wool trade in Florence see A. Doren, *Die florentiner Wollentuchindustrie vom vierzehnten bis zum sechzehnten Jahrhundert* (Stuttgart, 1901).

13. On Mariotto di Nardo see R. Offner, "The Mostra del Tesoro di Firenze Sacra," *Burlington Magazine* 63 (1933):169; M. Eisenberg, "A Flagellation by Mariotto di Nardo and Some Related Panels," *Record of the Princeton Art Museum* 8 (1949):6–14; Eisenberg, "An Addition to a Group of Panels by Mariotto di Nardo," *Record of the Princeton Art Museum* 18 (1959):61–64; Berenson, pp. 129–33; Fremantle, pp. 451–60.

14. On Jacopo di Cione see R. Offner, *Jacopo di Cione, Corpus of Florentine Painting*, IV, III (Glückstadt, 1965).

15. On Bicci di Lorenzo see Offner, "Mostra," 170; Berenson, pp. 27–32; Fremantle, pp. 471–82.

16. On Giovanni Toscani see Offner, "Mostra," 173; L. Bellosi, "Il Maestro della Crocifissione Griggs: Giovanni Toscani," *Paragone* 17 (1966):44–58; Fremantle, pp. 493–502; M. Eisenberg, "'The Penitent St. Jerome' by Giovanni Toscani," *Burlington Magazine* 118 (1976):275–83.

17. On the Straus Master see Offner, "Mostra," 169–70; Fremantle, pp. 303–12.

18. For Gentile da Fabriano see B. Molajoli, *Gentile da Fabriano* (Fabriano, 1934); L. Grassi, *Tutta la pittura di Gentile da Fabriano* (Milan, 1953); E. Micheletti, *L'opera completa di Gentile da Fabriano* (Milan, 1976).

19. On artistic contracts see Introduction, notes 5 and 6; and D. Chambers, *Patrons and Artists in the Italian Renaissance* (Columbia, S.C., 1971).

20. On Masolino see P. Toesca, *Masolino da Panicale* (Bergamo, 1908); E. Micheletti, *Masolino da Panicale* (Milan, 1959); L. Vayer, *Masolino és Róma* (Budapest, 1962); Berenson, pp. 136–37; M. Bianchini, *Masolino da Panicale* (Milan, 1965); Fremantle, pp. 483–92.

21. On Masolino's now destroyed frescoes in Empoli see B. Cole, "A Reconstruction of Masolino's True Cross Cycle in Santo Stefano, Empoli," *Mitteilungen des Kunsthistorischen Institutes in Florenz* 13 (1968):289–300.

22. For the documentation on Masolino see Micheletti, pp. 15–17; U. Procacci, "Sulla cronologia delle opere di Masaccio e di Masolino tra il 1425 e il 1428," *Rivista d'arte* 28 (1953):3–55; R. Fremantle, "Some New Masolino Documents," *Burlington Magazine* 117 (1975):658–59.

23. For the Empoli cycle see note 21.

III. The Beginnings of the New Century: Sculpture c.1390–1420

1. On the development of early Florentine painting see E. Garrison, *Italian Romanesque Panel Painting: An Illustrated Index* (Florence, 1949); R. Oertel, *Early Italian Painting to 1400* (New York, 1968); B. Cole, *Giotto and Florentine Painting 1280–1375* (New York, 1976).

2. On the development of early sculpture in Florence see, above all, J. Pope-Hennessy, *Italian Gothic Sculpture* (London, 1972), J. White, *Art and Architecture in Italy 1250–1400* (Harmondsworth, 1966).

3. On Orcagna see K. Steinweg, *Andrea Orcagna* (Strasbourg, 1929); H. Gronau, *Andrea Orcagna und Nardo di Cione* (Berlin, 1937); R. Offner, *Andrea di Cione, Corpus of Florentine Painting*, IV, I (Glückstadt, 1962); Pope-Hennessy, p. 196.

4. On the *Dormition*, now in Berlin, see A. Martindale and E. Baccheschi, *The Complete Paintings of Giotto* (New York, 1966), p. 112. Although this work seems to come from Giotto's shop, it is not completely autograph.

5. On Andrea Pisano see I. Toesca, *Andrea e Nino Pisano* (Florence, 1950); Pope-Hennessy, pp. 190–93.

6. On Jacopo di Piero Guidi see M. Wundram, "Jacopo di Piero Guidi," *Mitteilungen des Kunsthistorischen Institutes in Florenz* 13 (1968):195–222; L. Becherucci and G. Brunetti, *Il Museo dell'Opera del Duomo a Firenze* (Milan, 1969), vol. 1, p. 250.

7. For Giovanni d'Ambrogio see G. Brunetti, "Giovanni d'Ambrogio," *Rivista d'arte* 14 (1932):1–22; Becherucci and Brunetti, passim; M. Wundram, "Der Meister der Verkündigung in der Domopera zu Florenz," *Beiträge zur Kunstgeschichte, Festgabe für H. R. Rosemann* (Munich, 1960), pp. 109–25; G. Kreytenberg, "Giovanni d'Ambrogio," *Jahrbuch der Berliner Museen* 14 (1972):5–32; Pope-Hennessy, p. 197.

8. On Gaddi's designs for the Loggia dei Lanzi see B. Cole, *Agnolo Gaddi* (Oxford, 1977), pp. 68–69.

9. For this attribution see M. Wundram, "Der Meister," 109–25.

10. On Ghiberti see the comprehensive monograph by R. Krautheimer, *Lorenzo Ghiberti*, 2 vols. (Princeton, 1970); Pope-Hennessy, pp. 204–209; *Lorenzo Ghiberti: Materia e Ragionamenti* (Florence, 1978).

11. For editions of Ghiberti's *Commentari* see J. von Schlosser, *Lorenzo Ghibertis Denkwürdigkeiten*, 2 vols. (Berlin, 1912); O. Morisani, *I Commentari del Lorenzo Ghiberti* (Naples, 1947).

12. On the competition see Krautheimer, vol. 1, pp. 31–43; Pope-Hennessy, pp. 205–207.

13. On Brunelleschi see P. Sanpaolesi, *Brunelleschi* (Milan, 1962); H. Klotz, *Die Frühwerke Brunelleschis und die Mittelalterliche Tradition* (Berlin, 1970).

14. For the history of Or San Michele see W. and E. Paatz, *Die Kirchen von Florenz* (Frankfurt am Main, 1952), vol. 4, pp. 480–558.

15. On Lamberti see Becherucci and Brunetti, pp. 261–62; M. Wundram, "Niccolò di Pietro Lamberti und die florentinische Plastik um 1400," *Jahrbuch der Berliner Museen* 4 (1962):78–115; Pope-Hennessy, p. 220.

16. On Ciuffagni see Becherucci and Brunetti, p. 264; Wundram, "Niccolò di Pietro Lamberti."

17. On Donatello see H. W. Janson, *The Sculpture of Donatello*, 2 vols. (Princeton, 1963); Becherucci and Brunetti, passim; Pope-Hennessy, *Italian Renaissance Sculpture* (London, 1971), passim.

18. On this progression in early Trecento art see Cole, *Giotto*, passim.

19. Jacob Burckhardt, *The Civilization of the Renaissance in Italy*, 2 vols. (New York, 1958). For other theories on the development of the Renaissance see H. Baron, *The Crisis of the Early Italian Renaissance* (Princeton, 1966); G. Brucker, *The Civic World of Early Renaissance Florence* (Princeton, 1977).

20. For an excellent survey of the history of Quattrocento Florence see G. Brucker, *Renaissance Florence* (New York, 1969). An engrossing collection of documents is found in the same author's *The Society of Renaissance Florence* (New York, 1971).

21. On medieval and Renaissance town planning see W. Braunfels, *Mittelalterliche Stadtbaukunst in der Toskana* (Berlin, 1966); C. Westfall, *In This Most Perfect Paradise: Alberti, Nicholas V, and the Invention of Conscious Urban Planning in Rome, 1447–55* (University Park, Pa., 1974).

22. On Nanni di Banco see L. Planiscig, *Nanni di Banco* (Florence, 1948); P. Vaccarino, *Nanni* (Florence, 1951); L. Bellosi, *Nanni di Banco* (Milan, 1966); M. Wundram, *Donatello und Nanni di Banco* (Berlin, 1969); Pope-Hennessy, pp. 217–19.

23. For the story of the four saints see G. Kaftal, *Iconography of the Saints in Tuscan Painting* (Florence, 1952), pp. 383–84.

IV. Masaccio: Origins and the Early Panels

1. For San Giovanni Valdarno See E. Repetti, *Dizionario geografico, fisico, storico della Toscana* (Florence, 1843), vol. 5, pp. 54–60; and F. Polverini, *Memorie storiche della terra di S. Giovanni nel Valdarno Superiore* (San Giovanni Valdarno, 1914).

2. For the documents connected with Masaccio's life see H. Lindberg, *To the Problem of Masolino and Masaccio* (Stockholm, 1931), vol. 1, pp. 5–10; U. Procacci, *All the*

Paintings of Masaccio (New York, 1962), pp. 24–25; L. Berti, *Masaccio* (University Park, Pa., 1967); P. Volponi and L. Berti, *L'opera completa di Masaccio* (Milan, 1968), pp. 83–84; J. Beck, *Masaccio: The Documents* (Locust Valley, N. Y., 1978).

3. On Masaccio's brother see *Arte nell'aretino* (Florence, 1975), pp. 88–91; L. Bellosi, *Mostra d'arte sacra della diocesi di San Miniato* (San Miniato, 1969), pp. 56–57. For documentation on Masaccio's mother see R. Fremantle, "Some Documents Concerning Masaccio and His Mother's Second Family," *Burlington Magazine* 115 (1973):516–18.

4. On the Master of Figline see R. Offner, *Studies in Florentine Painting* (New York, 1927, 1972), pp. 49–57; A. Graziani, "Affreschi del Maestro di Figline," *Proporzioni* 1 (1943):65–79; Fremantle, *Florentine Gothic Painters from Giotto to Masaccio* (London, 1975), pp. 105–14.

5. On the veneration and replication of ancient images see B. Cole, "Old in New in the Early Trecento," *Mitteilungen des Kunsthistorischen Institutes in Florenz* 17 (1973):229–48.

6. For Mariotto see Fremantle, pp. 553–62; M. Boskovits, "Mariotto di Cristofano: un contributo all' ambiente culturale di Masaccio giovane," *Arte illustrata* 2 (1969):4–13.

7. On artists, guilds, and matriculation see Introduction, notes 5 and 6.

8. On Cascia see Repetti, vol. 1 (1833), 499–500.

9. On the development of the altarpiece shape see H. Hager, *Die Anfänge des italienischen Altarbildes* (Munich, 1962); M. Cämmerer-George, *Die Rahmung der toskanischen Altarbilder im Trecento* (Strasbourg, 1966).

10. For the church of Sant'Ambrogio see W. and E. Paatz, *Die Kirchen von Florenz* (Frankfurt am Main, 1940), vol. 1, pp. 21–43.

11. For a survey of Giotto's work see A. Martindale and E. Baccheschi, *The Complete Paintings of Giotto* (New York, 1966); B. Cole, *Giotto and Florentine Painting 1280–1375* (New York, 1976).

12. For a summary of the opinions on the Sant'Ambrogio altarpiece see Volponi and Berti, p. 87.

13. U. Procacci, *All the Paintings of Masaccio* (New York, 1962), p. 9.

14. On the relation between design and execution see U. Procacci, *Sinopie e affreschi* (Milan, 1961); B. Cole, "Some Sinopie by Taddeo Gaddi Reconsidered," *Pantheon* 34 (1976):99–102.

V. Masaccio: The Pisa Altarpiece

1. For example, Agnolo Gaddi, Mariotto di Nardo, and Bicci di Lorenzo all joined the Company of St. Luke after they had matriculated in the *Arte dei Medici e Speziali*. See D. Colnaghi, *A Dictionary of Florentine Painters* (London, 1928), passim.

2. For the fullest, most accurate account of the history of the Pisa altarpiece see M. Davies, *The Earlier Italian Schools* (National Gallery Catalogue; London, 1961), pp. 347–51.

3. For the payment documents for the Pisa altarpiece see L. Tanfani-Centofanti, *Notize di artisti tratte dai documenti pisani* (Pisa, 1897), pp. 178–80. The document of 15 October 1427 seems to indicate that Masaccio's brother, Giovanni, was also in Pisa.

4. For a similar contractual clause see D. Chambers, *Patrons and Artists in the Italian Renaissance* (Columbia, S.C., 1971), p. 14.

5. On Andrea di Giusto see B. Berenson, *Italian Pictures of the Renaissance: Floren-*

tine School (London, 1963), vol. 1, pp. 5–7; R. Fremantle, *Florentine Painting from Giotto to Masaccio* (London, 1975), pp. 513–22.

6. G. Vasari, *Le vite de più eccellenti pittori, scultori ed architettori*, edited by G. Milanesi (Florence, 1878) vol. 2, p. 292. The English translation is from *The Lives of the Painters, Sculptors and Architects by Giorgio Vasari*, translated by A. Hinds (London, 1927), vol. 1, pp. 265–66.

7. For the textual sources and for other representations of the SS. Julian and Nicholas stories see G. Kaftal, *The Iconography of the Saints in Tuscan Painting* (Florence, 1952), pp. 593–601 and 756–68, respectively.

8. Several critics have suggested this placement. See P. Volponi and L. Berti, *L'opera completa di Masaccio* (Milan, 1968), pp. 89–91.

9. For the provenance of these panels see Davies, pp. 350–51.

10. For an altarpiece with a Crucifixion at the center and half-lengths at the sides see R. van Marle, *The Italian Schools of Painting* (The Hague, 1925), vol. 5, p. 257, plt. 169. For reconstructions of the altarpiece see K. Steinbart, *Masaccio* (Vienna, 1948), p. 29; M. Salmi, *Masaccio* (Milan, 1948), plt. 35; U. Procacci, *All the Paintings of Masaccio* (New York, 1962), pp. 27–30; L. Berti, *Masaccio* (University Park, Pa., 1967), pp. 152–53; J. Shearman, "Masaccio's Pisa Altarpiece: An Alternate Reconstruction," *Burlington Magazine* 108 (1966):449–55.

11. Davies, p. 349.

12. See, for instance, several of Ambrogio Lorenzetti's children: G. Rowley, *Ambrogio Lorenzetti* (Princeton, 1958), vol. 2, plts. 13, 19, 25, 26.

13. For Ambrogio's *Annunciation*, now in the Siena Pinacoteca, see ibid., plt. 1.

14. On the Quaratesi altarpiece see E. Micheletti, *L'opera completa di Gentile da Fabriano* (Milan, 1976), pp. 90–91. The Marxist art historian F. Antal makes an interesting comparison between the Quaratesi altarpiece and Masaccio's London Madonna in his *Florentine Painting and Its Social Background* (London, 1975).

15. For this suggestion see Procacci, p. 14.

16. See, for example, the small panels in Neri di Bicci's altarpiece in Detroit or in Fra Angelico's San Marco altarpiece. For Angelico's picture see J. Pope-Hennessy, *Fra Angelico* (London, 1974), pp. 199–200.

17. Perhaps a possible prototype for the Magdalene may have existed in a now destroyed work by Giotto. A *Crucifixion* in the church of Ognissanti, Florence, by an artist working around 1340, contains a brilliantly conceived Magdalene that is so clearly Giottesque that it may have been copied from a picture by Giotto. Masaccio's Magdalene has, in turn, some stylistic connections with the Ognissanti figure.

18. On the influence of Giovanni Pisano on Masaccio in Pisa see E. Borsook, "A Note on Masaccio in Pisa," *Burlington Magazine* 103 (1961):212–15. On Giovanni Pisano see H. Keller, *Giovanni Pisano* (Vienna, 1942); M. Ayrton, *Giovanni Pisano* (London, 1969); E. Carli, *Giovanni Pisano* (Pisa, 1977).

VI. Masaccio: The Frescoes

1. On the Carmine and its history see U. Procacci, "L'incendio della chiesa del Carmine del 1771," *Rivista d'arte* 14 (1932):141–232; W. and E. Paatz, *Die Kirchen von Florenz* (Frankfurt am Main, 1952), vol. 3, pp. 188–303; P. Fadalti, *La Capella Brancacci nel Carmine di Firenze* (Florence, 1963).

2. On the history of the Brancacci Chapel see Fadalti; Paatz, pp. 196–97, 201–209, 224–26.

3. On the destroyed images of the vault see R. Longhi, "Fatti di Masolino e di Masaccio," *Crictica d'arte* 5 (1940):145–48.

4. On Filippino see A. Scharf, *Filippino Lippi* (Vienna, 1935); K. Neilson, *Filippino Lippi* (Cambridge, Mass., 1938); L. Berti and U. Baldini, *Filippino Lippi* (Florence, 1957).

5. For the theory that Masolino and Masaccio began the cycle together and for a review of other ideas on how the painting in the chapel proceeded see P. Volponi and L. Berti, *L'opera completa di Masaccio* (Milan, 1968), pp. 92–93.

6. On the possible relation between the 1427 *Catasto* and the *Tribute Money* see L. Berti, *Masaccio* (University Park, Pa., 1967), pp. 22–24; A. Molho, "The Brancacci Chapel: Studies in Its Iconography and History," *Journal of the Warburg and Courtauld Insitutes* 40 (1977):50–98.

7. For photographs of Giotto's Peruzzi chapel frescoes see L. Tintori and E. Borsook, *Giotto: The Peruzzi Chapel* (New York, 1965).

8. For some observations on the relation of Masaccio's painting — both in style and motif — to the art of antiquity see R. Offner, "Light on Masaccio's Classicism," *Studies in the History of Art Dedicated to William E. Suida on His Eightieth Birthday* (London, 1959), pp. 66–72. Masaccio's *Expulsion* is also close in spirit and form to a relief of the same subject on San Petronio, Bologna, by the Sienese sculptor Jacopo della Quercia (c.1374–1438). Quercia, who was a talented and innovative artist, may have exerted some influence on Masaccio, but this is by no means certain. For Quercia see J. Pope-Hennessy, *Italian Gothic Sculpture* (London, 1972), pp. 209–14.

9. For the suggestion that the figure is a Brancacci cardinal see P. Meller, "La Cappella Brancacci: Problemi ritrattistici ed iconografici," *Acropoli* 1 (1961):186–227, 273–312. Meller's article on the iconography and identification of portraits contains some interesting, if sometimes rather far-fetched, conclusions.

10. For a survey of the opinions on this fresco see Volponi and Berti, pp. 93–94.

11. On the history of Santa Maria Novella see Paatz, vol. 3, pp. 663–845; S. Orlandi, *S. Maria Novella e i suoi chiostri monumentali* (Florence, 1966). On the history of the *Trinity*, see L. Berti, *Masaccio* (University Park, Pa., 1967), pp. 157–58 n 270. On the fresco itself see Volponi and Berti, pp. 97–99; H. von Einem, *Masaccios Zingroschen* (Cologne, 1967); J. Polzer, "The Anatomy of Masaccio's Holy Trinity," *Jahrbuch der Berliner Museen* 13 (1971):18–59.

12. On the Daddi panel see L. Becherucci and G. Brunetti, *Il Museo dell'Opera del Duomo* (Milan, 1969), vol. 2, pp. 281–82; B. Cole, "A Popular Panel from the Early Trecento," *Apollo* 101 (1975):9–13.

13. On *memento mori* in Tuscan art and for some iconographic speculation on the *Trinity* see U. Schlegel, "Observations on Masaccio's Trinity Fresco in Santa Maria Novella," *Art Bulletin* 45 (1963):19–33.

14. For a Quattrocento representation, attributed to Carlo Braccesco, of a saint buried under an altar table see M. Laclotte and E. Mognetti, *Avignon-Musée du Petit Palais: Peinture italienne* (Paris, 1976), no. 44.

15. On Nardo's frescoes see R. Offner, *Nardo di Cione, Corpus of Florentine Painting*, IV, II (Glückstadt, 1960), pp. 47–60. For Andrea da Firenze see M. Meiss, *Painting in Florence and Siena after the Black Death* (New York, 1973), pp, 94–104.

16. See E. Lavagnino, "Masaccio: 'Dicesi è morto a Roma,'" *Emporium* 97 (1943):97–112; U. Procacci, "Sulla cronologia delle opere di Masaccio e di Masolino tra il 1425 e il 1428," *Rivista d'arte* 28 (1953):3–55.

17. For similar donors in late Trecento painting see B. Berenson, *Italian Pictures of the Renaissance: Florentine School* (London, 1963), vol. 1, plts. 314, 327, 334, 337.

18. For other representations of the Trinity see Schlegel, p. 26 n 49.

VII.   Florentine Art around 1430: New Directions

1. On the *Feast of Herod* see H. Janson, *The Sculpture of Donatello* (Princeton, 1957), vol. 2, pp. 65–75; J. Pope-Hennessy, *Italian Renaissance Sculpture* (London, 1971), pp. 257–58.

2. For Donatello in Padua see Pope-Hennessy, pp. 259–63; Janson, pp. 162–87.

3. For Donatello's later works see Pope-Hennessy, pp. 264–68.

4. On the second Baptistery doors see R. Krautheimer, *Lorenzo Ghiberti* (Princeton, 1970), vol. 1, pp. 159–202; Pope-Hennessy, pp. 208–209.

5. For the Frick picture and Gentile's later work see E. Micheletti, *L'opera completa di Gentile da Fabriano* (Milan, 1976), pp. 91–92.

6. On Masolino's work in Rome see L. Vayer, *Masolino és Róma* (Budapest, 1962).

7. For the Castiglione Olona cycle see E. Micheletti, *Masolino da Panicale* (Milan, 1959).

8. On Bicci di Lorenzo see B. Berenson, *Italian Pictures of the Renaissance: Florentine School* (London, 1963), vol. 1, pp. 27–32.

9. On Filippo Lippi see R. Oertel, *Fra Filippo Lippi* (Vienna, 1942); U. Baldini, *Filippo Lippi* (Milan, 1964); G. Marchini, *Fra Filippo Lippi* (Milan, 1975).

10. For comments on the Uffizi *Adoration* see M. Baxandall's extremely interesting *Painting and Experience in Fifteenth Century Italy* (Oxford, 1972), passim.

11. On Angelico see E. Morante and U. Baldini, *L'opera completa dell'Angelico* (Milan, 1970); J. Pope-Hennessy, *Fra Angelico* (London, 1974).

12. For a discussion of how contemporaries may have looked at Quattrocento paintings see M. Baxandall, passim.

13. On Piero see B. Berenson, *Piero della Francesco or the Ineloquent in Art* (New York, 1954); E. Battisti, *Piero della Francesco* (Milan, 1971), 2 vols.; K. Clark, *Piero della Francesca* (London, 1969); P. Murray and P. de Vecchi, *The Complete Paintings of Piero della Francesca* (New York, 1967).

14. On the important, but still mysterious, Domenico Veneziano see G. Pudelko, "Studien über Domenico Veneziano," *Mitteilungen des Kunsthistorischen Institutes in Florenz* 4 (1934):139–200; M. Salmi, *Paolo Uccello, Andrea del Castagno, Domenico Veneziano* (Milan, 1938); J. Pope-Hennessy, "The Early Style of Domenico Veneziano," *Burlington Magazine* 93 (1951):216–23; F. Hartt, *History of Italian Renaissance Art* (New York, n.d.), pp. 217–19.

15. On Michelangelo see C. de Tolnay, *Michelangelo* (Princeton, 1943–1960), 5 vols.; de Tolnay, *The Art and Thought of Michelangelo* (New York, 1964); H. Hibbard, *Michelangelo* (New York, 1974). On the sculpture see J. Pope-Hennessy, *Italian High Renaissance and Baroque Sculpture* (London, 1970), pp. 299–339.

16. On Michelangelo's drawing after Giotto see B. Berenson, *The Drawings of the Florentine Painters* (Chicago, 1938), vol. 2, pp. 207–208.

17. On Raphael see J. Crowe and G. Cavalcaselle, *Raphael, His Life and Works* (Lon-

don, 1882–1885), 2 vols.; J. Pope-Hennessy, *Raphael* (New York, 1970); J. Shearman, *Raphael's Cartoons in the Collection of Her Majesty the Queen* (London, 1972). See also Raphael's Masaccio-inspired study of two figures for the *Transfiguration* in Pope-Hennessy, plt. 66.

18. For a translation of Leonardo's statement see *The Notebooks of Leonardo da Vinci* translated by E. MacCurdy (New York, n.d.), vol. 2, p. 276.

19. On Leonardo see L. Heydenreich, *Leonardo da Vinci*, 2 vols. (New York, 1954); K. Clark, *Leonardo da Vinci* (Harmondsworth, 1967).

20. For Vasari's biography of Masaccio see *Le vite de più eccellenti pittori, scultori ed architettori*, edited by G. Milanesi (Florence, 1878), vol. 2, pp. 287–301. For an English translation see *The Lives of the Painters, Sculptors and Architects by Giorgio Vasari*, translated by A. Hinds (London, 1927), vol. 1, pp. 263–69.

21. Vasari, in fact, says that Masaccio "had been held in slight esteem during his life," ibid., p. 269.

22. For a survey of criticism on Masaccio see P. Volponi and L. Berti, *L'opera completa di Masaccio* (Milan, 1968), pp. 10–14.

Appendix

1. For the *Sagra* see P. Volponi and L. Berti, *L'opera completa di Masaccio* (Milan, 1968), p. 88; C. Gilbert, "The Drawings Now Associated with Masaccio's 'Sagra,'" *Storia dell'arte* 3 (1969):260–78.

2. G. Vasari, *Le vite de più eccellenti pittori, scultori ed architettori*, edited by G. Milanesi (Florence, 1878), vol. 2, pp. 295–97. English translation from *The Lives of the Painters, Sculptors and Architects by Giorgio Vasari*, translated by A. Hinds (London, 1927), vol. 1, p. 267.

3. For the drawings see Volponi and Berti; Gilbert.

4. For Bicci's fresco see B. Berenson, *Italian Pictures of the Renaissance: Florentine School* (London, 1963), vol.1, plt. 510.

Selected Bibliography

The following is a selected bibliography on the early Renaissance painters and sculptors discussed in this book. It is divided into three sections: *Historical Background*: works on economic, religious, and social history; *Early Renaissance Art*: general surveys covering, at least in part, the late Trecento and early Quattrocento, and writings on more particularized questions, such as iconography and artistic training; *Artists*: books and articles devoted specifically to the early Renaissance artists included in this book. Although not mentioned under individual artists, B. Berenson, *Italian Pictures of the Renaissance: Florentine School*, 2 vols. (London, 1963), is of fundamental importance for the reconstruction of each painter's work.

HISTORICAL BACKGROUND

Baron, H. *The Crisis of the Early Italian Renaissance*. Princeton, 1966.

Becker, M. *Florence in Transition*. 2 vols. Baltimore, 1967–1968.

Brucker, G. *Florence Politics and Society 1343–1378*. Princeton, 1962.

———. *Renaissance Florence*. New York, 1969.

———. *The Society of Renaissance Florence*. New York, 1971.

———. *The Civic World of Early Renaissance Florence*. Princeton, 1977.

Burckhardt, J. *The Civilization of the Renaissance in Italy*. 2 vols. [1860]. New York, 1958.

Burke, P. *Culture and Society in Renaissance Italy 1420–1540*. New York, 1972.

———. *Tradition and Innovation in Renaissance Italy*. London, 1974.

Davidsohn, R. *Geschichte von Florenz*. 4 vols. Berlin, 1896–1927.

Goldthwaite, R. *Private Wealth in Renaissance Florence*. Princeton, 1968.

Hay, D. *The Italian Renaissance in Its Historical Background*. Cambridge, England, 1977.

Hartt, F. "Art and Freedom in Quattrocento Florence." *Essays in Memory of Karl Lehmann*. New York, 1964.

Holmes, G. *The Florentine Enlightenment 1400–1450*. London, 1969.

Kent, F. *Family Worlds in Renaissance Florence*. Princeton, 1977.

Larner, J. *Culture and Society in Italy 1290–1420*. New York, 1971.

Martines, L. *The Social World of the Florentine Humanists 1390–1460*. Princeton, 1963.

Origo, I. *The Merchant of Prato*. New York, 1957.

Rubinstein, N. *The Government of Florence under the Medici 1434–1494*. Oxford, 1966.

———, ed. *Florentine Studies: Politics and Society in Renaissance Florence*. Evanston, 1968.

Schevill, F. *Medieval and Renaissance Florence*. 2 vols. New York, 1963.

Waley, D. *The Italian City-Republics*. New York, 1969.

EARLY RENAISSANCE ART

Antal, F. *Florentine Painting and Its Social Background*. London, 1975.

Baxandall, M. *Painting and Experience in Fifteenth Century Italy*. Oxford, 1972.

Berenson, B. *The Drawings of the Florentine Painters*. 3 vols. Chicago, 1938.

————. *Italian Painters of the Renaissance*. London, 1952.

————. *Italian Pictures of the Renaissance: Florentine School*. 2 vols. New York, 1963.

Borsook, *The Mural Painters of Tuscany*. London, 1960.

Cennini, C. *The Craftsman's Handbook* (*Il libro dell'arte*). Translated by D. V. Thompson, Jr. New Haven, 1933.

Cole, B. *Giotto and Florentine Painting 1280–1375*. New York, 1976.

Colnaghi, D. *A Dictionary of Florentine Painters*. London, 1928.

Crowe, J., and Cavalcaselle, G. *A History of Painting in Italy*. 3 vols. London, 1864.

Davies, M. *The Earlier Italian Schools* (National Gallery Catalogue). London, 1961.

Fremantle, R. *Florentine Gothic Painters from Giotto to Masaccio*. London, 1975.

Hartt, F. *History of Italian Renaissance Art*. New York, 1969.

Higson, J. *A Historical Guide to Florence*. New York, 1973.

Kaftal, G. *Iconography of the Saints in Tuscan Painting*. Florence, 1952.

Lanzi, L. *The History of Painting in Italy*. 3 vols. London, 1847–1852.

Marle, R. van. *The Development of the Italian School of Painting*. The Hague, 1923–1938.

Meiss, M. *Painting in Florence and Siena after the Black Death*. New York, 1973.

Neri di Bicci. *Le ricordanze*. Edited by B. Santi. Pisa, 1976.

Oertel, R. *Early Italian Painting to 1400*. New York, 1968.

Offner, R. *Studies in Florentine Painting*. New York, 1927; reprint 1972.

————. *A Critical and Historical Corpus of Florentine Painting*. Berlin, New York, and Glückstadt, 1930–.

Paatz, W. and E. *Die Kirchen von Florenz*. 6 vols. Frankfurt am Main, 1940–1954.

Panofsky, E. *Renaissance and Renascences in Western Art*. New York, 1972.

Pope-Hennessy, J. *Essays on Italian Sculpture*. London, 1968.

————. *Italian Renaissance Sculpture*. London, 1971.

————. *Italian Gothic Sculpture*. London, 1972.

Procacci, U. *Sinopie e affreschi*. Milan, 1960.

Seymour, C. *Sculpture in Italy 1400–1500*. Harmondsworth, 1966.

Toesca, P. *Il Trecento*. Turin, 1951.

Vasari, G. *Le vite de' più eccellenti pittori, scultori ed architettori*. 9 vols. Edited by G. Milanesi. Florence, 1878–1885.

————. *The Lives of the Painters, Sculptors and Architects*. 4 vols. Translated by A. B. Hinds. London, 1927.

Venturi, A. *Storia dell'arte italiana*. 11 vols. Milan, 1901–1937.

Wackernagel, M. *Der Lebensraum des Künstlers in der florentinischen Renaissance*. Leipzig, 1938.

White, J. *Art and Architecture in Italy 1250–1400*. Harmondsworth, 1966.

————. *The Birth and Rebirth of Pictorial Space*. New York, 1972.

Vavalà, E. Sandberg. *Uffizi Studies: The Development of the Florentine School of Painting*. Florence, 1948.

————. *Studies in the Florentine Churches*. Florence, 1959.

ARTISTS

Agnolo Gaddi

Cole, B. "The Interior Decoration of the Palazzo Datini in Prato." *Mitteilungen des Kunsthistorischen Institutes in Florenz* 13 (1967):61–82.

———. *Agnolo Gaddi*. Oxford, 1977.

Poggi, G. "La Cappella del Sacro Cingolo nel Duomo di Prato e gli affreschi di Agnolo Gaddi." *Rivista d'arte* 14 (1932): 355–76.

Salvini, R. *L'arte di Agnolo Gaddi*. Florence, 1936.

Thieme, U., and Becker, F., eds. *Allgemeines Lexikon der bildenden Künstler*. Leipzig, 1920. S.v. "Agnolo Gaddi," by O. Sirén.

Tosi, L. "Gli affreschi della Cappella Castellani in Santa Croce." *Bollettino d'arte* 9 (1929–1930):538–54.

Andrea da Firenze

Meiss, M. *Painting in Florence and Siena after the Black Death*. New York, 1973.

Oertel, R. *Early Italian Painting to 1400*. New York, 1968.

Toesca, P. *Il Trecento*. Turin, 1964.

Thieme, U., and Becker, F., eds. *Allgemeines Lexikon der bildenden Künstler*. Leipzig, 1908. S.v. "Andrea da Firenze," by J. B. Supino.

Andrea di Giusto

Thieme, U., and Becker, F., eds. *Allgemeines Lexikon der bildenden Künstler*. Leipzig, 1908. S.v. "Andrea di Giusto," by J. B. Supino.

Fra Angelico

Berti, L. *L'Angelico a San Marco*. Florence, 1965.

Douglas, L. *Fra Angelico*. London, 1902.

Morante, E., and Baldini, U. *L'opera completa dell'Angelico*. Milan, 1970.

Mostra delle opere di Fra Angelico nel quinto centenario della morte (1455–1955). Florence, 1955.

Pope-Hennessy, J. *Fra Angelico*. London, 1974.

Antonio Veneziano

Czarnecki, J. "A New Panel by Antonio Veneziano." *Burlington Magazine* 119 (1977):188–91.

Offner, R. "The Panels of Antonio Veneziano." *Studies in Florentine Painting*. New York, 1927; reprint 1972.

Thieme, U., and Becker, F., eds. *Allgemeines Lexikon der bildenden Künstler*. Leipzig, 1908. S.v. "Antonio Veneziano," by G. Fogolari.

Bernardo Ciuffagni

Becherucci, L., and Brunetti, G. *Il Museo dell'Opera del Duomo a Firenze*. 2 vols. Milan, 1969.

Lányi, J. "Le statue quattrocentesche dei Profeti nel Campanile e nell'antica facciata di Santa Maria del Fiore." *Rivista d'arte* 17 (1935):245–80.

Thieme, U., and Becker, F., eds. *Allgemeines Lexikon der bildenden Künstler.* Leipzig, 1912. S.v. "Bernardo Ciuffagni," by F. Schottmüller.

Wundram, M. "Donatello und Ciuffagni." *Zeitschrift für Kunstgeschichte* 22 (1959): 85–101.

Bicci di Lorenzo

Constable, W. G. "A Florentine Annunciation." *Bulletin of the Boston Museum of Fine Arts* 43 (1945):72–76.

Thieme, U., and Becker, F., eds. *Allgemeines Lexikon der bildenden Künstler.* Leipzig, 1909. S.v. "Bicci di Lorenzo," by G. Gronau.

Zeri, F. "Una precisazione su Bicci di Lorenzo." *Paragone* 9 (1958):67–71.

Brunelleschi

Battisti, E. *Filippo Brunelleschi.* Milan, 1976.

Bozzoni, C., and Carbonara, G. *Filippo Brunelleschi: Saggio di bibliografia.* Rome, 1977.

Fabriczy, C. von. *Brunelleschi, sein Leben und sein Werk.* Stuttgart, 1892.

Fanelli, G. *Brunelleschi.* Florence, 1977.

Klotz, H. *Die Frühwerke Brunelleschis und die mittelalterliche Tradition.* Berlin, 1970.

Saalman, H., ed. *The Life of Brunelleschi by Antonio di Tuccio Manetti.* University Park, Pa., 1970.

Sanpaolesi, P. *Brunelleschi.* Milan, 1962.

Domenico Veneziano

Gioseffi, D. "Domenico Veneziano: 'l'esordio masaccesco' e la tavola con i SS. Girolamo e Giovanni Battista della National Gallery di Londra." *Emporium* 135 (1962):51–72.

Longhi, R. "Un frammento della pala di Domenico Veneziano per Santa Lucia de' Magnoli." *L'arte* 28 (1925):31–35.

Muraro, M. "Domenico Veneziano at S. Tarasio." *Art Bulletin* 41 (1959):151–58.

Pope-Hennessy, J. "The Early Style of Domenico Veneziano." *Burlington Magazine* 93 (1951):216–23.

Pudelko, G. "Studien über Domenico Veneziano." *Mitteilungen des Kunsthistorischen Institutes in Florenz* 4 (1934):139–200.

Salmi, M. *Paolo Uccello, Andrea del Castagno, Domenico Veneziano.* Milan, 1938.

Shell, C. "Domenico Veneziano: Two Clues." *Festschrift U. Middeldorf.* Berlin, 1968. Pp. 150–54.

Wohl, H. "Domenico Veneziano Studies: The Sant'Egidio and Parenti Documents." *Burlington Magazine* 113 (1971):635–41.

Donatello

Castelfranco, G. *Donatello.* New York, 1965.

Cruttwell, M. *Donatello.* London, 1911.

Donatello e il suo tempo. Florence, 1968.

Encyclopedia of World Art. 1961. S.v. "Donatello," by L. Becherucci.

Hartt, F. *Donatello: Prophet of Modern Vision.* New York, 1973.

Herzner, V. "Donatello in Siena." *Mitteilungen des Kunsthistorischen Institutes in Florenz* 15 (1971):161–86.

———. "Die Kanzeln Donatellos in San Lorenzo." *Münchner Jahrbuch der bildenden Kunst* 23 (1972):101–64.

Janson, H. W. *The Sculpture of Donatello.* 2 vols. Princeton, 1963.

Kauffman, H. *Donatello: Eine Einführung in sein Bilden und Denken.* Berlin, 1935.

Lányi, J. "Le statue quattrocentesche dei Profeti nel Campanile e nell'antica facciata di Santa Maria del Fiore." *Rivista d'arte* 17 (1935):121–59; 245–80.

———. "Tre rilievi inediti Donatello." *L'arte* 6 (1935):284–97.

———. "Zur Pragmatik der Florentiner Quattrocento Plastik." *Kritische Berichte* 1932–1933 (1936):126–31.

———. "Problemi della critica Donatelliana." *Critica d'arte* 5(1940):9–23.

Middeldorf, U. Review of Kauffmann's *Donatello: Eine Einführung in sein Bilden und Denken. Art Bulletin* 18 (1936):570–85.

Morisani, O. *Studi su Donatello.* Venice, 1952.

Pope-Hennessy, J. *Italian Renaissance Sculpture.* London, 1971.

———. "The Medici Crucifixion of Donatello." *Apollo* 101 (1975):82–87.

———. "The Madonna Reliefs of Donatello." *Apollo* 103 (1976):172–91.

———. "Donatello and the Bronze Statuette." *Apollo* 105 (1977):30–33.

———. "The Evangelist Roundels in the Pazzi Chapel." *Apollo* 106 (1977):262–69.

Rosenauer, A. *Studien zum frühen Donatello: Skulptur im projektiven Raum der Neuzeit.* Vienna, 1975.

Tanfani-Centofanti, L. *Donatello in Pisa.* Pisa, 1887.

Filippino Lippi

Berti, L., and Baldini, U. *Filippino Lippi.* Florence, 1975.

Neilson, K. *Filippino Lippi.* Cambridge, Mass., 1938.

Scharf, A. *Filippino Lippi.* Vienna, 1935.

Filippo Lippi

Baldini, U. *Filippo Lippi.* Milan, 1964.

Marchini, G. *Filippo Lippi.* Milan, 1975.

Oertel, R. *Fra Filippo Lippi.* Vienna, 1942.

Strutt, E. *Fra Filippo Lippi.* London, 1901.

Gentile da Fabriano

Colasanti, A. *Gentile da Fabriano.* Bergamo, 1909.

———. "Le prime opere di Gentile da Fabriano." *Rassegna marchigiana* 12 (1934):180–85.

Grassi, L. *Tutta la pittura di Gentile da Fabriano.* Milan, 1953.

Micheletti, E. *L'opera completa di Gentile da Fabriano.* Milan, 1976.

Molajoli, B. *Gentile da Fabriano.* Fabriano, 1934.

Thieme, U., and Becker, F., eds. *Allgemeines Lexikon der bildenden Künstler.* Leipzig, 1920. S.v. "Gentile da Fabriano," by B. C. Kreplin.

Giovanni d'Ambrogio

Becherucci, L., and Brunetti, G. *Il Museo dell'Opera del Duomo a Firenze.* 2 vols. Milan, 1969.

Brunetti, G. "Giovanni d'Ambrogio." *Rivista d'arte* 14 (1932):1–22.

Kreytenberg, G. "Giovanni d'Ambrogio." *Jahrbuch der Berliner Museen* 14 (1972):5–32.

Lisner, M. "Zu Jacopo della Quercia und Giovanni d'Ambrogio." *Pantheon* 34 (1976):275–79.

Pope-Hennessy, J. *Italian Gothic Sculpture.* London, 1972.

Wundram, M. "Der Meister der Verkündigung in der Domopera zu Florenz." *Beiträge zur Kunstgeschichte: Festgabe für H. R. Rosemann.* Munich, 1960. Pp. 109–25.

Giovanni del Biondo

Cole, B. Review of Offner and Steinweg *Giovanni del Biondo, Corpus of Florentine Painting. Art Bulletin* 52 (1970):200–202.

Offner, R., and Steinweg, K. *Giovanni del Biondo, Corpus of Florentine Painting.* IV, V, Pts. 1 and 2. Glückstadt, 1967; 1969.

Thieme, U., and Becker, F., eds. *Allgemeines Lexikon der bildenden Künstler.* Leipzig, 1921. S.v. "Giovanni del Biondo," by J. Kurzwelly.

Zeri, F. "Due profeti di Giovanni del Biondo e la loro origine." *Bollettino d'arte* 49 (1964):127–30.

Giovanni da Milano

Castelfranchi-Vegas, L. *Giovanni da Milano.* Milan, 1965.

Gregori, M. *Giovanni da Milano alla Cappella Rinuccini.* Milan, 1965.

Marabottini, A. *Giovanni da Milano.* Florence, 1950.

Procacci, U. "Il primo ricordo di Giovanni da Milano a Firenze." *Arte antica e moderna* 13/16 (1961):49–66.

Thieme, U., and Becker, F., eds. *Allgemeines Lexikon der bildenden Künstler.* Leipzig, 1921. S.v. "Giovanni da Milano," by W. Suida.

Giovanni Toscani

Bellosi, L. "Il Maestro della Crocifissione Griggs: Giovanni Toscani." *Paragone* 17 (1966):44–58.

Eisenberg, M. "'The Penitent St. Jerome' by Giovanni Toscani." *Burlington Magazine* 118 (1976):275–83.

Offner, R. "The Mostra del Tesoro di Firenze Sacra." *Burlington Magazine* 63 (1933):166–78.

Thieme, U., and Becker, F., eds. *Allgemeines Lexikon der bildenden Künstler.* Leipzig, 1950. S.v. "Meister der Griggs Kreuzigung," by H Vollmer.

Jacopo di Cione

Gronau, H. D. "The San Pier Maggiore Altarpiece: A Reconstruction." *Burlington Magazine* 86 (1945):139–44.

Offner, R. *Jacopo di Cione, Corpus of Florentine Painting*. IV, III. Glückstadt, 1965.

Steinweg, K. "Die Kreuzigung Petri des Jacopo di Cione in der Pinacoteca Vaticana." *Atti della Pontificia Accademia Romana di Archeologia* 30–31 (1957–1958; 1958–1959):231–44.

Jacopo di Piero Guidi

Becherucci, L., and Brunetti, G. *Il Museo dell'Opera del Duomo a Firenze*. 2 vols. Milan, 1969.

Thieme, U., and Becker, F., eds. *Allgemeines Lexikon der bildenden Künstler*. Leipzig, 1925. S.v. "Jacopo di Piero Guidi," by K. Rathe.

Wundram, M. "Der Meister der Verkündigung in der Domopera zu Florenz." *Beiträge zur Kunstgeschichte: Festgabe für H. R. Rosemann*. Munich, 1960. Pp. 109–25.

———. "Jacopo di Piero Guidi." *Mitteilungen des Kunsthistorischen Institutes in Florenz* 13 (1968):195–222.

Leonardo da Vinci

Clark, K. *Leonardo da Vinci*. Harmondsworth, 1967.

Gould, C. *Leonardo: The Artist and the Non-Artist*. Boston, 1975.

Heydenreich, L. *Leonardo da Vinci*. 2 vols. New York, 1954.

Richter, J. P. *The Notebooks of Leonardo da Vinci*. 2 vols. New York, 1970.

Lorenzo Ghiberti

Krautheimer, R. "Ghibertiana." *Burlington Magazine* 71 (1937):68–80.

———. *Ghiberti's Bronze Door*. Princeton, 1971.

Krautheimer, R., and Krautheimer-Hess, T., *Lorenzo Ghiberti*. 2 vols. Princeton, 1970.

Krautheimer-Hess, T. "More Ghibertiana." *Art Bulletin* 46 (1964):307–21.

Middeldorf, U. "Additions to Lorenzo Ghiberti's Work." *Burlington Magazine* 113 (1971):72–79.

Morisani, O., ed. *I Commentari del Lorenzo Ghiberti*. Naples, 1947.

Pope-Hennessy, J. *Italian Gothic Sculpture*. London, 1972.

Schlosser, J. von. *I Commentari (Lorenzo Ghibertis Denkwürdigkeiten)*. 2 vols. Berlin, 1912.

———. *Leben und Meinungen des florentinischen Bildners Lorenzo Ghiberti*. Basel, 1941.

Lorenzo Monaco

Baldini, U. "Note brevi su inediti toscani: Lorenzo Monaco: Crocifisso." *Bollettino d'arte* 40 (1955):81–82.

Bellosi, L. *Lorenzo Monaco*. Milan, 1965.

Berenson, B. "Un nuovo Lorenzo Monaco." *Rivista d'arte* 6 (1909):3–6.

Davies, M. "Lorenzo Monaco's 'Coronation of the Virgin' in London." *Critica d'arte* 8 (1949):202–10.

Eisenberg, M. "A Crucifix and a Man of Sorrows by Lorenzo Monaco." *Art Quarterly* 18 (1955):45–49.

―――. "Un frammento smarrito dell' 'Annunciazione' di Lorenzo Monaco nell' Accademia di Firenze." *Bollettino d'arte* 41 (1956):333–35.

―――. "An Early Altarpiece by Lorenzo Monaco." *Art Bulletin* 39 (1957):49–52.

Golzio, V. *Lorenzo Monaco*. Rome, 1931.

González-Palacios, A. "Indagini su Lorenzo Monaco." *Paragone* 21 (1970):27–36.

Gronau, H. "The Earliest Works of Lorenzo Monaco." *Burlington Magazine* 92 (1950):183–88; 217–22.

Meiss, M. "Four Panels by Lorenzo Monaco." *Burlington Magazine* 100 (1958):191–96.

Montebello, P. de. "Four Prophets by Lorenzo Monaco." *Metropolitan Museum of Art Bulletin* 25 (1966):153–69.

Pudelko, G. "The Stylistic Development of Lorenzo Monaco." *Burlington Magazine* 73 (1938):237–48; 74 (1939):76–81.

Sirén, O. "Di alcuni pittori fiorentini che subirono l'influenza di Lorenzo Monaco." *L'arte* 7 (1904):337–55.

―――. *Don Lorenzo Monaco*. Strasbourg, 1905.

Toesca, P. "Nuove opere di Don Lorenzo Monaco." *L'arte* 7 (1904):171–74.

Zeri, F. "Investigations into the Early Period of Lorenzo Monaco." *Burlington Magazine* 106 (1964):554–58; 107 (1965):3–11.

―――. "Aggiunta a una primizia di Lorenzo Monaco." *Bollettino d'arte* 51 (1966):150–51.

Lorenzo di Niccolò

Cole, B. "A New Work by the Young Lorenzo di Niccolò." *Art Quarterly* 33 (1970):114–19.

Fahy, Everett. "On Lorenzo di Niccolò." *Apollo* 108 (1978):374–81.

Thieme, U., and Becker, F., eds. *Allgemeines Lexikon der bildenden Künstler*. Leipzig, 1920. S.v. "Lorenzo di Niccolò Gerini," by O. Sirén.

Mariotto di Cristofano

Boccia, L. G. *Arte nell'aretino*. Florence, 1974.

Boskovits, M. "Mariotto di Cristofano: un contributo ail' ambiente culturale di Masaccio giovane." *Arte illustrata* 13–14 (1969):4–13.

Cohn, W. "Maestri sconosciuti del Quattrocento fiorentino." *Bollettino d'arte* 43 (1958):64–68.

Mariotto di Nardo

Boskovits, M. "Mariotto di Nardo e la formazione del linguaggio tardo-gotica a Firenze negli anni intorno al 1400." *Antichità Viva* 7 (1968):21–31.

―――. "Sull'attivitá giovanile di Mariotto di Nardo." *Antichità Viva* 7 (1968):3–13.

Eisenberg, M. "A Flagellation by Mariotto di Nardo and Some Related Panels." *Record of the Princeton Art Museum* 8 (1949):6–14.

―――. "A Partial Reconstruction of a Predella by Mariotto di Nardo." *Allen Memorial Art Museum Bulletin* 9 (1951):9–16.

―――. "An Addition to a Group of Panels by Mariotto di Nardo." *Record of the Princeton Art Museum* 18 (1959):61–64.

———. "The Coronation of the Virgin by Mariotto di Nardo." *Minneapolis Institute of Arts Bulletin* 55 (1966):9–24.

Offner, R. "The Mostra del Tesore di Firenze Sacra." *Burlington Magazine* 63 (1933):166–78.

Pouncey, P. "An Initial Letter by Mariotto di Nardo." *Burlington Magazine* 88 (1946):71–72.

Salmi, M. "Lorenzo Ghiberti e Mariotto di Nardo." *Rivista d'arte* 30 (1955):147–52.

Masaccio

Antal, F. *Florentine Painting and Its Social Background.* London, 1948.

Baldini, U. "Masaccio." *Mostra di Quattro Maestri del Primo Rinascimento.* Florence, 1954. Pp. 11–17.

Beck, J. *Masaccio: The Documents.* Locust Valley, N. Y., 1978.

Berti, L. "Masaccio 1422." *Commentari* 12 (1961):84–107.

———. "Masaccio a San Giovenale di Cascia." *Acropoli* 2 (1962):149–65.

———. *Masaccio.* University Park, Pa., 1967.

Bologna, F. *Masaccio: La cappella Brancacci.* Milan, 1969.

Borsook, E. "A Note on Masaccio in Pisa." *Burlington Magazine* 103 (1961):212–15.

Brockhaus, H. "Die Brancacci-Kapelle in Florenz." *Mitteilungen des Kunsthistorischen Institutes in Florenz* 3 (1930):160–82.

Campani, E. "Newly Discovered Frescoes in Santa Maria Novella." *Burlington Magazine* 47 (1925):191–95.

Chiarini, M. "Una citazione della 'Sagra' di Masaccio nel Ghirlandaio." *Paragone* 13 (1962):53–56.

Coolidge, J. "Further Observations on Masaccio's 'Trinity.'" *Art Bulletin* 48 (1966):382–84.

Creutz, M. *Masaccio.* Berlin, 1901.

Davies, M. *The Earlier Italian Schools.* London, 1961.

Einem, H. von. *Masaccios Zingroschen.* Cologne, 1967.

———. "Zur Deutung von Masaccios 'Zingroschen.'" *Acta historiae artium* 13 (1967):187–90.

Filangeri di Candida, A. "Un quadro acquistato dalla Galleria del Museo Nazionale di Napoli." *L'arte* 4 (1901):74.

Fremantle, R. "Some Documents Concerning Masaccio and His Mother's Second Family." *Burlington Magazine* 115 (1973):516–18.

———. *Florentine Gothic Painters from Giotto to Masaccio.* London, 1975.

———. "Ricerche documenti di archivio: Note sulla parentela di Mariotto di Cristofano con la famiglia di Masaccio." *Antichità vivà* 17 (1978):52–53.

Gherardi-Dragomanni, F. *Memorie della terra di San Giovanni del Valdarno superiore.* Florence, 1834.

Gigioli, O. H. *Masaccio.* Florence, 1921.

———. "Masaccio." *Bollettino del Reale Instituto di Architettura e Storia dell'Arte* 3 (1929):55–101.

Gilbert, C. "The Drawings Now Associated with Masaccio's 'Sagra.'" *Storia dell'arte* 3 (1969):260–78.

Janson, H. W. "Ground Plan and Elevation in Masaccio's Trinity Fresco." *Essays in the History of Art Presented to R. Wittkower.* London, 1967. Pp. 83–88.

Lavagnino, E. "Masaccio: 'Dicesi è morto a Roma.'" *Emporium* 97 (1943):97–112.

Lindberg, H. *To the Problem of Masolino and Masaccio.* 2 vols. Stockholm, 1931.

Linnenkamp, R. "Zu Masaccios 'Dreifaltigkeit' in S. Maria Novella zu Florenz." *Pantheon* 25 (1967):126–27.

Longhi, R. *Fatti di Masolino e di Masaccio e altri studi sul Quattrocento.* Florence, 1975.

Magherini-Graziani, G. *Masaccio: Ricordo delle onoranze rese in San Giovanni Valdarno nel di 25 ottobre 1903.* Florence, 1904.

Meiss, M. "London's New Masaccio." *Art News* 51 (1952):24–25; 50–51.

———. "Masaccio and the Early Renaissance: the Circular Plan." *Studies in Western Art.* vol. 2. (Acts of the 20th International Congress of the History of Art). Princeton, 1963. Pp. 123–45.

Meller, P. "La Cappella Brancacci: Problemi ritrattistici e iconografici." *Acropoli* 1 (1961):186–227; 273–312.

Mesnil, J. "Per la storia della cappella Brancacci." *Rivista d'arte* 8 (1912):34–40.

———. *Masaccio et les débuts de la Renaissance.* The Hague, 1927.

Molho, A. "The Brancacci Chapel: Studies in Its Iconography and History." *Journal of the Warburg and Courtauld Institutes* 40 (1977):50–98.

Oertel, R. "Die Frühwerke des Masaccio." *Marburger Jahrbuch für Kunstwissenschaft* 7 (1933):191–289.

———. "Masaccio und die Geschichte der Freskotechnik." *Jahrbuch der preussischen Kunstsammlungen* 55 (1934):229–40.

———. "Wandmalerei und Zeichnung in Italien." *Mitteilungen des Kunsthistorischen Institutes in Florenz* 7 (1940):217–314.

Offner, R. "Light on Masaccio's Classicism." *Studies in the History of Art Dedicated to William E. Suida on His Eightieth Birthday.* London, 1959. Pp. 66–72.

Paatz, W. and E. *Die Kirchen von Florenz,* vol. 3. *Frankfurt am Main, 1940–1954.*

Pittaluga, M. *Masaccio.* Florence, 1935.

Polzer, J. "The Anatomy of Masaccio's Holy Trinity." *Jahrbuch der Berliner Museen* 13 (1971):18–59.

Pope-Hennessy, J. "The Santa Maria Maggiore Altarpiece." *Burlington Magazine* 94 (1952):31.

Procacci, U. "Documenti e ricerche sopra Masaccio e la sua famiglia." *Rivista d'arte* 14 (1932):489–503; 17 (1935):91–111.

———. "L'incendio della chiesa del Carmine del 1771." *Rivista d'arte* 14 (1932):141–232.

———. "Sulla cronologia delle opere di Masaccio e di Masolino tra il 1425 e il 1428." *Rivista d'arte* 28 (1953):3–55.

———. *All the Paintings of Masaccio.* New York, 1962.

Rivista storica carmelitana. (On the occasion of the fifth centenary of the death of Masaccio.) Florence, 1929.

Salmi, M. *Masaccio.* Milan, 1948.

———. "Gli scomparti della pala di Santa Maria Maggiore acquistati dalla National Gallery." *Commentari* 3 (1952):14–21.

Schlegel, U. "Observations on Masaccio's Trinity Fresco in Santa Maria Novella." *Art Bulletin* 45 (1963):19–33.

Shearman, J. "Masaccio's Pisa Altarpiece: An Alternative Reconstruction." *Burlington Magazine* 108 (1966):449–55.

Somaré, E. *Masaccio*. Milan, 1924.

Steinbart, K. *Masaccio*. Vienna, 1948.

Tanfani-Centofanti, L. *Notizie di artisti tratte dai documenti pisani*. Pisa, 1897.

Thieme, U., and Becker, F., eds. *Allgemeines Lexikon der bildenden Künstler*. Leipzig, 1930. S.v. "Masaccio," by O. H. Gigioli.

Volponi, P., and Berti, L. *L'opera coompleta di Masaccio*. Milan, 1968.

Watkins, L. B. "Technical Observations on the Frescoes of the Brancacci Chapel." *Mitteilungen des Kunsthistorischen Institutes in Florenz* 17 (1973):65–74.

Wood-Brown, J. *The Dominican Church of Santa Maria Novella*. Edinburgh, 1902.

Masolino

Argenti, M. *Masolino da Panicale: Il battistero di Castiglione Olona*. Bergamo, 1975.

Beenken, H. "Masaccios und Masolinos Fresken von San Clemente in Rom." *Belvedere* 11 (1932):7–13.

Bianchini, M. *Masolino da Panicale*. Milan, 1965.

Cole, B. "A Reconstruction of Masolino's True Cross cycle in Santo Stefano, Empoli." *Mitteilungen des Kunsthistorischen Institutes in Florenz* 13 (1968):289–300.

Eiko-Wakayama, M. L. "Novità di Masolino a Castiglione Olona." *Arte lombarda* 16 (1971):1–16.

Fremantle, R. "Some New Masolino Documents." *Burlington Magazine* 117 (1975): 658–59.

Longhi, R. *Fatti di Masolino e di Masaccio e altri studi sul Quattrocento*. Florence, 1975.

Micheletti, E. *Masolino da Panicale*. Milan, 1959.

Offner, R. "A Saint Jerome by Masolino." *Art in America* 8 (1920):68–76.

Poggi, G. "Masolino e la Compagnia della Croce a Empoli." *Rivista d'arte* 3 (1905):46–53.

Procacci, U. "Sulla cronologia delle opere di Masaccio e di Masolino tra il 1425 e il 1428." *Rivista d'arte* 28 (1953):3–55.

Salmi, M. "Gli affreschi nella Collegiata di Castiglione Olona." *Dedalo* 8 (1927–1928):227–44; 9 (1928–1929):1–30.

Toesca, P. *Masolino da Panicale*. Bergamo, 1908.

———. "Frammenti di un trittico di Masolino." *Bollettino d'arte* 3 (1923):3–6.

———. *Masolino a Castiglione Olona*. Milan, 1946.

Vayer, L. *Masolino és Róma*. Budapest, 1962.

Master of the Bambino Vispo

Boskovits, M. "Il Maestro del Bambino Vispo: Gherardo Starina o Miguel Alcaniz?" *Paragone* 26 (1975):3–15.

Longhi, R. "Un'aggiunta al Maestro del Bambino Vispo (Miguel Alcaniz?)." *Paragone* 16 (1965):38–40.

Oertel, R. "Der Laurentius-Altar aus dem florentiner Dom." *Studien zur toskanischen Kunst; Festschrift für L. H. Heydenreich*. Munich, 1964:205–20.

Pudelko, G. "The Master of the Bambino Vispo." *Art in America* 26 (1938):47–63.

Sirén, O. "Di alcuni pittori fiorentini che subirono l'influenza di Lorenzo Monaco." *L'arte* 7 (1904):349–55.

Thieme, U., and Becker, F., eds. *Allgemeines Lexikon der bildenden Künstler.* Leipzig, 1950. S.v. "Meister des Bambino Vispo," by H. Vollmer.

Van Waadenoijen, J. "A Proposal for Starnina: Exit the Maestro del Bambino Vispo?" *Burlington Magazine* 116 (1974):82–91.

Volpe, C. "Per il completamento dell'altare di San Lorenzo del Maestro del Bambino Vispo." *Mitteilungen des Kunsthistorischen Institutes in Florenz* 17 (1973):347–60.

Master of 1419

Cohen, W. "Notizie storiche intorno ad alcune tavole fiorentine del '300 et '400." *Rivista d'arte* 31 (1956):49–52.

Francis, H. S. "Master of 1419." *Bulletin of the Cleveland Museum of Art* 43 (1956):211–13.

Nicolson, B. "The Master of 1419." *Burlington Magazine* 96 (1954):181.

Pouncey, P. "A New Panel by the Master of 1419." *Burlington Magazine* 96 (1954):291–92.

Michelangelo

De Tolnay, C. *Michelangelo.* 5 vols. Princeton, 1943–1960.

———. *Michelangelo.* Princeton, 1975.

Einem, H. von. *Michelangelo.* London, 1973.

Hartt, F. *Michelangelo.* New York, 1965.

Hibbard, H. *Michelangelo.* New York, 1974.

Pope-Hennessy, J. *Italian High Renaissance and Baroque Sculpture.* London, 1970.

Nanni di Banco

Bellosi, L. *Nanni di Banco.* Milan, 1966.

Brunetti, G. "I profeti sulla porta del campanile di Santa Maria del Fiore." *Festschrift U. Middeldorf.* Berlin, 1968. Pp. 106–11.

Herzner, V. "Donatello und Nanni di Banco: Die Prophetenfiguren für die Strebefeiler des Florentiner Domes." *Mitteilungen des Kunsthistorischen Institutes in Florenz* 17 (1973):1–28.

Lányi, J. "Le statue quattrocentesche dei Profeti nel Campanile e nell' antica facciata di Santa Maria del Fiore." *Rivista d'arte* 17 (1935):121–59; 245–80.

Planiscig, L. *Nanni di Banco.* Florence, 1946.

Pope-Hennessy, J. *Italian Gothic Sculpture.* London, 1972.

Seymour, C. "The Younger Masters of the First Campaign of the Porta della Mandorla, 1391–1397." *Art Bulletin* 41 (1959):1–17.

Vaccarino, P. *Nanni.* Florence, 1951.

Wundram, M. *Donatello und Nanni di Banco.* Berlin, 1969.

Nardo di Cione

Gronau, H. D. *Andrea Orcagna und Nardo di Cione.* Berlin, 1937.

Middeldorf, U. "Ein neuer Nardo di Cione." *Mitteilungen des Kunsthistorischen Institutes in Florenz* 7 (1956):169–72.

Offner, R. "Nardo di Cione and His Triptych in the Goldman Collection." *Art in America* 12 (1924):99–112.

———. "Nardo di Cione." *Studies in Florentine Painting.* New York, 1927; reprint 1972.

———. *Nardo di Cione, Corpus of Florentine Painting.* IV, II. Glückstadt, 1960.

Procacci, U. "L'affresco dell'Oratorio del Bigallo ed il suo maestro." *Mitteilungen des Kunsthistorischen Institutes in Florenz* 17 (1973):307–24.

Thieme, U., and Becker, F., eds. *Allgemeines Lexikon der bildenden Künstler.* Leipzig, 1931. S.v. "Nardo di Cione," by H. Gronau.

Neri di Bicci

Laget, E. "Contribution aux recherches sur les 'Ricordanze' de Neri di Bicci: Un panneau de 1454 fragmenté au 20ᵉ siècle." *Annali della Scuola Normale Superiore di Pisa* 3 (1973):189–93.

Santi, B. "Dalle 'Ricordanze' di Neri di Bicci." *Annali della Scuola Normale superiore di Pisa* 3 (1973):169–93.

———, ed. *Neri di Bicci: Le ricordanze.* Pisa, 1976.

Thieme, U., and Becker, F., eds. *Allgemeines Lexikon der bildenden Künstler.* Leipzig, 1909. S.v. "Bicci — Neri di Bicci," by G. Gronau.

Niccolò di Pietro Gerini

Baldini, U. *La Cappella Migliorati nel San Francesco di Prato.* Florence, 1965.

Bisogni, F. "Una rara scena della Leggenda di S. Andrea di Niccolò di Pietro Gerini." *Mitteilungen des Kunsthistorischen Institutes in Florenz* 17 (1973):195–200.

Cole, B. "The Interior Decoration of the Palazzo Datini in Prato." *Mitteilungen des Kunsthistorischen Institutes in Florenz* 13 (1967):61–82.

Offner, R. "Niccolò di Pietro Gerini." *Studies in Florentine Painting.* New York, 1927; reprint 1972.

Niccolò di Pietro Lamberti

Becherucci, L. "Una statuetta del Bargello." *Antichità viva* 15 (1976):9–13.

Becherucci, L., and Brunetti, G. *Il Museo dell'Opera del Duomo a Firenze.* 2 vols. Milan, 1969.

Brunetti, G. "Osservazioni sulla Porta dei Canonici." *Mitteilungen des Kunsthistorischen Institutes in Florenz* 8 (1957):1–12.

Fiocco, G. "I Lamberti a Venezia — I. Niccolò di Pietro Lamberti." *Dedalo* 8 (1927–1928):287–314.

Goldner, G. "Two Statuettes from the Doorway of the Campanile of Florence." *Mitteilungen des Kunsthistorischen Institutes in Florenz* 18 (1974):219–26.

————. *Niccolò and Pietro Lamberti.* New York, 1977.

————. "Niccolò Lamberti and the Gothic Sculpture of San Marco in Venice." *Gazette des Beaux Arts* 89 (1977):41–50.

Kreytenberg, G. "Zwei Marienstatuen über der Porta dei Cornacchini des Florentiner Doms." *Pantheon* 34 (1976):183–90.

Pope-Hennessy, J. *Italian Gothic Sculpture.* London, 1972.

Seymour, C. "The Younger Masters of the First Campaign of the Porta della Mandorla, 1391–1397." *Art Bulletin* 41 (1959):1–17.

Wundram, M. "Albizzo di Piero: Studien zur Bauplastik von Or San Michele in Florenz." *Das Werk des Künstlers, Studien zur Ikonographie und Formgeschichte. H. Schrade zum 60. Gerburtstag.* Stuttgart, 1960. Pp. 161–76.

————. "Niccolò di Pietro Lamberti und die Florentiner Plastik um 1400." *Jahrbuch der Berliner Museen* 4 (1962):78–115.

————. "Der heilige Jacobus an Or San Michele in Florenz." *Festschrift K. Oettinger.* Erlangen, 1967. Pp. 193–207.

Orcagna [Andrea di Cione]

Gronau, H. D. *Andrea Orcagna und Nardo di Cione.* Berlin, 1937.

Meiss, M. *Painting in Florence and Siena after the Black Death.* New York, 1973.

Offner, R. *Andrea di Cione, Corpus of Florentine Painting.* IV, I. Glückstadt, 1962.

Steinweg. K. *Andrea Orcagna.* Strasbourg, 1929.

————. "Rekonstruktion einer orcagnesken Marienkrönung." *Mitteilungen des Kunsthistorischen Institutes in Florenz* 10 (1961):122–27.

Thieme, U., and Becker, F., eds. *Allgemeines Lexikon der bildenden Künstler.* Leipzig, 1932. S.v. "Orcagna, Andrea di Cione," by H. D. Gronau.

Valentiner, W. R. "Orcagna and the Black Death of 1348." *Art Quarterly* 12 (1949):48–72, 113–28.

Piero della Francesca

Bianconi, P. *Piero della Francesca.* New York, 1962.

Clark, K. *Piero della Francesca.* London, 1969.

Hendy, P. *Piero della Francesca and the Early Renaissance.* New York, 1968.

Longhi, R. *Fatti di Masolino e di Masaccio e altri studi sul Quattrocento.* Florence, 1975.

Murray, P., and Vecchi, P. de. *The Complete Paintings of Piero della Francesca.* New York, 1967.

Raphael

Colacicchi, P. *All the Paintings of Raphael.* 2 vols. New York, 1963.

Crowe, J., and Cavalcaselle, G. *Raphael: His Life and His Works.* 2 vols. London, 1882–1885.

Dussler, L. *Raphael: A Critical Catalogue of His Pictures, Wall-Paintings and Tapestries.* London, 1971.

Müntz, E. *Raphael, His Life, Works and Times.* London, 1882.

Oppé, A. *Raphael.* New York, 1970.

Pope-Hennessy, J. *Raphael.* New York, 1970.

Prisco, M. *L'opera completa di Raffaello.* Milan, 1966.

Rossello di Jacopo Franchi

Colnaghi, D. *A Dictionary of Florentine Painters*. London, 1928.

D'Ancona, M. Levi. *Miniatura e miniatori a Firenze dal XIV al XV secolo*. Florence, 1962.

Thieme, U., and Becker, F., eds. *Allgemeines Lexikon der bildenden Künstler*. Leipzig, 1916. S.v. "Franchi, Rossello di Jacopo."

Spinello Aretino

Bellosi, L. "Da Spinello Aretino a Lorenzo Monaco." *Paragone* 16 (1965):18–43.

Donati, P. "Contributo a Spinello Aretino e la sua scuola." *Antichità viva* 3 (1964):11–24.

Fehm, S. "Notes on Spinello Aretino's So-called Monte Oliveto Altarpiece." *Mitteilungen des Kunsthistorischen Institutes in Florenz* 17 (1973):257–72.

Gombosi, G. *Spinello Aretino*. Budapest, 1926.

González-Palacios, A. "Due proposte per Spinello." *Paragone* 16 (1965):43–51.

Longhi, R. Il più bel frammento dagli affreschi del Carmine di Spinello Aretino." *Paragone* 11 (1960):33–35.

Masetti, A. R. *Spinello Aretino giovane*. Florence, 1973.

Thieme, U., and Becker, F., eds. *Allgemeines Lexikon der bildenden Künstler*. Leipzig, 1937. S.v. "Spinello di Luca Spinelli," by F. M. Perkins.

Straus Master

Asano Fabbi, D. "Artisti fiorentini nel territorio di Norcia." *Rivista d'arte* 34 (1959):109–22.

Offner, R. "The Mostra del Tesoro di Firenze Sacra." *Burlington Magazine* 63 (1933):166–78.

Thieme, U., and Becker, F., eds. *Allgemeines Lexikon der bildenden Künstler*. Leipzig. 1950. S.v. "Meister des Straus-Madonna."

Wilkins, D. "A Florentine Diptych." *Carnegie Magazine* 47 (1972): 158–61.

Zeri, F. "Italian Primitives at Messrs. Wildenstein." *Burlington Magazine* 107 (1965):252–56.

Index